GLOBAL CARE WORK

Global Care Work

Gender and Migration in Nordic Societies

Lise Widding Isaksen (Ed.)

NORDIC ACADEMIC PRESS

Nordic Academic Press
P.O. Box 1206
S-221 05 Lund, Sweden
info@nordicacademicpress.com
www.nordicacademicpress.com

Typesetting: Stilbildarna i Mölle, Frederic Täckström, www.sbmolle.com
Cover: Maria Jörgel Andersson
Cover images: www.istockphoto.com
Print: ScandBook AB, Falun 2010
ISBN: 978-91-85509-48-5

Contents

Foreword

Some chapters in this book were presented in draft form at the workshop on 'Global Care Chains: Nordic Experiences' held in the spring of 2008 at the University of Bergen, Norway. This workshop was an outcome of collaboration between Ellinor Platzer and myself on issues such as gender, migration and domestic work since the beginning of this millennium.

This first workshop brought together researchers from Sweden and Norway. Later, funding from the Nordic Research Council, NordForsk, made it possible to expand the group and form a Nordic research network with members from four of the Nordic countries (for several reasons no members from Iceland were able to join the network this time). We have held workshops at universities in Sweden, Denmark and Norway. We have commented on one another's drafts and critically examined relevant ideas, concepts and theoretical perspectives. It has been a great pleasure to work in a network with scholars from different generations. Masters students, doctoral students and professors have worked together in a very productive way.

The project budget has been administered by SKOK, the Centre for Gender and Women's Research at the University of Bergen, Norway. Tone Lund-Olsen and Signe Solberg have been unstinting with their support and help throughout.

Annika Olsson and Charlotte Merton of Nordic Academic Press have given us valuable advice in the editing process.

Lise Widding Isaksen

CHAPTER I

Introduction

Global care work in Nordic societies

Lise Widding Isaksen

Outsourcing gender-equality problems

Balancing work and family is today a global issue and creates great tensions in modern societies. International migration is now dominated by women, and the beginning of the twenty-first century is marked by changing family roles. Demographic changes and women's integration in the labour market have led to increased demands for care services. Given the fact that care work is closely connected with femininity, women have become more active in the new processes of labour migration.

One consequence is a change in family roles in sender countries as well as in receiver countries: in many societies the male breadwinner family has largely been replaced by a dual-earner family or a female breadwinner model. Another is the emergence of new social organizations of care in the interaction between different nations, ethnic groups and social classes. Hochschild (2000) has conceptualized this phenomenon as 'global care chains', which she defines as 'a series of personal links between people across the globe based on the paid and unpaid work of caring' (ibid. 131). In studies of global care chains, North American research has mainly focused on domestic care work as a commodity bought and sold on the global market and leading to a commodification of motherhood (Ehrenreich & Hochschild 2002). Parreñas (2001) has shown how globalization includes the emergence of transnational families, and how the refinement of modern technology makes it possible to do motherhood from afar. European research, as opposed to the North American, has focused more on how different welfare regimes regulate the sharing of responsibility between the family and the state (Williams 2007; Lutz 2009). The intention with this book is to bring the example of the Nordic societies to the European and North American debate.

When it comes to social equality and gender equality, Nordic countries have been ahead of many other European welfare states. Social policy has traditionally been made within the framework of a tripartite system of the state, the trade unions and the market. The Nordic model is a social-democratic welfare-state model based upon core values such as gender equality, social equality and international solidarity. Given the fact that the production of care services is largely a public concern in Scandinavia, a global-care-chain approach that is limited to the domestic care sector and the commercialization of care in the household sphere would be too narrow. Here we will argue that extending the concept of global care chains to other care sectors and spaces, particularly nursing and other institutional kinds of care for children and the elderly, will enhance the concept's analytical and explanatory power. Using this extended model of the global care chain, we explore how international migration and global care chains influence equalitarian norms and values in social-democratic welfare states. We explore the way in which global markets affect social policies on such things as work–family balance, and the important role migration now plays in the provision of care services. Our studies consider Sweden, Finland, Denmark and Norway.

It is tempting to understand the globalization of care mainly as market-driven processes determined by the principles of 'supply and demand'. When affluent countries experience a care deficit and poorer regions suffer from unemployment, migration for care work can easily be pictured as a 'win–win' situation. Behind this picture there exist complex social realities. The everyday lives of migrants and their families might be lived in transnational spaces, while many Scandinavian families struggle to live a gender-equal family life in which care and housework is fairly shared. In the Nordic welfare states, the increasing employment of migrant women in private households and in public services can be related to a change in political and social ideas of how gender and social equality can be achieved. In Denmark the au-pair programme is presented by politicians as a strategy to make individual work–family balances more flexible and to support professional women's career development in the labour market. Migrant women are expected to 'do' the gender equality in the family while 'native' women take care of the gender equality in the labour market. Gender equality in the private sphere is 'outsourced' to the global market.

Migration and the incomplete revolution

The Nordic countries have traditionally shared care responsibilities between the state and the family.[1] In the public discourse the provision of care services is a cornerstone in the welfare system, and care work is no longer seen as a 'natural' job for women.

Nowadays Nordic people have internalized a picture of themselves as modern citizens in women-friendly societies. Esping-Andersen (2009) argues that there has been a revolution in women's lives and work roles. This has provoked fundamental changes in how people make decisions and behave in relation to marriage, education, parenting and employment. But the revolution is still incomplete because it has been led by well-educated middle-class women, and according to Esping-Andersen the quest for gender equality tends to produce social inequality as long as it is a middle-class affair. He understands new stratification patterns and the acceptance of greater social inequalities between well-paid, highly-educated parents and low-paid, low-educated parents as an outcome of well-educated women's struggle to be fully integrated in the labour market. He primarily deals with the intersection between national welfare states and gender, and ignores the significant role migration plays in these differentiation processes. Here we argue that social inequalities emerge as a combination of new social and political meanings attached to gender equality and female-dominated international migration patterns.

An experienced lack of gender equality among the middle classes has become an important drive in the increased demand for affordable care services. Studies of global care chains and new intersections of welfare, gender and migration reveal new complexities in work/care reconciliation policies. Men's reluctant participation in the gender-equality project plays a central role in the social distribution of local care deficits. 'Daddy leave', or the extended parental welfare benefits to parents with newborn babies, is designed to increase male participation in families' care work; it is a strategic state intervention intended to engineer a greater degree of gender equality in household work. In reality, women's full-time work has increased without much increase in men's participation in housework. The persisting unequal distribution of care and housework creates a cultural lag that opens for the outsourcing of care services and domestic duties to the global market. Contemporary welfare states do not only produce 'politics against markets' (Esping-Andersen 1985). Social-democratic welfare states also increasingly operate as actors in global markets to deal with national gender-equality problems expressed as care deficits in public and private contexts.

As the welfare states have expanded, the provision of services has become more costly. One strategy to keep costs down has been to hire migrant workers as a part of a cost-minimization strategy. The ageing population and increased fertility rates have been important as a driving force in developments of intersecting welfare and migration politics. How to combine welfare, gender, and migration policy in line with social-democratic visions of justice, social equality and women's emancipation is a major challenge.

Many professional middle-class women, in Scandinavia as in many other parts of Europe, have difficulties combining flexible working hours with the fixed opening hours of public child-care. Even if many young spouses and partners participate in care and housework, there are an increasing number of women who prefer and need different solutions. The au-pair programme makes the 'outsourcing' of housework and child-care to markets possible because it gives access to low-paid migrant care workers. The programme was originally meant to promote cultural exchange between countries, but has become an immigration channel that facilitates the legal incorporation of 'students' as care workers. While domestic work is constructed in the programme as a basis for entry in the 'labour' migration, it remains partly unprotected by labour law and offers only restricted access to citizenship rights.

In eldercare the gap between supply and demand for services has led to a more rational and effective organization of care work. The industrialized production of care services has led to an emotional cooling off in care work, and staff problems in nursing homes and services to the homebound elderly are seen as arising from new demands for more cost-effective care. Adult daughters and sons largely depend on the supply of public eldercare services when elderly parents need daily help and support. Family members of both genders and different generations now increasingly rely on skilled and unskilled migrant care workers to deal with the reconciling of work and eldercare. In Norway today, every third care worker in public eldercare in Oslo comes from a non-Western country (Høst & Homme 2009).

Public and private care work

Migrant women such as au pairs, skilled and unskilled care workers in the public sector, legal and illegal cleaners, nannies and housemaids, and mail-order brides have made the provision of care services more diverse. Migration theorists have pointed to the fact that domestic care work is 'not just another labour market'; it is work marked by characteristics such as intimacy, privacy and femininity, and the relationship between employer and employee is highly emotional and personalized (Lutz 2008). The work is performed in private homes and families, and is embedded in different cultures of care.

In Scandinavia, however, public child-care and extended parental leave still keeps the demand for domestic workers low. Sweden, for instance, has fewer migrant domestic workers than Spain and Britain because of its public commitment to child-care (Williams & Gavanas 2008). Even if public child-care services are more or less available to everyone, an increasing number of families in Norway and Denmark need additional help and prefer to hire an au pair (see Stenum and Bikova in this volume). In Nordic families, public child-care has a hegemonic position because of its reputation as being professional and having educative qualities. When families hire migrant care workers, it is not primarily the care that is outsourced, but gendered housework such as cleaning and cooking.

Not so many years ago migration for care work evoked ideas of bourgeois families with a servant class. The image was often accompanied by a perception of an old-fashioned pre-industrial society. Now we face a new servant class that is related to an increasingly female-dominated international migration, and the new 'migrant-in-the-family' model is an expression of how problems in Nordic gender-equality politics can contribute to new social inequalities.

In her analysis of migration and domestic work in Europe, Lutz (2008) presents an intersectional perspective consisting of three different regimes at the heart of migrant domestic work. Firstly, she writes, *'gender regimes* in which the household and care work organization can be seen as the expression of a specifically gendered cultural script. Secondly, *care regimes* as part of the welfare regime, concerning a multitude of state regulations according to which the responsibility for the wellbeing of national citizens is distributed between the state, the family and the market. Thirdly, *migration regimes,* which for various reasons either promote or discourage the employment of migrant domestic workers' (Lutz 2008, 2). She uses the term 'regime' as it is defined by Esping-Andersen (1990) – the organization and the corresponding cultural codes of social policy and social practice in which the relationship between social actors (state, labour market, and family) is articulated and negotiated.

Fiona Williams (2007) presents another theoretical approach to understanding the employment of migrant women in home-based care work in Europe and how global care chains are related to this practice. She thinks that the employment of migrant women is in some countries a significant strategy in work–care reconciliation policies. But policies make few references to the boundaries of the welfare state, even if child-care now exists in a global market and is part of a transnational movement of care labour and capital. The transnational political economy of care is based on (*i*) the fact that nation-states are caught up and operate in a situation of unequal geopolitical interdependence, and (*ii*) the unrecognized centrality of care policies to the quality of life in all countries. She proposes that an analysis of these dimensions could be enhanced by new works on global justice and the ethics of care. Hanne Marlene Dahl and Marlene Spanger (in this volume) consider some of the complexities of global social policy issues and discuss how sex workers in Denmark might have a different ethics of care than expected.

Both Lutz's (2008) and Williams's (2007) perspectives stress the role of the state in global transformation processes. While Lutz in particular claims that studies of care and gender regimes have to be more closely connected to a broader understanding of the migration regime, Williams calls for a broader understanding of the welfare states in the new transnational economies of care. Minna Zechner (in this volume) looks into how migration regimes and the welfare state have determined the rules for immigration and subsequent return.

Both authors have developed their analyses based on studies of domestic child-care services. Public care and institutional spaces that are of great importance in the Nordic provision of care, such as kindergartens, public after-school programmes, nursing homes and services to the homebound elderly and families in need of extra support, are given less attention. However, their perspectives can be of relevance for explorations of public care work. This now increasingly operates in the intersections between gender, migration and welfare policy. While nannies, maids and au pairs find jobs in families with small children, skilled and unskilled care workers for the sick and elderly are employed in publicly regulated workplaces. Unlike domestic workers, professional nurses and other care workers in welfare institutions have access to social citizenship and their own trade unions, and they are protected by labour laws. Their problems are related to discriminatory practices, differences in the acceptance of qualifications, and gender and ethnic hierarchies in welfare institutions. Lise Widding Isaksen (in this volume) shows how welfare states recruit nurses internationally and become a part of the new transnational economies of care.

Contextualizing care and migration

Care and migration are nothing new. In earlier historical periods welfare was provided in households by migrant domestic workers. However, migration for care work in Scandinavia has changed from being an internal matter to becoming one of international migration. In general the period from 1880 to 1920 was in Europe a time when it was considered 'normal' among urban middle and upper classes to have a maid (Sarti 2008). In Denmark paid domestic work was then a 'normal' job for a young woman (Vammen 1987). In Sweden rural women were considered suitable maids because of their subservience (Moberg 1978). Historical studies of domestic workers in this period show that they mainly migrated from rural to urban areas. They were live-in workers in the employers' households: they worked long hours and many had to sleep with the children of the family. They were socially invisible and it was difficult for them to develop a political voice, such as obtaining representation in the trade unions. However, in contrast to present-day domestic workers such as au pairs, they were at least allowed to join their own union and obtain a modicum of bargaining power. Moreover, they were a part of the general labour force and had access to citizenship rights.

Today, au pairs work as caregivers but are not legally constructed as workers (see Calleman in this volume). In public discourse there is currently a struggle over the definition of power between the political authorities and public opinion. Politicians claim that au pairs are 'students' participating in a cultural exchange programme. Among the public, as it is expressed in the media, the common opinion is that au pairs work as low-paid housemaids (Stenum 2010). In the Nordic countries, as elsewhere in Europe, the new global servants are well-educated, and when at home might well have the same middle-class status as their employers (Stenum 2010). These characteristics were not present in previous patterns of migration for care work either in Europe (Lutz 2008) or in the Nordic regions.

Domestic workers can also be skilled care workers employed by the national health services. In the Swedish nation-building process after the Second World War, a home-help programme was implemented to create social equality among families in need of support (see Carlsson in this volume). The normal family model in the 1950s and 1960s was the male breadwinner family. When housewives fell ill or for other reasons were unable to take proper care of their family, the care work could be done by a publicly employed care worker. These care workers had their own trade unions, education systems and career opportunities. Domestic work was an important political issue, but while it was related to political visions of social equality and justice, it was less so to gender equality and work–care reconciliation policies.

In 2007 new legislation introduced a tax deduction for private households' domestic services. In order to get the tax credit, a company is supposed to provide the service to a house-owner. Companies from other countries are included; employees who are citizens in other countries can work legally in Sweden, but in general they work under very different conditions than Swedish workers. Even if the public discourse stresses the political intention to turn illegal cleaning into legal work, and as such to create greater social equality between groups of workers, it is also related to a shift in the meaning of gender equality. Politicians openly state that paying for cleaning services will promote women's professional careers and create more gender equality in the labour market (see Platzer in this volume).

The purchase of cleaning services can also be related to subjectively internalized ideas of gender equality. As Tove Fjell (in this volume) shows, people buy cleaning services as part of a construction of a gender-equality image. Through the 'outsourcing' of gender-equality conflicts, families can pretend to have realized a gender-equality culture. Couples combine gender-equality ideals with traditional divisions of labour and exaggerate men's contribution to the housework. Many men prefer to hire cleaners to do their part of the housework.

For trade unions, illegal cleaners represent a political challenge. Trade unions have to develop new meanings of international solidarity (see Lise Lotte Hansen in this volume) and ensure their strategies include the invisible groups of immigrant workers such as au pairs and illegal cleaners. Lack of citizenship among migrant workers is an important democratic issue.

The chapters in this book show that immigrant women are actively involved in the making of their own lives. They receive support from social movements even if it still is on a small scale. In many other countries trade unions have largely ignored the living and working conditions of migrant domestic workers and illegal cleaners. It is to be hoped that the Nordic trade unions' interest in the unacceptable working conditions of many migrant care workers can contribute to putting these issues higher on the public agenda. As the chapters in this book show, taking the Nordic welfare states as a case-study reveals how social-democratic ideals such as gender equality, social equality and international solidarity have become related to and challenged by international migration and a global economy of care.

In 2010, the International Labour Organization arranged an international conference on 'Decent Work for Domestic Workers' in Geneva. The intention was to produce an international convention to support the legal regulation of domestic work on the national level. Nordic trade unions negotiated to get au pairs included in the definition of domestic work. Professional nurses' trade unions are already internationally organized and have given priority to developing a political strategy to deal with the ethics of international nurse recruitment.

The European Union has recently initiated (in 2010) a research project to explore how member states use au pairs. It is clear that a European discussion on the role and status of au pairs needs to be pursued in many institutional contexts and at many levels. Domestic and public care work have become global issues, and many insightful studies will be needed to explore the complexities of this global phenomenon in the future.

Notes

1 By 'Nordic countries' and 'Scandinavia' we mean Norway, Sweden, Finland and Denmark. Although Iceland is also a Nordic country, for a variety of reasons it could not be included in our project.

References

Ehrenreich, Barbara & Hochschild, Arlie R. (2002), *Global Women. Nannies, Maids, and Sex Workers in the New Economy* (New York: Metropolitan Books).

Esping-Andersen, Gøsta (1985), *Politics Against Markets. The Social Democratic Road to Power* (New Jersey: Princeton University Press).

Esping-Andersen, Gøsta (1990), *The Three Worlds of Welfare Capitalism* (London: Polity Press).

Esping-Andersen, Gøsta (2009), *The Incomplete Revolution: Adapting to Women's New Roles* (Cambridge: Polity Press).

Hochschild, Arlie R. (2001), 'Global Care Chains and Emotional Surplus Value' in A. Giddens & W. Hutton (eds.), *On The Edge. Living with Global Capitalism* (London: Vintage).

Høst, Håkon & Homme, Anne (2009), 'Hvem pleier de gamle i Oslo?' [Who cares for the elderly in Oslo?] (Report; Bergen: Rokkan Research Centre).

Lutz, Helma (ed.) (2008), *Migration and Domestic Care Work. A European Perspective on a Global Theme* (Hampshire & Burlington: Ashgate).

Moberg, Kerstin (1978), *Från tjenstehjon til hembitrede. En kvinnlig lågtlønegrupp I den fackliga kampen 1903 – 1946* (Uppsala: Historiska Institutionen, Uppsala University).

Øien, Cecilie (2009), 'On Equal terms? An Evaluation of the Norwegian Au Pair Scheme' (Fafo report 2009:29; Oslo).

Parreñas, Rachel (2001), *Servants of Globalization. Women, Migration and Domestic Work* (Stanford: Stanford University Press).

Stenum, Helle (2010), 'Fortidens tjenestepiger og nutidens Au Pairs? Har de noget til felles?' (Victorian servants and au pairs – Do they have something in common?), *Arbejderhistorie* 2.

Williams, Fiona (2007), 'How do we theorise the employment of migrant women in home-based care work in European welfare states?' Paper presented at RC19 Conference, University of Florence, 6–8 September.

Williams, Fiona & Gavanas, Anna (2008), 'The Intersection of Childcare Regimes and Migration Regimes: A Three Country Study,' in H. Lutz, (ed.), *Migration and Domestic Work. A European Perspective on a Global Theme* (Hampshire & Burlington: Ashgate).

I
DOMESTIC WORK
AND IMAGES OF EQUALITY

CHAPTER 2

Au-pair migration and new inequalities

The transnational production of corruption

Helle Stenum

Contemporary au-pair arrangements in Denmark and Norway, which largely involve Filipina women, entail a range of ambiguities and contradictions in the transnational and national space in which au-pair migrants are organized and positioned. Ambiguities, contradictions and discomforts are part of the social construct that is the au-pair system – some of these phenomena are visible and others less visible.

Au-pair migration is managed and regulated migration, but migration management is not only about nation-states claiming their sovereign right to admit or refuse non-citizens at their borders. Migration management, especially migration from economically poor to economically rich countries, also operates in transnational chains. The legalizing and illegalizing of different types of migration and migrant statuses are important tools in governing the non-citizen population and in separating desired from unwanted migrants.

Based on an empirical study of the lived experience of Filipina live-in domestic workers who have formal status as au pairs, this chapter analyses au-pair migration from the Philippines to Denmark in the light of the legality and illegality produced by the nation-states involved in the shape of migration management regulations, and the position of the au pairs reflected in political and media discourse.

The Danish context

Danish estate agents advertising exclusive homes have found a new way to describe unused basement space: an 'au-pair room'. In one advertisement the first few lines of the description of a € 2 million (DKK 15 million) house in Copenhagen run as follows: 'Five-storey townhouse, 362 m², dining area in high-ceilinged cellar and door to the garden, au-pair girl bedroom, bathroom.'[1] In another, the description of a € 0.9 million (DKK 6 million) house notes that 'In the basement there is a lot of space for teenagers, the au-pair girl or guests from abroad.'

These advertisements reflect two new trends in modern Danish life. Firstly, it is increasingly common to find an au-pair living with middle- and upper-class families, as the popular media coverage of middle-class lifestyles shows. Secondly, au pairs are relegated to the basement, reflecting their upstairs–downstairs position as not part of the family, but rather as someone who serves or helps the family from a subordinate position, quite literally beneath them in the physical space of the basement area.[2]

Formally, Danish regulations are based on the Council of Europe's European Agreement on 'au pair' Placement (Strasbourg, 24 November 1969), which states that an au pair is not an employee but a private person taking part in a cultural exchange. The concept of au pairing is highly gendered, as it is historically rooted in a mixture of domestic work, family control and cultural education.

Au-pairing is a managed migration system – one that has undergone a largely unremarked change in Scandinavia in recent years. In the past decade, Denmark has experienced a remarkable increase in the number of au pairs.[3] The statistics show that in 2007 2,205 individuals were granted residence permits as au pairs, of whom 1,509 came from the Philippines, 105 from the Ukraine, 80 from Russia, 49 from Brazil, 34 from Thailand and 429 from other countries; in 2008, 2,939 individuals were granted au-pair permits, of whom 2,165 were from the Philippines, 104 from the Ukraine, 75 from Russia, 57 from Brazil, 40 from Thailand, and 498 from other countries.[4] The increase in the number of Filipina au pairs in Denmark in the same decade has been remarkable: in 1999 only

Table 1: Au-pair residence permits issued in Denmark, 1996–2008.

	1996	1997	1998	1999	2000	2001	2002	2003	2004	2005	2006	2007	2008
Filipinas				21	45	83	157	246	490	612	979	1509	2165
All au pairs	318	438	478	528	865	1018	1156	1233	1500	1471	1793	2205	2939
Filipinas %				4	5	8	14	20	33	42	55	68	73

Source: Danish Immigration Service 2009.

Table 2: Au-pair residence permits issued in Norway, 1996–2007.

	1996	1997	1998	1999	2000	2001	2002	2003	2004	2005	2006	2007
Filipinas	77	88	74	39	38	54	69	138	235	423	587	1103
All au pairs	202	261	293	382	277	666	743	948	1019	1209	1243	1760
Filipinas %	38	34	25	10	14	8	9	15	23	35	47	63

Source: UDI 2008.

21 residence permits for au pairs were issued to Filipinas; by 2007 the figure was 1,509 out of a total of 2,205, or 68 per cent; while in 2008 fully 2,165 of a total of 2,939 (73 per cent) were from the Philippines.[5] Although some male au pairs came to Denmark, the vast majority were female.

Norway seems to have seen a parallel development, with a significant increase from 2006 to 2007. In a report from 2009 (Øien 2009) the number of residence permits is higher than the figures provided to me by the Norwegian Directorate of Immigration in 2008, possibly because of the difference between the number of identified persons and the number of residence permits. Moreover, according to Øien (ibid.), in 2008 a total of 2,090 Filipinas were granted au-pair residence permits in Norway.

In Denmark, 'migration management' in the past decade has focused on refusing entry to non-white, non-Western, Muslim, low-skilled immigrants by tightening the requirements for asylum permits and family unification regulations, by introducing a strictly selective labour immigration policy, and by adding new stipulations for obtaining permanent residence status and Danish citizenship. Several parliamentary election campaigns have revolved around the 'toughness' of anti-immigration policy. In the latest campaign, in November 2007, a key theme was fear of 'the influx of refugees' because of a limited proposal by the left-wing opposition parties to allow asylum seekers to work while awaiting a decision on their applications. In this political climate it would seem something of a paradox that Filipina immigration to Denmark has increased in the same period, along with a slight increase in the number of family unifications (marriage).[6] Meanwhile, at the same time as the tightening of migration legislation, middle- and upper-class families in Denmark experienced a very prosperous period, with rising home equity values, increasing salaries, low inflation, cheap loans and mortgages, and increasing consumption (AE, 2008).

The idea of the welfare state and the egalitarian society, despite increasing inequality, is still a central ideal of the nation.[7] Gender equality, while often labelled a 'Danish value' – especially when linked to immigration issues – is assumed to be a reality in Denmark. Very often men with immigrant backgrounds are singled out as one of the few problems left to be dealt with.[8] Responding to repeated criticism from the EU Commission for not meeting the requirements of the EU Gender Equality Directives, the minister for equality, Inger Støjberg, recently stated: 'Yes, by and large I think we have gender equality in Denmark, but there is one area lagging far behind, and that is immigrant women.'[9] However, academic research and the Danish government's own report on gender equality (SFI 2004) all conclude that gender equality has not been achieved in Denmark.[10] Furthermore, the Danish labour market is heavily gender divided. In the World Economic Forum's Gender Gap Index for 2007 (World Economic Forum 2007), Denmark ranked eighth, well behind the other Nordic countries (Sweden, Norway, Finland and Iceland ranked first, second, third, and fourth respectively). More specifically relevant to the study of au-pairing is the general increase in domestic work. Hence, in 1987, 281 minutes per day were spent on domestic work, with women accounting for 65 per cent of this time. By 2001, the amount of daily domestic work had increased to 356 minutes, with women carrying out 59 per cent of this work (SFI 2002, 53).

Ethnic equality is a difficult subject in Denmark. Legislation has been tightened to live up to the EU equality directive of 2002, but only as a minimum solution. The Danish government has been repeatedly criticized by international institutions and organizations for ethnic discrimination and ethnic inequality.

The Philippine context

The Philippines has more than 25 years' experience of comprehensive migration management: the country has systematically been exporting labour to North America, the Middle East, Europe and Southeast Asia. In 2001, Filipinas abroad sent home more than US$6 billion via formal channels, equivalent to 8.4 per cent of the Philippine GDP (O'Neil 2004), and in 2005 remittances increased 25 per cent over those in 2004 to more US$10 billion (POEA 2005). The Philippines has turned itself into a 'labor-brokering nation' (Ong 2006, 199), dependent on remittances, and promoting 'the great Filipina worker' who is 'born with a natural ability to adapt to many cultures' (government statement, quoted in Ong 2006, 200). Filipinas are especially promoted as flexible, docile workers. In 2004, some 8 million Philippine citizens were working abroad. Of these, 3.2 million were permanent residents abroad, 3.6 million were temporary workers, and 1.2 million were irregular residents (O'Neil 2004). The government tries to manage and keep track of irregular migrants as well as regular migrants.

The regulated temporary labour migration is organized through the Philippines Overseas Employment Administration (POEA). This government agency provides labour directly to foreign employers, agencies and governments.[11] When migrating via official channels, migrants obtain a number of benefits, such as pre-migration training, life insurance, pension plans, and medical insurance. The government also tries to manage irregular migration by prohibiting its citizens from overstaying visas and keeping a list of workers banned from future contracts. A considerable number of female migrants are hired for household jobs. Some of these migrant workers are on formal contracts, but probably a large number migrate irregularly.

The fact that a significant part of the Philippine population is working abroad naturally affects the structure and conditions of family life. Due to the feminization of migration, many Filipina transnational families subsist with the help of a mother who works abroad and sends money home. Many Philippine migrants work as domestic workers, taking care of children and the elderly in affluent families while leaving their own children and family behind. But as Parreñas (2002, 49) notes, this care deficit is assigned to women: 'While a great number of children with migrant fathers receive full-time care from stay-at-home mothers, those with migrant mothers do not receive the same amount of care'. The Philippines is thus exporting care and is dependent on remittances from migrant care workers. The situation has been characterized as a veritable 'care crisis'.

In the World Economic Forum's Gender Gap Index, the Philippines is ranked sixth, and there are significant parallels with the situation in Denmark, where women are still expected to take the prime responsibility in the family while also being expected to take an active part in the labour market and contribute to the economic support of the family. According to Parreñas (2008, 23), laws in the

Philippines maintain 'the gender ideology of women's domesticity even as the economy promotes the labour market participation'. Meanwhile, in 1996, the Philippine government ratified the UN Convention on the Protection of the Rights of All Migrant Workers and Members of Their Families.[12]

National and transnational spaces of migration and migrant residency

According to one school of thought among social scientists (for example, Wimmer & Glick-Schiller 2002; and Beck 2006), it is necessary to break with the 'methodological nationalism' that has been so influential in the social sciences since the birth of the nation-state. Migration studies have often been linked with this nation-state perspective, transforming migration studies into knowledge production in the service of the state and overlapping with the perspective of the nation-state (De Genova 2005; Goldberg 2002). Studying the migration process as lived experience is one way of achieving a more transnational perspective on human mobility and residency. However, state management of migration must be analysed as both a national and a transnational process. As Nina Glick-Schiller (2007, 65) observes:

> We need to study and popularize concepts of the migration process that is part of global forces experienced by people who move and who do not move. This means migration scholars must enter into public debate about social cohesion by identifying the forces of globalization that are restructuring lives of migrants and non-migrants alike and speaking of the common struggle of most of the people of the world for social and economic justice and equality.

Just as chain migration is a well-known concept of transnationalized social mobility, the reach of government now extends to chains of national and transnationalized human mobility and residence, connected in chains of (migration) management. A key element in nation-state migration management is the ability to legalize and illegalize certain types of migration. Migration regulations are not the only determining conditions of migration, however: family policy, welfare arrangements, labour market structure, and policies in sending, transit and receiving countries all have an impact. All these elements form the space of migration.

To simplify the transnational scope of au-pair migration, we reduce it here to the relationship between Denmark and the Philippines – the analytical focus of this paper. This perspective establishes the framework for the co-production of migrant legality and illegality. However, the perspective of analysing the transnationalized control of au-pair migration could be widened to include other facets of government – for example, other nation-states that 'export' au-pair migrants, and other nation-states that 'import' au-pair migrants, or to regionalized government, such as the EU or the Council of Europe.

The position of Filipina au-pair migrants is brought home in Figure 1 (p. 31), which brings together the national and transnational spaces of migration. Au pairs are dependent on social structures and practices linked to the nation-state: (*i*) migration regulations in sending and receiving countries, viz. the conditions that prompt emigration (the Philippines) and immigration (Denmark); (*ii*) labour market regulations and conditions in sending and receiving countries, such as the employment situation, employee rights, working conditions etc.; and (*iii*) welfare and family policy in the two countries, and more specifically whether there is a care deficit – and thus a market – for au pairs or domestic workers (Denmark), and whether the care deficit is addressed privately or publicly (the Philippines). Likewise, the migrants' social position and transnational mobility are linked to social relations and networks of family, kinship, au-pair agencies, host families in the receiving countries, and care of the au pairs' own children in their home communities. In both sending and receiving countries there are specific gender and ethnic hierarchies that permeate formal regulations, policies and social practice.

In sum, au pairs are often placed within a transnational social reality, which, while it can be equally coherent and non-coherent, still often reflects the societal spaces and social relationships that are framed by nation-states and local communities.

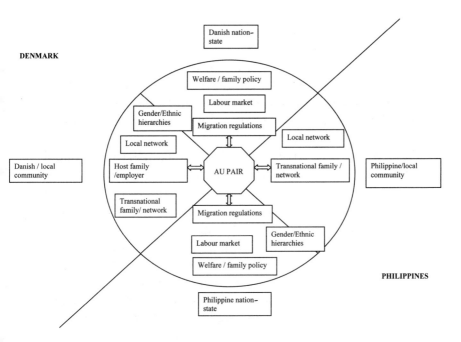

Au pairing as a system

The Philippines: illegalizing emigration

In 1998, the Philippine government banned Filipina migrant workers from being employed through the services of the so-called au-pair programme in Europe.[13] The media had reported on cases in Europe of exploitation, excessive working hours, abuse, discrimination and prostitution, and the government chose to react by reducing 'domestic insecurities' (Robyn 2004) in order to prevent its young people from migrating as au pairs.[14]

The Philippine embassy in the Netherlands stated in 1999 that 'the au pair, as far as Filipinas are concerned, has been understood to mean domestic helper – not a cultural exchange visitor as originally envisaged by the 1969 agreement' (Anderson 2000, 25). The implications for Filipinas who choose to migrate as au pairs to Europe are that they are not covered by the POEA and thus have migrated illegally. Such 'illegal emigrants' cannot appeal to their embassies abroad in cases of abuse without risking being placed on the list of workers banned from migration through the POEA. If they outstay their permits or for other reasons are deported from Europe to the Philippines, they risk facing difficulties in obtaining new travel documents from the Philippine authorities.

In my research on au-pair life primarily among Filipina migrant workers in Denmark (Stenum 2008),[15] they were quite aware of their situation as 'illegal emigrants'. One of my informants, Evelyn, expressed the situation in the following way:

> Because in the Philippines ... This programme it really depends ... the Philippine government doesn't allow its citizens to go out as au pairs. Except for overseas workers ... Yes, it's a lot of money, because au pairs also ... it's also bad because [she] doesn't have papers from the POEA – the Philippines Overseas Workers, because you should also apply or else you can't go out of the country ... So instead of not leaving the Philippines, most people rather need money to get out. Because it is also difficult to get a visa, and it's also difficult to travel on a tourist visa if you don't have much money. And if you need help, there's nothing to be done about it.

In spite of the ban and the Philippine government's stated concern about the abuse of Filipina au pairs, it is an ambiguous agenda. The Philippine state is aware of the au-pair traffic to Scandinavia, and in reality accepts it, if only for the sake of the remittances sent home by labour migrants, regardless of their status.

In order to travel from the Philippines to Denmark or Norway as an au pair, a Filipina needs proper travel documents. Indeed, the border in fact begins at the airport of embarkation, with border controls in Europe being enforced by air carriers under the threat of possible sanctions. Airline companies and immigration officials often charge the au pairs going to Denmark and Norway an extra sum of money for overlooking the fact that the women are travelling on au-pair visas and without the proper POEA certificates. The bribery payments are apparently highly systematic,[16] even though the specific amounts vary. In my research I found a wide range of sums, ranging from ₱8,000 (€ 122) up to ₱80,000 (€ 1,221), depending on the individuals' contacts and networks in the state administration. The average bribe paid to border officials in order to emigrate for work as an au pair was ₱15,000–25,000 (€ 228–389).

Both the regulations on illegal emigration per se and their actual enforcement create burdens and extra expenses for such migrants, while also generating corrupt practices among Philippine officials. Financing the bribe is often a problem for au pairs coming to Denmark, especially in view of the modest minimum 'pocket money', DKK 2,500 (€ 335), that they are likely to receive.[17] All of my au-pair informants travelling from the Philippines had paid an exit bribe, although for some their host family covered their expenses prior to departure. (Not that this is self-evident. One host family told me that they had sent their au pair to Manila for the Christmas holidays when they discovered that she had a child in the Philippines. They had paid her airfare, but had not realized that the exit bribe was just as much part of the travel costs – they knew nothing about the ban.) Other au pairs had borrowed the money and had to pay back the loan out of their 'pocket money'. The bribe amounts to the individual's investment in au-pairing.

An obvious consequence of living as an illegal emigrant is the knowledge that no support will be forthcoming from the embassy in cases of abuse or detention, or indeed any other problem. In cases where they overstay their residence permits, or where they are faced by criminality, sickness, and death, there is in principle no assistance offered by the Philippine state. Furthermore, the Filipina migrants' ability to complain about their situation or demand improvements in their conditions is greatly inhibited by their 'irregular' emigrant status. Amy explains her situation in this way: 'because we came over and that is something that they don't recognize, so I don't know if the Philippine embassy can help us because we're leaving the country illegally and they don't accept it.'

The Nordic co-production of corruption and illegality

The Philippine ban on au-pair migration to Europe is not made much of in Denmark. It is certainly not a topic of public discussion: while all the Filipina au pairs I interviewed were clearly aware of the ban, none of the host families I interviewed knew about it. Sweden and Finland have chosen to respect the ban and do not grant residence permits to Filipina au pairs; a regulation clearly stated in the guidelines on their immigration websites.[18] This is a kind of migration management chain in which emigration restrictions or illegalized emigration in one ('sending') nation-state produce immigration restrictions or illegalize immigration in another ('receiving') nation-state directed specifically at nationals of the sending country.

The Netherlands (Oosterbek-Latoza 2007) permits Filipina au pairs, while Germany apparently does not. In Norway, the authorities have at least discussed the issue: in a report published after a media debate on fair conditions for au pairs there, the Norwegian Directorate of Immigration (UDI) concludes that as regards Filipina au pairs, the area needs to be more regulated. Furthermore, the UDI states that

> it could be desirable for the group to be excluded until the outward journey situation is addressed in domestic legislation. This would be in line with what other countries do, for example Sweden, which does not grant permits to Philippine au pairs because this is held to be contrary to the laws of their home country. However, it has been decided to continue with the previous arrangement. (UDI 2006)

The Philippine state, by banning au-pair migration to Europe, compels potential emigrants to use illicit or illegal methods to emigrate. Denmark, Norway and the Netherlands, by ignoring the ban and offering Filipinas au-pair visas, effectively offer an incentive for Filipina au-pair migrants to obtain visas by corrupt means. The typical migration career is that of an individual who leaves their country of origin legally, but enters illegally; the situation in Denmark is the reverse, for Filipinas enter the country legally, but have left the Philippines illegally – legal entry, illegal exit.

Illegalized emigration (by the sending state, the Philippines) is here linked to legalized immigration (by the receiving states, Denmark and Norway) in a transnational space, with the upshot that corrupt practices are sustained and a market for private care and cleaning is generated. Corruption and an irregular market thus make up the framework for the rights, living conditions and migration circumstances of Filipina au-pair migrants, with all the limitations and personal insecurities that entails.

In the transnationalized social space, host families hire au pairs in the Philippines. This is a precondition for the au pair managing to obtain a residence permit in Denmark or Norway. Officials at the Norwegian Embassy in Manila issue residence permits in full knowledge of the necessary bribes to travel out of the Philippines. Private networks, agents or money-lenders lend the au pairs the money to pay the bribe, and immigration officers and officials at the airport are paid by the au pairs. Once in Denmark and Norway, the au pairs then start to pay off their debt – forced on them by the transnationalized production of corruption – and keep it a secret from the host family because of the illegality of corruption and their experiences as illegal emigrants.

States as well as individuals take part in this transnationalized social process of corruption. The 'import' of Filipina au pairs to Denmark has increased significantly since the ban was implemented, despite the severe tightening on non-EU immigration to Denmark in general. In addition, both the total number and the proportion of Filipinas are larger in Denmark than Norway and the Netherlands. In Denmark, the inconsistency in all this seems to be mainly unproblematic, managed as it is through the questionable construct of au-pair work being defined as a 'cultural exchange' rather than as employment. In a response to parliament in 2008, the Danish minister for immigration stated that the ministry

> is aware that Philippine citizens are denied departure from the Philippines, when it is found at the border control, that the citizen concerned is going to work as an au pair abroad. ... The background for these rules ... is to protect Philippine citizens and to ensure the best possible working conditions. ... I find that the concerns of the Government of the Philippines are dealt with according to the parliamentary decision of 28 March 2007, by which a period of suspension for abusive host families was introduced.[19]

The Danish state – illegalizing employment

In light of Danish immigration policy and discourse, the Filipina au pair might actually be the ideal migrant from the global South: temporary, highly skilled,[20] poorly paid, and with limited rights, a Christian and an English speaker, and, thanks to their illegality and cultural representations, reduced to a state of social invisibility.

Au-pairing is officially about cultural exchange.[21] The rules formulated by the Danish immigration authorities tie each residence permit to a specific family. Domestic work is rephrased as household 'chores'. Au-pairing is constructed as something other than 'employment', as not-employment. In an explanatory text that comes with the family au-pair contract, it is stated that 'It should be noted that an au pair in not an inexpensive maid. The participation of the au pair in the family household is not the type of work which requires a work permit.' Yet if one compares the Danish and the Norwegian au-pair contracts with the 'Employment Contract for a Domestic Helper Recruited from outside Hong Kong'(Human Rights Watch (2005:115) – Hong Kong being a major destination for migrant domestic workers – there are striking similarities in the way in which immigration and domestic work are linked: in conditions for live-in staff, duration, minimum wages, the task specifications, and penalties for employers and domestic helpers alike. The main difference between the Hong Kong version and the Scandinavian is the lack of maximum working hours in the Hong Kong version.

The Danish state has defined domestic work as non-work and non-employment. At the same time, another kind of (domestic) work is defined as 'illegal work' and highlighted on the Immigration website in the guideline sections for au pairs:

> Consequences of illegal work: If you work illegally in Denmark, you risk deportation, and may be banned from re-entering the country again for a set period of time (usually one year). If you are an EU citizen, however, you cannot be deported for working illegally in Denmark. You also risk a fine or imprisonment, as does your employer.[22]

The link between illegalized work and deportation of non-EU citizens is clearly expressed. The Danish government website aimed at au pairs defines 'illegal work' as 'working for the host family before being granted a residence permit, working more than 30 hours a week for the host family and any kind of work for others than the host family.'[23]

Living in migrant illegality

There are two main dimensions in migrant illegality, which we can call 'residence illegality' and 'employment illegality'. When it comes to employment the situation for au-pair migrants is unambiguous: it is illegal to exceed working hours, to work outside the family, or to work without reporting to the tax authorities. In my findings, the au pairs are typically the breadwinners for their families back home; they often have some kind of education and often become au pairs because of an unexpected turn of events with economic consequences (becoming a single parent, a death or illness in the family, unemployment, bankruptcy in the family, and so on). They are often interested in earning additional income over and above their au-pair allowance, and are thus are willing to work as domestic help – sometimes low-paid, but often well-paid – for other families than their host family. Around half the au pairs I interviewed had broken the immigration rules on overtime and working outside the home, while others had sought out extra jobs but were either prohibited by their employers or had not (yet) been able to find extra work.

The comparison between the conditions and wages for legal and illegal work reveals the paradoxical situation in which au-pairs in Denmark find themselves. Normally, illegalized work is associated with low pay and hard working conditions, but in the case of the au pairs who work 'extra' in the informal household economy, there seems to be a tendency to have better hourly wages and occasionally better working conditions for illegal work than for legal work. The net hourly wage for cleaning in affluent homes is often close to or above the minimum wage, whereas a 30-hour week at DKK 2,500 (€ 335) a month gives an hourly wage that falls well below any regulated hourly wage on the open labour market.[24]

Being defined as not-worker makes it difficult to organize, complain, contact labour unions, or go public with stories of abuse, so this illegalizing of work maintains the fragile discursive framework around the au-pair arrangement as a 'cultural exchange', leaving the 'working au pair' very vulnerable. The vulnerability lies in the fact that by working illegally the au pair can lose her residence permit, and thereby her ability to provide for her family, if she were to publicly complain about her working conditions.

Liberating the white, middle-class woman

There are different perspectives on the au-pair system in the political discourse, and different rationalizations, but one key construct in recent years that might help explain the extraordinary increase in au pairs – and Philippine au pairs in particular – despite Denmark's generally restrictive immigration policies, could be the willingness with which the notion of domestic help has been pressed into the service of the liberation of white middle-class women from domestic drudgery. In a country that imagines itself to be egalitarian, non-colonial,[25] endowed with gender equality, non-racist, socially equal, democratic and advanced, it seems reasonable to ask why so many families can bring themselves to employ migrant, live-in domestic workers under a state regulation that allows them as the host family to pay DKK 2,500 a month, or approximately one-fourth of the comparable minimum wage. How is this possible?

Slight, if coherent, the political discourse on domestic workers construed as au pairs was illustrated very clearly in a newspaper interview with the Danish minister of family affairs, Carina Christensen, in March 2007.[26] This interview also illustrates the elements of a powerful discourse that serves to support the fragile au-pair concept: white (middle-class) gender equality and the biological reproduction of the nation (Yuval-Davis 1997).

> C. C.: There are too many expectations placed on families these days. Many have the image of the perfect mother, who bakes bread rolls and always deals with everything. Why isn't it OK to hire an au pair? Or to a greater extent let the husband take over and be responsible for a larger share of the household?

Interviewer: But you are saying that Mum and Dad should relax more? What is it that they should stop doing?

C. C.: You could for instance buy the bread rolls instead of baking them. You could pay for some cleaning help. It should be OK to have an au pair. There can be many reasons for choosing not to have children, because you don't feel that you match the ideal. I think that especially women are good at spinning themselves up. We have to break that down.

The interview pushed the overall message that women in Denmark should raise 3 children, because the current reproduction rate of 1.8 was too low. It started a huge media and political discussion, but mainly as a criticism of the state ordering people to reproduce on a specific scale. There were no comments about the au-pair part of the interview. Women are often constructed as symbolic border guards of ethnic and national collectives (Yuval-Davis 2005), and the future national collective is here defined as solely depending on the national birthrate. If the issue were only about the national dependency ratio, an extended 'influx' of permanent immigrants could solve the problem.

The Christensen interview reflects the fact that an increasing number of middle-class families employ or 'have' an au pair as a strategy to manage a dual-career lifestyle and as a tool to achieve gender equality within the family. The minister is not talking about having an au pair because of the cultural exchange perspective, but exclusively as a hired help to do domestic work, primarily to 'liberate' the mother of the family from household chores.

What it also reveals is the extent of the moral disciplining of women in Denmark for not reproducing adequately. Mirroring the Philippines (and illustrated in many studies on hired domestic work) it becomes a feminized problem. The au-pair solution lets men off the hook, as it maintains the gender imbalance. Domestic chores in Danish middle-class households are still carried out by the 'woman of the house' – except the woman is now 'the au-pair girl' living in the basement.

Another example of the quite open connection drawn between liberating the white, Danish career woman and having an au pair is an interview with the then minister of social affairs in October 2007, in which she discusses how she manages her job as minister and being the mother of small children: 'Where many mothers take pride in kissing their children goodnight, Eva Kjer Hansen has to leave this to her husband and the au-pair girl, because her working days are in Copenhagen far away from her family in South Jutland, where she only returns at weekends.'[27] The question of gender equality and liberation from domestic chores precludes any mention of the au-pair dilemma in this context. The gender-equality issue is limited to equality within the Danish career family and its reproduction as a well-functioning unit where household duties can be done effectively while career goals are achieved.

Some are more equal than others

Another example of the relationship between the Danish career woman and the (non-European) au pair is the efforts in the City of Copenhagen to increase the number of high-level female administrators. The City has announced it will help its female executives by subsidizing the expenses of having an au pair. Under the headline 'Diversity in every corner', the Social Democratic mayor of Copenhagen, Ritt Bjerregaard, wrote in 2007 the following commentary in the leading magazine for municipal policy and administration:

> But it is not even necessary for modern women to be faced by the dilemma of family and career. ... In special cases, the local council can even offer a subsidy for au-pair and cleaning services as part of the salary package. We will create good possibilities for more female executives. We simply have to make it possible for women to make it to the top.[28]

The rapid transnationalization of domestic care (Lutz 2004) is illustrated by an enthusiastic proposal from the minister of social affairs about extending au-pair arrangements to include eldercare:

> Many families with small children appreciate the au-pair system, because it means a helping hand in a busy working day. 'Why

shouldn't elderly people have the same opportunity?', she says, being a mother of small children herself and having had an au-pair girl at home. 'The arrangement is meant as a cultural encounter for both the elderly Danish person as well as the young person from abroad, and of course it must not in any way replace public home-care assistance help. But there are tasks that the public home-care help cannot carry out', she says. (*Jyllandsposten*, 9 November 2007)

Even the extreme right-wing, anti-immigration Danish Peoples' Party (Dansk Folkeparti) spoke positively about the au-pair proposal.

Newspaper articles such as these tend to mention au pairs in generic terms. No specific reference is made to Filipinas, but politicians have been praising Filipina au pairs as devoted heroines in busy family life and Filipinas have appeared in the media as au pairs.[29] Au pair is becoming synonymous with Filipina. Phrases such as 'my Filipina' or 'my Fili' are used among host families, and the Filipina is constructed as gifted with 'care genes', docile, smiling, and so on.[30]

In the Nordic welfare-state mentality of government, equality is still a main theme, but in Danish immigration policy 'gender equality' most often produces national, white-imagined sameness (Gullestad 2006) and constructs a cultural homogeneity in the face of the Other. 'Gender equality' unites white women, white men and the white classes, connected as it is to national identity and sameness. The term 'au-pair girl', the term most commonly used in Denmark, supports the suspension of gender as in 'woman' or adult citizen. The infantilization of the migrant as a 'girl' draws both on colonial subjectification (the colonized subject with the colonizer as parent) and establishes her position in a family context.

In public and political debate, there is no effort to extend the gender-equality debate to include Philippine gender equality and the position of Filipinas coming to Denmark, despite their being women who are often single mothers and providers for a whole family. Gender equality is made irrelevant to the life of the au pairs – it is only relevant for the career women for whom the au pair is essential everyday support. Geopolitical inequality suspends the logic of class relations, keeping au pairs out of arenas where they could press claims to equality, and reinforcing a particular kind of social invisibility.

Migrant domestic and care workers in Europe are officially treated to a large extent as temporary residents; some are positioned as 'illegals', with the permanent threat of deportation, while others are 'legals', with a time-limited residence or work permit. The temporariness of their residence is a key element in understanding their position as invisible subjects with no or limited rights, and the suspension of their existence within the recognized power relationships along the lines of gender, ethnicity and class.

In a nation-state such as Denmark, which has focused on preventing citizens from the global South from entering the country as permanent residents, and is so preoccupied with categories of difference and imagined sameness, it seems puzzling as to why this 'influx' of Filipina au pairs has been widely accepted. The Filipinas have even been 'allowed in' to take care of Danish children, who according to the dominant ethno-nationalistic emphasis on 'Danishness' are meant to grow up in a universe of 'Danish values' and 'Danish language'. Filipinas are not portrayed as cultural or economic threats, which is the usual image of the immigrant from the global South. Rather, they are most often portrayed as hardworking, kind, fond of children – and as victims of abuse.

This 'tolerance' (Brown 2006) is founded on the reality of their migrant status and the limitations of their residence permits – the temporariness of their stay. The chances are virtually non-existent for au pairs to transform their position by successfully applying as independent migrants for permanent residence. Their permits, and their lives, are tied legally as well as physically to their specific host families, and a breach in this relationship can lead to their being deported. The possibilities for claiming any rights are very limited. Temporary residence is a key device in governing foreign (economically poor) migrants in Europe.

A Filipina au pair in Denmark is offered the roles of docile servant, grateful poor, and abused victim, genetically and culturally predisposed to provide care – but not the roles of migrant worker, independent woman, or political subject.

Conclusion

The background for young Filipinas coming to Denmark as au pairs is the colonial geopolitical power imbalance and racialization of global South women delivering care and domestic work to global North families, plus the privilege-defending immigration policies of the North. Illegalizing migration in the shape of emigration illegality[31], residence illegality and employment illegality are key elements in migration management: migrants are governed through their relationship to the nation-state, and the nature of this relationship is decisive for their ability to assert or exercise rights. Illegalizing migration, residence and employment produces and maintains the permanent insecurity and the fluidity of the migrant workers' position in Europe.

The au-pair system in Denmark is a specific version of the fluidity between legality and illegality which frames the position of migrant domestic workers. Both Denmark and the Philippines appear to be preoccupied with au-pair welfare. The Philippine state is apparently trying to protect migrant workers from potential abuse, but at the same time generates new forms of corruption in the obtaining of exit permits. The Danish state pays lip-service to a 'cultural exchange, not-employment' construct, well aware that au pairs are working more hours than permitted and taking extra jobs on the side.

In both nation-states, the reproduction of the population (in the Philippines through remittances and in Denmark through reproduction of a family lifestyle of middle- and upper-class citizens) is a central element in maintaining au-pair migration and the ambiguous Danish political construct, whereby gender equality and dual careers are achieved by having a 'girl' living in the basement.

Notes

1 *Berlingske Tidende*, 15 November 2009. Au pairs are most often in Denmark referred to as 'au pair girls' (*au pair piger*). The connotations are obvious.

2 As described in my study of au-pair life in Denmark (Stenum 2008), the basement was the commonest place for the au pair to live – to have her room. Generally, most basements in Denmark do not meet the legal requirements for human habitation.

3 For a more detailed description of the formal regulations in Denmark, see

Calleman (2010) and Stenum (2008); for experiences of being an au pair in Denmark, see Stenum (2008).

4　The Danish Immigration Service (2009).

5　Compared with the numbers of asylum seekers granted permanent status as 'refugees': 1,147 in 2005; 1,095 in 2006; 1,278 in 2007; and 1,441 in 2008 (The Danish Immigration Service 2009).

6　It should be observed, however, that this family immigration is between Danish citizens (presumably men) and Filipinas.

7　See Petersen et al. (2007).

8　The Minister for Gender Equality (2007). Annual Report (2006) / Perspective and Action Plan for (2007) in the section on actions regarding 'Employment, participation and equal opportunities' includes several initiatives that aim to change attitudes within the ethnic minority group.

9　*Dagbladet Information*, 9 September 2009.

10　Examples: The difference between male and female salaries is 12–19 per cent; in 2005, 80–82 per cent of top executives in public administration were men (Minister for Equal Opportunity 2007). Until the end of 2009, Denmark had been one of the few EU countries without the institutionalized monitoring of gender equality.

11　In February 2007, the Philippine government concluded an agreement with the French government on migration of highly skilled labour to France (*Manila Bulletin*, 12 February 2008). Nurses are a highly sought-after group in many parts of the world and often dealt with within bilateral agreements. Between 1992 and 1999, the government deployed more than 45,000 nurses abroad (Parreñas 2002).

12　No receiving Western countries have yet ratified this convention, despite its position as one of seven UN core conventions.

13　Other sending countries (for example, Bangladesh) have also implemented explicit or implicit gendered emigration restrictions (Oishi 2005; Piper 2009).

14　The ban was issued by the Philippine embassy in The Hague. The reported cases of abuse apparently took place in the Netherlands and other European countries, 'in particular Scandinavia' (Anderson 2000). The Philippine embassy reported that 'the concomitant irregularities and complaints have come about, such as under-compensation, excessive hours, over-work, culture shock, etc. There have been reported cases of abuse, discrimination, runaways and even prostitution' (ibid. 24).

15　My research (Stenum 2008) is based on a number of qualitative semi-structured interviews, conducted between October 2007 and June 2008 with 24 au pairs in Greater Copenhagen, of whom 21 were from the Philippines, plus 1 each from Russia, Nepal and Uganda. I also interviewed six host families in Greater Copenhagen who had had between 2 and 8 au pairs in their homes, and 8 persons involved in au pair arrangements in their capacity as government officials, NGO representatives and priests. All those interviewed have been anonymized; the interviews lasted from 30 minutes to 2¾ hours. Some were interviewed more than once, and some of the interviewees sent me written accounts/comments before or after the interviews. In addition, I have had many informal conversations with people who take different approaches to au pair arrangements, be they au pairs, employers/host family members, Filipina migrants in Denmark, neighbours of host families, and so on. Parallel with my research I have participated in the 'au pair network', which was established in 2007 as a collaboration between the Trade Union FOA, Filipino organizations in Denmark and interested individuals.

16 According to Transparency International, which ranks countries according to the perceived prevalence of corruption, the Philippines ranked 131 out of 180 countries in their corruption perceptions index (<www.transparency.org>, accessed on 10 August 2008).

17 Since July 2009, the minimum 'pocket money' allowance is now DKK 2,900.

18 The Swedish Migrationsverket's advice is as follows: 'Philippine citizens may not apply. The Philippines does not allow its citizens to travel to Europe to work as au pairs. There is therefore no point submitting an application for a work permit for this purpose' (<http://www.migrationsverket.se/info/172_en.html 010210>, accessed on 1 February 2010). The Finnish Immigration Service, under the heading 'Entry into Finland as an au pair', states: 'Citizens of the Philippines: The Philippines does not permit its citizens to travel to Europe as au pairs, and they are advised not to apply for a residence permit for this purpose' (<http://www.migri.fi/netcomm/content.asp?article=3557&search=true>, accessed on 1 February 2010).

19 Besvarelse af spørgsmål 171 stillet af Folketingets arbejdsmarkedsudvalg til ministeren for flygtninge, indvandrere og integration den 20. maj 2008 (Answer to Question 171 of the Folketing's labour market committee to the minister for refugees, immigrants and integration, 20 May 2008).

20 In my study, 17 out of 24 informants had a full or interrupted higher education; among them were a veterinary surgeon, an engineer, an accountant, a biologist, a midwife, a nurse, a teacher, and one with a BA in literature.

21 For more specific regulations on the Danish au-pair system, see Calleman's chapter on au-pair regulations in four Nordic countries in this volume.

22 Danish Immigration Service: 'New to Denmark. Au pairs', <http://www. nyidanmark.dk/en-us/coming_to_dk/au_pairs/au_pairs.htm> (accessed 10 October 2008).

23 Ibid.

24 According to the tax authorities (see Stenum 2008, 44) the au pair must pay tax on both pocket money and the value of free room and board. At the minimum rate of DKK 2,500 a month, the calculation for 2007 is as follows: pay (pocket money) DKK 30,000; board DKK 23,725 (365 days at DKK 65 a day); room for 12 months DKK 7,680. With basic rate personal tax starting at DKK 39,500, this means that an au pair who receives DKK 2,500 a month must pay social security contributions at a rate of 8 per cent, corresponding to DKK 2,400 a year. In addition, the employer must pay ATP (contributions to supplementary labour market pension). Accordingly, based on these calculations, the total monthly minimum expense/total pay generated by an

au pair employment relationship is DKK 5,117. Converted to an hourly rate, including the value of room and board, and with a working week of 30 hours, this results in an hourly rate of approximately DKK 42.

25 For example, considerable efforts in the reproduction of national identity are made to maintain the amnesia of the Danish colonial past in the slave trade, the Virgin Islands and Greenland.

26 *Berlingske Tidende*, 7 March 2007.

27 *Ekstrabladet*, 14 October 2007.

28 Danmarks Radio, 13 August 2007, 10: 42 Copenhagen, and *Danske Kommuner* 17 April 2008.

29 See, for example, comments by Edith Tingstrup, priest and politician, 'Au pair girls are the heroines of our time. The world's most effective development aid' *Berlingske Tidende*, 14 May 2006; and Malene Lei Raben, lawyer and commentator, 'Hands off my au pair', *Politiken*, 1 November 2008.

30 The migrant domestic workers from the Philippines are racialized within a hierarhcy of constructions of non-whiteness, as analysed for example by Andall (2003), Anderson (2000), Hondagneu-Soleto (2001) & Parreñas (2001).

31 On 22 October 2010, the Philippine Embassy in Norway announced on their website on the basis of a decree from POEA of 6 October 2010, that the ban 'on au pairs bound to Denmark' had been lifted due to an agreement with the Danish government on a 'repatriation clause in the contract'. On 9 June 2010 the ban on au pairs to Norway was lifted by the Philippines authorities.

References

AE, or Arbejderbevægelsens Erhvervsråd (2008), *Fordeling og Levevilkår 2008*. (Copenhagen : Arbejderbevægelsens Erhvervsråd).

Anderson, Bridget (2002), 'Just another Job? The Commodification of Domestic Labour', in Ehrenreich, Barbara & Arlie Russell Hochschild (eds.). *Global Woman. Nannies, Maids and Sex Workers in the New Economy.* New York: Metropolitan/Owl Books.

Anderson, Bridget (2000*), Doing the Dirty Work* (London and New York: Zed Books).

Beck, Ulrich (2006), *Cosmopolitan Vision* (Cambridge: Polity Press).

Berlingske Tidende, 7 March 2007. 'Familieministeren har selv for travlt til børn – andre skal have tre' (Bjarne Steensbeck).

Bjerregaard, Ritt (2008), 'Mangfoldighed I alle hjørner', *Danske Kommuner*, 17 April.

Bonke, Jens (2002), *Tid og velfærd* (SFI 02:26; Copenhagen: SFI).

Brown, Wendy (2006), *Regulating Aversion. Tolerance in the Age of Identity and Empire* (Princeton and Woodstock: Princeton University Press).

Deding, M. et al. (2006), *Børnefamiliernes balance mellem arbejdsliv og familieliv* (SFI 06:32; Copenhagen: SFI).

De Genova, Nicholas (2005), *Working the Boundaries* (Durham & London: Duke).

DR, 'Lokker kvindelige chefer med deltid', 13 August 2007 10.42, Copenhagen.

Gavanas, Anna (2006), 'Jämlikhet, "svenskhet" och privata hushållstjänster i pigdebattens Sverige', in Paulina de los Reyes (ed.), *Arbetslivets (o)synliga murar* (Utredningen om Makt, Integration och Strukturell Diskriminering; Stockholm: Statens Offentliga Utredningar, SOU 2005:4).

Glick Schiller, Nina (2007), 'Beyond the Nation-State and its Units of Analysis: Towards a New Research Agenda for Migration Studies', in Karin Schittenhelm (ed.) (2007), *Concepts and Methods in Migration Research. Conference Reader*, <www.cultural-capital.net>, accessed on 7 September 2008.

Goldberg, Theo (2002), *The Racial State* (Malden: Blackwell Publishing).

Gullestad, Marianne (2006), *Plausible Prejudices* (Oslo: Universitetsforlaget).

Høgsholm, Filomenita Mongaya (ed.) (2007), *Views of Filipino Migrants in Europe* (Quezon City: Philippines Social Science Council).

Human Rights Watch (2006), 'Swept Under the Rug. Abuses against Domestic Workers Around the World', *HRW*, 18/7(c).

Human Rights Watch (2005) '"Maid to Order". Ending Abuses Against Migrant Domestic Workers in Singapore', *HRW*, 17/10(c).

Immigration Service (2009), Statistics on au pairs. <http://www.nyidanmark. dk/resources.ashx/Resources/Statistik/statistik/uk/seneste_tal_udlaendinge-omraadet_en.xls#'S2'!A1>, and <http://www.nyidanmark.dk/NR/rdonlyres/ EFB2567D-6C5F-4E4B-A6EF-3AE5F1ACEDDC/0/statisticaloverview2007. pdf>, accessed on 17 March 2009.

Isaksen, Lise Widding, Sambasivan, Devi, Hochschild, Arlie Russel (2008): 'Global Care Crisis: A Problem of Capital, Care Chain, or Commons?' *American Behavioral Scientist*, Volume 52 No 3, Nov. 2008, 405–425.

Jyllandsposten, 'V-forslag om au pair-piger til ældre', 9 November 2007.

Lutz, Helma (2004), 'Life in the Twilight Zone: Migration, Transnationality and Gender in Private Households', *Journal of Contemporary European Studies*, 12/1 (April).

Ministeriet for Flygtninge (2008), *Tal og Fakta på Udlændingeområdet 2007* (Copenhagen).

Minister for Gender Equality (2007), *The Minister for Gender Equality's Annual Report 2006 / Perspective and Action Plan for 2007* (Copenhagen).

Øien, Cecilie (2009), *On Equal Terms? An Evaluation of the Norwegian Au Pair Scheme* (Oslo: Fafo).

Oishi, Nana (2005), *Women in Motion. Globalization, State Policies, and Labour Migration in Asia* (Stanford: Stanford University Press).

O'Neil, Kevin (2004), *Labor Export as Government Policy: The Case of the Philippines*; Migration Policy Institute, January (Washington: MPI).

Ong, Aihwa (2006), *Neoliberalism as Exception. Mutations in Citizenship and Sovereignty* (Durham & London: Duke University Press).

Oosterbeek-Latoza, Diana (2007), 'The Filipina Au Pairs in The Netherlands', in F. Høgsholm (ed.), *In De Olde Worlde* (Quezon City: Philippines Social Science Council).

Parreñas, Rachel Salazar (2002), 'The Care Crisis in the Philippines: Children and Transnational Families in the New Global Economy', in Barbara Ehrenreich & Arlie Russel Hochschild (eds.), *Global Women* (London: Granta Books).

Parreñas, Rachel Salazar (2008), *The Force of Domesticity. Filipina Migrants and Globalization* (New York: New York University Press).

Petersen, J. H. et al. (eds.) (2007), *13 værdier bag den danske velfærdsstat* (Odense: Syddansk Universitetsforlag).

Platzer, Ellinor (2002), 'Kulturellt utbyte eller billig arbetskraft? Au pair i Sverige', *Sociologisk Forskning*, 3–4 (Uppsala).

POEA 2005, *Philippines Overseas Employment Administration: Annual Report 2005* <http://www.poea.gov.ph/ar/AR2005.pdf>, accessed on 4 September 2008.

Raben, M. L. (2008), 'Snitterne væk fra min au pair', *Politiken* (1 November).

Rodriguez, Robyn M. (2004), 'Domestic Insecurities: Female Migration from the Philippines, Development and National Subject-Status'. Working paper, University of California, Berkeley.

Stenum, Helle (2008), *Cheap Labour or Cultural exchange?* (Copenhagen: FOA).

Tingstrup, Edith (2006), 'Au pair-piger, vor tids heltinder.' 'Verdens mest effektive ulandsbistand', *Berlingske Tidende*, 14 May.

UDI (2006), *Utredning af au pair ordningen* (Oslo).

Williams, F. & Gavanas, A. (2008), 'The Intersection of Childcare Regimes and Migration Regimes: A Three-Country Study', in Helma Lutz (ed.), *Migration and Domestic Work* (Hampshire & Burlington: Ashgate).

Wimmer, Andreas & Schiller, Nina Glick (2002a), 'Methodological Nationalism and Beyond Nation-state Building, Migration and the Social Sciences', *Global Networks*, 2(4), 301–34.

World Economic Forum: Gender Gap Index 2007 <http://www.weforum.org/en/initiatives/gcp/Gender%20Gap/index.htm>, accessed on 5. October 2008.

Yuval-Davies, Nira, Anthias, Floya & Kofman, Eleonore (2005), 'Secure borders and safe haven and the politic of gendered politics of belonging: Beyond social cohesion', *Ethnic and Racial Studies*, 28/3 (London: Rautledge).

Yuval-Davies, Nira (1997), *Gender and Nations* (London: Sage).

CHAPTER 3

The snake in the grass of gender equality

Au-pairing in women-friendly Norway

Mariya Bikova

Norway, like the other Nordic countries, is internationally recognized as a social welfare state intent on the well-being and equality of its citizens. The welfare state has been dubbed an agent of modernity, with its state feminism policies to promote family patterns that favour the reconciliation of work and family life and a more equal division of care work and household chores between parents. Given the wide availability of state-subsidized child-care, the generous parental leave legislation, and the family-friendliness of the Norwegian labour market, Norway has even been referred to as 'the professional women's paradise' (*BT*, 28 October 2008). Still, despite excellent public child-care, an increasing number of Norwegian families are now turning to private solutions, alone or in combination with a public day care. In addition to the traditional use of private childminders, the so-called '*dagmamma*',[1] it has now become common to use au pairs to supplement, and sometimes to replace, public child-care.

Research on au pairs as an institution in the other Scandinavian countries has shown that of the families who hire au pairs, the majority are middle-class and upper-middle-class, dual-income families looking for greater flexibility in their everyday and professional lives (Hovdan 2005; Bertelsen 2007; Platzer 2007; Bikova 2008; Stenum 2008; Øien 2009). Research results indicate that au-pairing has lost much of its original focus on cultural exchange and is now used chiefly as a channel for the import of cheap labour. International research, meanwhile, views the au-pair system as a part of the transnational redistribution of care work, by which women from poorer regions of the world migrate to economically advantaged countries to provide better life chances for themselves and their families at home (Anderson 2000, 2002; Cox 2006, 2007; Ehrenreich & Hochschild 2002; Hess & Puckhaber 2004; Rotkirch 2001). The new feminist orientation on the globalization of care that emerged a decade ago describes this phenomenon as the commodification of care (Ehrenreich & Hochschild 2002). Much of the current research on the globalization of care, however, has focused on 'global care chains', and is mostly related to North American experiences (Ehrenreich & Hochschild 2002; Parreñas 2001; Hochschild 2000), and less attention has been given to the different institutional framings of the global economy of care. The au-pair system, being a small but important part of the global economy of care, is the subject in hand here.

Based on interviews with employers of au pairs in Norway (Bikova 2008) and on prior research on the au-pair institution, this chapter will elaborate on the cultural, demographic and political mechanisms that create the need for au pairs among certain types of Norwegian families, and will discuss the status of au pairs in these families. It will be argued that the 'stalled revolution' (Hochschild 1989) in the Norwegian nuclear family and the 'incomplete revolution' in women's roles (Esping-Anderesen 2009) creates a cultural lag that opens for the outsourcing of care work and household chores, and encourages the initiation of global care chains. The chapter also discusses the particularity and applicability of the concept of global care chains in the context of the Norwegian welfare state.

Au-pairing in Norway

Historically, au-pairing was a European phenomenon that started at the end of the nineteenth century when a large number of young Swiss women moved away from home to work in the big cities. Concerned for the morals of these young women, the Church encouraged them to live with local families where they could also acquire household skills. With the placing of German-speaking Swiss girls with French-speaking families, the language-learning element of au-pair placements developed (Griffith & Legg 1997). Though cultural in its origins, au-pairing soon shifted focus from language-learning to domestic duties and child-care. Being a guest teacher implied an egalitarian relationship of sorts between the au pair and the host family. This balance changed when the au pair started serving the host family's members rather than teaching them.

In Norway the phenomenon became popular after the Second World War, when many young women travelled to English-speaking countries to learn languages and culture. However, it was not until the end of the 1990s that au-pairing in Norway started changing rapidly. From being primarily a sending country, Norway became a receiving country for au pairs from all over the world. Especially for young women from Eastern Europe and Asia, Norway has become an attractive cultural exchange destination. While only 277 au pairs came to Norway in 2000, their number was ten times higher in 2008. According to the Norwegian Immigration Authorities' official statistics, as many as 2,865 au pairs came to Norway in 2008 – and in that year 72 per cent of all au-pair visas were granted to Filipinas despite the fact that the Philippine authorities do not permit their citizens to take au-pair jobs in Norway (UDI 2009).

The original intention with au-pairing was to enable young adults to experience a different culture and to increase their linguistic and professional abilities through participation in a foreign family's everyday life. In the official discourse, however, the au pairs are constructed neither as workers nor as migrants, but as guests of a host family on a temporary visit. Au pairs are supposed to be on equal terms with the members of the host family, and as such they receive free board and lodging. In return they are expected to help with child-care and light housework (Council of Europe 1969). The use of kinship terms to define the relationship between au pair and host family reinforces a view of care work as a gift one gives to family members. Care work is thus indirectly defined as a 'labour of love' (Øien 2009). Though legally and discursively constructed as non-workers, au pairs pay tax on the amount of money and the lodging they receive from the host family, thus accumulating welfare to be consumed by the local citizens. The work of the au pairs generates benefits for the Norwegian welfare state.

In 2008 I conducted a study among Norwegian families who had participated in the au-pair scheme, with the objective of understanding why, despite the improving public arrangements for parents with care responsibilities, an increasing number of Norwegian families hire au pairs.[2] The study is based on ten qualitative interviews. Because of its scope, rapid development and controversial nature, au-pairing has been extensively debated in Norwegian academia and the media in recent years. Newspaper headlines such as 'The new servants' (*DN*, 6/7 March 2004), 'The family threatened me' (*Klassekampen*, 3 November 2007), and 'We are dependent on Anna' (*DB*, 1 April 2004) signalled that au pairs in Norway might have been overworked, but also that certain types of Norwegian families are growing increasingly dependent on having an au pair. Especially career-oriented women in high-status jobs were in the public eye, seen as outsourcing housework and child-care to au pairs. As a result of this negative media attention, host families have been reluctant to share experiences with researchers and journalists. Aware of this, I deployed different recruitment channels. Having been an au pair in Norway myself, I had a personal network of au pairs and host families that I mobilized for the study, and in addition a local language school for foreigners who want to learn Norwegian and commercial agencies placing au pairs in Norwegian families were contacted. Through these channels I recruited ten families who had employed au pairs. Two of the families were single-parent families; the rest were two-parent, two-career families. The informants were aged 30–45 at the time the study was conducted in 2008, all of them gainfully employed, and all had a university or a postgraduate education.[3] All ten interviews were conducted in the host families' homes. Based on their occupations and the material standard of their homes, the majority of the families would be rated as belonging to the middle class and upper middle class, except for the two single-parent families who had a modest standard of living.

In line with prior studies on the institution of the au pair (Hovdan 2005; Bertelsen 2007; Platzer 2007; Bikova 2008; Stenum 2008; Øien 2009), my research findings indicate that au pairs are hired to enhance career families' flexibility in terms of work and family life, and to outsource conflicts related to the redistribution of domestic work, which in many of the families was gender-conservative, or 'stalled' (Hochschild 1989). Another important finding is that thanks to the flexibility au pairs bring, Norwegian middle-class families achieve a particular kind of gender equality that is based on contributions to the family budget rather than on the equal sharing of care and domestic work. One of the main conclusions of the study is that the au-pair scheme in Norway has lost its cultural character and is now used as a channel for the import of cheap domestic labour.

Norway – the professional women's paradise?

Although the Norwegian welfare state has been slow to respond to parents' needs for kindergarten places, kindergarten coverage has improved considerably in the last few years, and by late 2008 was close to universal: as of December 2008, 87 per cent of all children aged 1–5 had kindergarten places (SSB 2009). Norway also has generous parental leave legislation that institutes legal rights for working parents to give priority to child-care over paid work. Working parents are entitled to 44 weeks' leave with full income compensation or 54 weeks with 80 per cent income compensation (NAV 2009). The use of parental leave is widely accepted by employers, and parents in both the public and the private sector take parental leave without risking their jobs. The parental leave scheme may also be combined with a time-account scheme that allows the prolonging of the period of leave for up to three years, thus enabling a combination of child-care and paid work (Arbeidstilsynet 2007; NAV 2009).

Families with children under the age of three, whose children do not attend public child-care institutions, are entitled to cash benefits for child-care, the so-called '*kontantstøtte*'; a sum corresponding to the cost to the government if the child had attended kindergarten (NAV 2009). This cash benefit is meant to compensate for the loss of income when parents choose to stay at home with their children. However, as the size of the benefit is relatively small and does not fully compensate for lost income, many parents use the cash benefit to finance private childminders rather than staying at home with the children themselves. The Norwegian state is thus indirectly encouraging the use of private child-care solutions. Child-care, then, may be described as a public–private mix. In addition, both sexes are expected and encouraged to take their share of child-care.

In order to mobilize men as carers and to ensure a more equal division of child-care and domestic work, a father's quota was introduced in 1993 (Brandth & Kvande 2003). The quota gives fathers a legal right to take leave of absence – currently up to ten weeks – and to stay at home with their children with income compensation (NAV 2009). Being a father has always been an important part of the masculinity and male identity of Norwegian men (Brandth & Kvande 1992). Brandth and Kvande (1999, 2003; Brandth 2007), in their extensive research on fathers, found that that Norwegian fathers did not view staying at home with a child as a threat to their masculine identity, but rather as an attribute – and an opportunity for personal growth. However, the quota did not have a significant effect on fathers' share of the housework. Fathers who took paternal leave did more housework than those who did not take the leave, but the fathers on leave did exactly as much or as little housework as they had done before the birth of the child (Brandth & Kvande 1999, 2003).

These developments might be an indication that the revolution in couples' roles remains 'incomplete' as long as they continue to do gender in a traditional way. This gender-conservative and unequal redistribution of care responsibilities and domestic work creates a cultural lag that opens for their outsourcing to migrant workers. It is here that au pairs appear an attractive option for time-pressed middle-class couples who need help in managing with the housework and having more quality time with their children.

The stratified revolution

The long-term developments in female employment patterns, with a shift from housewifery to lifelong employment, have been an extraordinary, all-embracing and revolutionary transformation (Esping-Andersen 2009). The new female cohorts, especially in the industrialized countries, embrace a lifelong commitment to employment. This is also the case in the Scandinavian countries, where female participation in the labour market is higher than the rest of Europe (Esping-Andersen 2009). Economically speaking, the life course of Scandinavian women has become masculinized. One of the indicators of the 'revolution' is the way women make their employment choices. From being secondary earners who only supplement their husbands' income, women have now become independent earners who choose their occupations almost exclusively on the basis of their own preferences and perceived opportunities. This female revolution, Esping-Andersen (2009) argues, has evolved in a stratified manner, beginning with higher educated middle-class women. It is among this group of women that the au-pair scheme is getting increasingly popular.

Some fifty years ago, families with small children would have received child-care help from their parents. However, due to the changing demographic structure of the population, many of the older generation are not only gainfully employed until their late sixties, but often have parents of their own who need care. According to a recent report by Statistics Norway, 65 per cent of adults aged 55 to 64 were active in the labour market in 2004. The percentage is highest for highly-educated women aged 58 or more (SSB 2006/9). This places contemporary grandparents in a 'sandwich' position between the requirements of work and those of their own families, and makes them less available to care for their grandchildren. Another factor that influences grandparents' availability is a new trend in Norwegian senior culture called 'retirement migration' (Hovland & Aagedal 2003; Martinsen 2007). An increasing number of Norwegian grandparents live in retirement communities in Spain and other warmer countries during the winter or most of the year. The changing demographic structure of the population and the masculinization of women's life courses create a care deficit that is met by migrant care workers such as the au pairs.

Having an au pair is mostly a middle-class phenomenon (Hovdan 2005; Bertelsen 2007; Platzer 2007; Bikova 2008; Stenum 2008; Øien 2009). Families who hire au pairs often occupy prestigious and well-paid positions in the post-industrial, knowledge-intensive economy where they produce knowledge and services rather than material goods. Some of these parents' jobs require them to leave early in the morning or work late or at night. Many of them travel a great deal, often abroad. Even when not required, face time is still preferable in many occupations. Work means a lot to these professionals. Parts of the 'new' or post-industrial economy, and especially the knowledge-intensive, middle-class professions of the majority of informants in my study, offer workers good opportunities for self-realization and personal growth. Having children is an important part of the ethic of self-fulfilment, and relates to the hope of discovering oneself through one's children (Beck & Beck-Gernsheim 1995, 2002). However, in order for these working parents to be able to build careers and develop professional identities, they need to liberate themselves from some of their care and housework responsibilities.

In the post-industrial economy, employees with zero drag or few family obligations are more attractive than those with a high drag coefficient (Halrynjo 2007, 86; Hochschild 1997, xviii–xx). Although the Norwegian collective work culture is recognized for its family-friendliness, it bears many similarities with the individualistic and competitive American work culture as described by Hochschild (1997) in her study of the American company Amerco. This is especially the case when it comes to the norms and rules for career advancement (Halrynjo 2007). A recent study of Norco, an avowedly family-friendly Norwegian company, revealed that despite the company's strong emphasis on flexibility, innovation and career advancement programmes, its internal career paths followed a traditional hierarchical ladder, where those with fewer family obligations and greater face time were the ones who were allowed to climb the company's career ladder. Long hours, flexibility, and availability were absolutely necessary if one was to progress at work (Halrynjo 2007).

These career advancement patterns might imply that for aspiring employees with a high drag coefficient, the inflexibility of state-subsidized child-care arrangements might mean that it was not always an adequate solution. However, with the help of an au pair to drop off and pick up the children from kindergarten, career-oriented parents can still place their children in public day care and continue working longer hours when so required.

A labour of love?

According to the formal regulations of the au-pair programme, the main duties of an au pair are restricted to child-care and light housework. The au pair should not be engaged in child-care and housework for more than 5 hours a day, 6 days a week, and the total time worked should not exceed 30 hours per week. The au pair is only supposed to help with child-care and housework, and not to be responsible for the daily care of the children or for the daily running of the household (Council of Europe 1969; UDI 2008). However, research has shown that many au pairs carry out a considerable amount of housework (Øien 2009; Bikova 2008; Bertelsen 2007; Hovdan 2005; Hemsing 2003).

The working day of the au pairs in the families in my study started between 6.30 and 7.30 a.m. Often at least one of the parents has left the house by that time. The au pair's job is to help the children get dressed and eat breakfast, prepare their packed lunch, clear away breakfast, and take the children to kindergarten. Other duties include vacuum-cleaning, dusting, emptying the dishwasher and washing machine, washing floors and cleaning bathrooms. Au pairs are also expected to prepare dinner for the family and spend time with the children while waiting for the parents to come home from work. Sometimes the au pairs are also expected to help clear away dinner. Some of the au pairs in my study chose to leave the house after dinner or spend the rest of the evening on their own.

Although the au pairs' working day is very busy, few of them complain at the amount of housework. Some of the au pairs in my study did more housework than required and even expressed gratitude for the opportunity to work as au pairs:

> She cleaned everything. I came home and I was, … what have you done? [Laughing] It's fantastic but … 'No, no, I want, I want', she answers. 'You are so kind to me; that is why I want to do it'. (Host mother, family 4)[4]

Many au pairs come from economically disadvantaged countries where levels of unemployment are high and living conditions are hard (Bikova 2008; Bertelsen 2007; Hovdan 2005). The structural adjustment policies that international financial institutions such as the IMF and the World Bank impose on poorer countries often have detrimental effects on the local economies (Ehrenreich & Hochschild 2002, 8). Unemployment and low wages push citizens from poor countries into involuntary migration, while the hard currencies of the industrialized countries pull them. For many young women from poorer countries, working as an au pair is an opportunity to earn money and appears a stepping-stone for a better future (Bikova 2008; Hovdan 2005).

In Norway au pairs are legally defined as non-workers. They only have temporary work permits that allow them to work only for a specified host family. Should an au pair want to change host family, she has to find another employer or leave the country (UDI 2007). This places au pairs in a vulnerable position as for many of them au-pairing is an investment in a better future. Being dependent on the host family, the au pairs might disregard their own feelings and put up a front of loyalty, obedience and even enthusiasm (Bikova 2008; Anderson 2000; Parreñas 2001). This 'emotional labour', Hochschild (1983) points out, emphasizes employers' authority over the worker and reveals how the employers' control penetrates into the bodily functions of the worker (Rollins 1985, in Parreñas 2001).

Yet, according to the Council of Europe's (1969) formal regulations on the au-pair scheme, au pairs should be treated 'like one of the family' and be included in the host family's day-to-day activities. This implies not only the delegation of domestic duties and care responsibilities, but also inclusion in the family's everyday practices. However, for many host families the au pair is just a person who lives in the house and is not one of the family. As one of the host mothers in my study puts it:

> I don't think they can ever be a part of the family, because you're kind of the wrong age and you're in a way an adult. So you can never be a part of the family, but you can be a part of the wider family. But we have never considered them … they have never been, we have never thought of them as of housemaids or something like that. No, it's simply a person who lives in the house and whom we get along with,who has an independent life here in Norway. (Host mother, family 7)

Focusing on cooperation and independence, this informant recalls local equality ideals according to which family members are equal. At the same time, placing the au pair in the wider family rather than in the immediate or nuclear family, this informant defines the au pair as not a family member. According to the social anthropologist Marianne Gullestad (1981), the family is defined by the biological bonds between its members, while the household includes all the persons occupying the same dwelling – parents, children, domestic workers.

For both au pairs and host families, the family-member scenario is unnatural and difficult to put in practice. Knowing their place and role in the host family's everyday life, the au pairs often choose to withdraw from family gatherings and spend the evenings on their own. Similarly, viewing the au pairs as strangers who simply deliver a wanted service, the host families often prefer that au pairs do not participate in the family's quality time. As one of the informants in my study mentions:

> The au pair has her private life when we have our private life. I think that if [she] were to sit between me and [my husband] at the weekends and watch TV, I wouldn't like it. That's the way it is. (Host mother, family 8)

The example above illustrates a common attitude towards au pairs: they are not seen as part of the family and are not welcome to share the family's quality time. Still, this is not the case for all types of host families. The au pairs in the single-parent families I studied had a somewhat different status. For the single mothers in my study, the au pairs were not simply persons whom they cooperate with, but rather wanted and needed family members.

The fact that au pairs, like maids, cleaners, and other types of domestic workers, are often unwanted and spatially segregated from the rest of the family only emphasizes their status as not family members. At the same time, the use of kinship terms to define the relationship between the au pair and the host family reinforces a view that the work done by the au pair is a 'labour of love', not recognizing the emotional labour put in by the au pair and the welfare produced through that emotional labour.

The au pairs produce welfare in a several ways. Though legally and discursively constructed as non-workers, the au pairs pay taxes for the amount of money and the lodging they receive by the host family. This accumulates welfare that is consumed by the local citizens. Liberating the host family from some of the housework and care responsibilities, the au pairs not only produce welfare in the families they work for, but also enable these families to contribute to the production of social welfare by participating in the labour market. The work of the au pairs, then, generates benefits for the Norwegian welfare state. Still, their labour is officially defined as a 'labour of love' (Øien 2009).

Answering cultural norms

For career-oriented middle-class mothers, hiring an au pair is more than a way of dealing with the stalled revolution at home (Hochschild 1989). Finding a reliable au pair who successfully takes over the household chores and part of the child-care is also a way of answering the local cultural norms of what makes good motherhood. Thanks to the au pair, career-oriented mothers can continue being good mothers – by paying another woman to perform part of their duties. That is why finding the 'right' au pair becomes an important job for which professional agents, friends, family members and sometimes the au pair's own networks are mobilized.

Racial, ethnic and bodily classifications are drawn upon in the selection of the 'right' au pair (Bikova 2008). For example, English-speaking au pairs are said not to be independent enough to manage an au-pair's duties. Girls from Russia and the Ukraine are known for their bad morals and poor work ethic. Polish, Hungarian and Romanian girls are seen as not good enough at housework duties. German-speaking au pairs and girls from the Baltic countries, on the other hand, are welcomed in Norwegian homes as they are said to be adaptable and to share similar views on child-care as the Norwegians (Adequate Assistance 2007).

The host families also have preferences as to the au pair's physique. The au pair should be healthy and fit enough to carry out physically demanding household duties, but not overtly physically attractive, because that would threaten the host mother's status in the family.

At the same time, the families in my study wanted the au pair to be 'someone like us' – someone who is educated, responsible and reliable – and preferred to look at the au pair as a young person on a cultural exchange rather than as a migrant worker in need (Bikova 2008). The image of the adventurous and culturally curious young person seemed to better suit the local equality ideals to which my informants conform.

Still, for the majority of families in my study, the most important qualification that made an au pair a *good* au pair is gender. The 'right' au pair is always a female au pair. Though positive to the increasing number of male assistants in Norwegian kindergartens, Norwegian parents are not willing to let unknown men from a foreign culture take care of their children in the intimate atmosphere of the private home (Bikova 2008). Stereotypes of women as biologically better caregivers and of foreign men as sexual predators are invoked to justify the scepticism to male au pairs. Asking my informants whether they would consider a male au pair, they usually answered in the negative. As one of the host mothers explained, 'I actually think that my husband wouldn't really want me to choose a male [au pair]' (Host mother, family 7). The purity of the conjugal relationship would be threatened by the presence of another male in the home, but also the local notion of good motherhood is incompatible with letting an unknown man taking care of small children,

> Well, no … [thinking for a while], I think it might be some kind of conservatism in this. But we had small children and … [hesitating for a while] one hears things. There have been some episodes … so I didn't want to make that choice … (Host father, family 7)

The employment of au pairs enables career-oriented parents to conform with yet another local cultural norm: the strong Scandinavian norm that the family should meet its needs by relying on its own resources with support from the welfare state. This is not violated when the person assisting the family in its daily routines is defined as someone who is 'on cultural exchange'. The ideology of cultural exchange obscures the fact that the majority of au pairs are hired to do the housework, while the child-care is delegated to professional staff at the public kindergartens. Having someone who is on cultural exchange, who is 'more like us' and whom 'we work with', creates the impression that the au pairs and host families are equal parties with common interests, and conceals the power and status discrepancy in their relationship, while it also helps families evade the discomfort of having a domestic help in a society with strong norms of social and gender equality.

At the same time, hiring educated women from poorer countries to do the housework that local women do not have time to do means that local families are participating in a global process of 'housewifization' that devalues migrant women's labour and professional qualifications (Mies, Thomson & Werlhof 1988).[5] The families who hire au pairs often view the employment of an au pair as an act of charity:

> I know that she likes it here and that I can give her something to make it even better. Because I know that where she comes from they are not doing well in terms of social environment, safety, money ... all this. (Host mother, family 8)

In her research on domestic work, however, Bridget Anderson (2002) argues that the employment of a domestic worker is not an act of sisterhood, but a discriminatory practice by which female employers assert their status as affluent women.

Local troubles – glocal issues

The introduction of state-subsidized domestic services such as cleaning, childminding, gardening, and so on has been discussed as a possible solution to the 1990s' unemployment crisis in Denmark, Sweden and Norway, but has also been promoted politically as a gender-equality policy (Platzer 2002). It has been argued that the engagement of weaker societal groups in the delivery of domestic services will help reduce the unemployment figures, transform the illegal purchase of domestic services into legal work, and improve the daily welfare of many households (Platzer 2002; Kitterød 2002). For female professionals, paying someone to take over part of the household chores and care responsibilities is an opportunity to participate in the labour market on equal terms with men. At the same time, the increased use of home-based services was said to strengthen the social inequality between the well-off and the not so well-off women (Holtsmark 1994; Cappelen et al. 1995; Selvaag 1995; Isaksen 1995; Ruud 1996, in Kitterød 1998, 188).

The home-service scheme was made permanent in Denmark in 1997. Sweden did not allow it until 2007 (Platzer 2007). Experience from Denmark shows that it is the affluent, two-career families who consume most of the state-subsidized home-based services, despite the fact that they can afford to buy them at a market price (Platzer 2002). In Norway, because of the strong equality norms that weaker social groups should not be used as cheap labour, a home-service scheme has not yet been introduced, although the idea is popular among right-wing political parties. At the same time, these services are delivered by some of the Norwegian society's weakest groups – the au pairs, who, because they are defined as non-workers, are paid pocket money to produce market services.

The use of au pairs means that housework and housework-related conflicts are outsourced, but likewise the opportunity for achieving gender equality in the nuclear middle-class Norwegian family. Equality is achieved on the basis of the contributions to the family budget rather than equal participation in the domestic chores. Equality in this case is primarily a *financial* equality achieved at the expense of the housewifization of migrant women. By hiring women rather than men to do the care work and domestic work, the traditional gender division of labour in the host family and society is reproduced and cemented.

Turning to the full implications of au-pairing on what Robertson (1995) has so aptly termed the glocal level, as international monetary politics makes the currencies of the industrialized countries more valuable than local currencies, millions of women and men from poorer countries leave their home countries in hope of better opportunities and higher pay. This is true of many of the young women who become au pairs in Norwegian families. Many of them are university graduates and promising professionals, so this outflow of highly qualified labour power, the 'brain drain' of the literature, often creates a shortage of qualified professionals in the migrants' countries of origin (Hochschild 2002; Parreñas 2002). In addition, the outflow of qualified labour causes the 'brain waste' of professional abilities, for migrant workers seldom have the opportunity to utilize their formal training in the receiving countries. Many of the au pairs coming to Norwegian families have university degrees or other professional training (Bikova 2008; Bertelsen 2007; Hovdan 2005). Taking up low-paid and low-skilled au-pair jobs, these women return to the kitchen, but as housewives rather than as qualified professionals. Still, for many au pairs the financial gains of this housewifization are too important to leave the global kitchen.

The outflow of labour from economically poor countries also causes care deficit in the migrant workers' countries of origin. When affluent families in economically rich countries hire au pairs to deal with entrenched gender divisions of labour and absent fathers, a new problem emerges – that of the absent mothers and daughters in the au pairs' home cultures. Leaving behind their own families to provide care for families in Norway, the au pairs activate global care chains that start at the au pairs' countries of origin and end at the homes of affluent Norwegian families. At the top of the care chain one finds the families who buy flexibility by hiring au pairs. In order for au pairs to be able to sell their care work, they in turn need to be freed from their own care responsibilities. The care of an au pair's children and siblings is delegated to a lower link in the chain – a grandmother, sister, aunt or a care worker. The women who provide care for the au pairs' children delegate the care for their own children to family members or local care workers, thus initiating a local care chain. At the bottom of the care chain one finds the children of the au pairs – and the children of the women providing care for the au pair's children.

For Hochschild (in Yeates 2004), the concept of global care chains reflects a basic inequality of access to material resources, but also a global inequality in the redistribution of care resources, particularly emotional care. The emotional labour involved in caring for children of parents further down the chain is displaced onto children of parents living further up, as a result of which 'emotional surplus value' is extracted (Hochschild in Yeates 2004, 373). However, as the majority of Norwegian children attend full-time or part-time kindergartens, the au pairs in Norwegian homes seldom have the opportunity to develop strong emotional bonds with their charges. Hence, emotional surplus value is not produced and extracted in the same way as described by Ehrenreich and Hochschild (2002) and Parreñas (2001) in their studies of care workers in North America and Europe.

Thus Norway does participate in the production of global care chains, but these chains take on another social form as they are integrated in the public–private mix particular to contemporary dual-income families. The difficulties affluent Norwegian families have with the work–family balance with the resources provided by the welfare state enhance structural inequalities at both the local and the global level, as the women performing domestic and care work in these affluent homes often leave behind them social networks of their own that need the same type of work. Brain drain; brain waste; the housewifization of educated women; the reproduction of traditional gender roles; and the activation of chains of power and privilege in the shape of global care chains: these are only some of the glocal issues related to the international division of labour, of which the institution of the au pair is a small but important part.

Notes

1 Childminders ('dagmamma') are state-subsidized private individuals who provide child-care in their homes.
2 'A family member or a family servant? Why Norwegian families hire au pairs' is the title of the study of Norwegian families I conducted in 2008 as a part of my Master's degree in sociology at the University of Bergen.
3 Family 1 consists of a single mother with three children. Family 2 is a two-parent family with three children, with both parents working. Family 3 is a two-parent family with one child, with both parents working. Family 4 is a two-parent family with three children, with both parents working. Family 5 is a single mother with two children; she was a student at the time of the interview. Family 6 is a two-parent family with three children, with both parents working. Family 7 is a two-parent family with two children, with both parents working. Family 8 is a two-parent family with two children, with both parents working. Family 10 is a two-parent family with three children, with both parents working.
4 All the interviews quoted in this chapter are taken from Bikova 2008.
5 The term 'housewifization' incorporates several aspects of women's work. It might be paid or unpaid, skilled or unskilled, often unregulated, low-paid and occupationally segregated. It is used here to describe the process by which

educated women from poorer countries are brought back to affluent families' kitchens and there defined as 'cheap labour' associated with the type of work they conduct (Mies, Thomson & Werlhof 1988).

References
Literature

Anderson, Bridget (2000), *Doing the Dirty Work. The Global Politics of Domestic Labour* (London & New York: Zed Books).

Anderson, Bridget (2002), 'Just another Job? The Commodification of Domestic Labour', in Barbara Ehrenreich & Arlie Russell Hochschild (eds.), *Global Woman. Nannies, Maids and Sex Workers in the New Economy* (New York: Metropolitan/ Owl Books), 104–114.

Beck, Ulrich & Beck-Gernsheim Elisabeth (1995), *The Normal Chaos of Love* (Cambridge: Polity Press).

Beck, Ulrich & Beck-Gernsheim, Elisabeth (2002), *Individualization* (London: Sage).

Bikova, Mariya (2008), 'A family member or a family servant. A qualitative study' (Master's thesis; Bergen: Institute of Sociology, University of Bergen).

Bertelsen, Marte (2007), Au pair-ordningen i søkelyset (Master's thesis in the sociology of law; Oslo: Institutt for kriminologi og rettssosiologi, Juridisk fakultet, University of Oslo).

Brandth, Berit & Kvande, Elin (1992), 'Changing masculinities – the reconstruction of fathering', paper presented at the conference 'Family Sociology – Developing the Field', Voksenåsen, 2–4 March 1992 (University of Trondheim).

Brandth, Berit & Kvande, Elin (1999), 'Flexible work and flexible fathers', *Work, Employment and Society*, 15/2, 251–267.

Brandth, Berit & Kvande, Elin (2003), *Fleksible fedre – maskulinitet, arbeid, velferdsstat* (Oslo; Universitetsforlaget).

Brandth, Berit (2007), 'Fedres selvutvikling og grensene mellom jobb og hjem', in Elin Kvande & Bente Rasmussen (eds.), *Arbeidslivets klemmer. Paradokser i det nye arbeidslivet* (Bergen: Fagbokforlaget), 273–289.

Council of Europe ([1969]1972), *Explanatory Report on the European Agreement on Au Pair Placement. (Council of Europe, Strasburg 1972. European Agreement on Au Pair Placement)* (Strasbourg, 24 November 1969).

Cox, Rosie (2006), *The Servant Problem. Domestic Employment in a Global Economy* (London & New York: I. B. Taurius).

Cox, Rosie (2007), 'The Au Pair Body: Sex Object, Sister or Student?', *European Journal of Women's Studies*, 14/3, 281–296.

Ehrenreich, Barbara & Hochschild, Arlie Russell (2002), 'Introduction', in id. (eds.), *Global Woman. Nannies, Maids and Sex Workers in the New Economy* (New York: Metropolitan/Owl Books), 1–13.

Esping-Andersen, Gøsta (2009), *The Incomplete Revolution: Adapting to Women's New Roles* (Cambridge: Polity Press).

Griffith, Susan & Legg, Sharon (1997), *The Au Pair and Nanny's Guide to Working Abroad* (Oxford: Vacation Work).

Gullestad, Marianne (1981), *Sosialantropologiske perspektiver på familie og hushold* (Bergen: Sosialantroplogisk institutt, University of Bergen).

Halrynjo, Sigtona (2007), 'Alltid beredt? Arbeids og familiedilemmaer i møte med formelle og uformelle spilleregler i et stort konsern', in Elin Kvande & Bente Rasmussen (eds.), *Arbeidslivets klemmer. Paradokser i det nye arbeidslivet* (Bergen: Fagbokforlaget), 81–103.

Hess, Sabine& Puckhaber, Annette (2004), '"Big sisters"' are better domestic servants?! Comments on the booming au pair business', *Feminist Review*, 77, 65–78.

Hochschild, Arlie Russell (1983), *The Second Shift. Working Parents and the Revolution at Home* (New York: Penguin Books).

Hochschild, Arlie Russell (1989), *The Managed Heart: Commercialization of Human Feeling* (Berkeley: University of California Press).

Hochschild, Arlie Russell (1997), *The Time Bind: When Work Becomes Home and Home Becomes Work* (New York: Metropolitan Books).

Hochschild, Arlie Russell (2000), 'The nanny chain', *The American Prospect*, 11/4, 32–36.

Hochschild, Arlie Russell (2002), 'Love and Gold', in Barbara Ehrenreich & Arlie Russell Hochschild (eds.), *Global Woman. Nannies, Maids and Sex Workers in the New Economy* (New York: Metropolitan/Owl Books), 15–30.

Hovland, Brit Marie & Aagedal, Olaf (eds.) (2003), *Det norske Spania – i sol og skygge. En konferanserapport om den nye norske utvandringsbølgen, og om norsk velferd i utlendighet* (Oslo: DHS).

Hovdan, Marianne (2005), *Au Pair in Norway. A Qualitative Study* (Bergen: Institute of Sociology, University of Bergen).

Kitterød, Ragni Hege (1998), 'Kjøp av rengjøringstjenster – større sosial ulikhet blant kvinner?', *Sosiologisk tidsskrift* 3/1998, 185–208.

Kitterød, Ragni Hege (2002), 'Få har rengjøringshjelp, men stor variasjon mellom grupper', *Samfunnsspeilet* 4–5/2002. <http://www.ssb.no/samfunnsspeilet/> Published 22 May 2002, accessed on 9 March 2009.

Martinsen, John-Tore (2007), *Til Spania for å finne det gode liv. Norske pensjonisters forsøk på å skape et meningsfylt liv i nye omgivelser* (Hovedoppgave i sosialantroplogi; Tromsø: Samfunnsvitenskapelige fakultetet, University of Tromsø).

Mies, Maria, Bennholdt-Thomson, Veronika & von Werlhof, Claudia (1988), *Women: The Last Colony* (London: Zed).

Øien, Cecilie (2009. *On Equal Terms? An Evaluation of the Norwegian Au Pair Scheme.* (FAFO report 2009, 29; Oslo).

Parreñas, Rhacel Salazar (2001), *Servants of Globalization. Women, Migration and Domestic Work* (Stanford, Calif.: Stanford University Press).

Parreñas, Rhacel Salazar (2002), 'The Care Crisis in the Philippines: Children and Transnational Families in the New Global Economy', in Barbara Ehrenreich & Arlie Russell Hochschild (eds.), *Global Woman. Nannies, Maids and Sex Workers in the New Economy* (New York: Metropolitan/Owl Books), 39–54.

Platzer, Ellinor (2002), *Domestic Service and the Division of Labour. The Example of the Danish Home Service Scheme* (Human Netten 10; Växjö: Institutionen for Humanoria, Vaxjo University), also available at <http://www.vxu.se/hum/pub/humanetten/nummer10/art0207.html>.

Platzer, Ellinor (2007), *Från folkhem till karriarhushåll. Den nya huslige arbeitsdelingen* (Doctoral thesis, Lund University, Sweden; Lund: Arkiv forlag).

Rotkirch, Anna (2001), 'The Internationalisation of Intimacy: A Study of the Chains of Care', paper presented at the 5th Conference of the European Sociological Association, Visions and Divisions, Helsinki, 28 August–1 September.

Robertson, Roland (1995), 'Glocalisation: Time–Space and Homogenity–Heterogenity', in Mike Featherstone, Scott Lash & Roland Robertson (eds.), *Global Modernities* (London: Sage), 25–44.

Stenum, Helle (2008), *Au pair in Denmark: Billig arbeidskraft eller kulturell utveksling?* (Copenhagen: FOA).

Yeats, Nicola (2004), 'Global Care Chains: Critical Reflections and Lines of Enquiry'. *International Feminist Journal of Politics*, Volume 6, number 3, 369–391.

Internet sources

Adequate Assistance AS (2007), <http://www.leaps.no/2+91NFoppslag.htm>, accessed on 2 December 2007.

Arbeidstilsynet (Labour Inspection) (2007), *Tidskonto* <http://www.arbeidstilsynet.no/c26976/faktaside/vis.html?tid=28501>, accessed on 9 December 2007.

NAV (The Norwegian Labour and Welfare Administration) (2009), *Foreldrepenger ved fødsel* <http://www.nav.no/1073744316.cms>, accessed on 6 December 2009.

SSB (Statistics Norway) (2006), *Dette er Kari og Ola* <http://www.ssb.no/locate>, accessed on 10 May 2008.

SSB (Statistics Norway) (2009), *Barnehager. Foreløpige tall, 2008* <http://www.ssb.no/emner/04/02/10/barnehager/>, accessed on 13 January 2009.

UDI (Norwegian Directorate of Immigration) (2007), *Circular 2007-020* <http://www.udi.no/upload/Rundskriv/2007/RS%202007-020-en.doc>, accessed on 1 December 2007.

UDI (Norwegian Directorate of Immigration) (2008), *Tall of Fakta 2007* <http://www.udi.no/templates/Page.aspx?id=9152>, accessed on 9 April 2008.

UDI (Norwegian Directorate of Immigration) (2009), *Tall of Fakta 2009* <http://www.udi.no/upload/Pub/Aasrapport/2008/UDI_Tall_og_fakta_web_rettet_versjon.pdf>.

Newspaper articles

BT, 28 October 2008, 'Yrkeskvinnenes paradis' <http://www.bt.no/na24/article431142.ece>, accessed on 22 May 2009.

DB, 1 April 2004, 'Vi er avhengig av Anna' (Tone Vassbø) <http://www.dagbladet.no/dinside/2004/04/01/394880.html>, accessed on 15 May 2008.

DagensNæringsliv, 6–7 March 2004, 'Det nye tjenesteskapet' (Eva Grinde and Ingvild H. Rishøi), 22–26.

Klassekampen, 3 November 2007, 'Den filippinkse au pair-en "Susan" (25) Stakk av fra vertsfamilie i Bærum – Familien truet meg' (Åse Brandvold), 6–7.

CHAPTER 4

Cultural exchange
or cheap domestic labour?

Constructions of 'au pair' in four Nordic countries

Catharina Calleman

This chapter deals with the regulation of au-pair work – a gender-coded, low-wage occupation on the outskirts of the labour market, which is, by definition, performed by foreigners. The regulation of au-pair work is particularly interesting today, as its social context has changed dramatically in the last few decades, most importantly as a result of the deregulation and globalization of the labour market and the development of Internet-based employment agencies.

Whereas earlier au-pair placements took place between countries with similar economic standards of living, the exchange now increasingly takes place between countries where very different material conditions prevail.[1] Today, au pairs often go abroad not primarily to travel, see another country and learn a language, but from economic necessity. Thus the au-pair form of work has become a loophole used to meet the demand for certain types of domestic labour, as general policy concerning labour immigration is very restrictive. Within the EU, citizens of non-EU countries are not granted work permits as long as there is labour available within the EU.

The regulation of au-pair work is strongly influenced by the fundamental limit in law between private and public. Firstly, as the au pair is seen as a family member, the regulation of au-pair placement is affected by the special treatment in law of family matters. Protecting private life and the family from intrusion and intervention on the part of the state is a crucial objective of the legal order,[2] which may imply that the family or family members are exempted from certain legislation or that the laws are applied differently in cases concerning the inner life of the family. This in turn implies protection for the stronger party in cases of conflict within the family. Secondly, au-pair regulation is influenced by the special legal treatment of paid domestic work, which builds not only on the low status attached to gender-coded, unpaid domestic work, but also on the protection of private life mentioned above. Thus employment regulation usually either excludes such work or entitles it to considerably weaker protection than other work, simultaneously implying an extension of the prerogative of the employer.[3] Thirdly, possibly as a consequence of the private nature accorded the relationship between the parties, the sources of law that determine the status of au-pair work may be said to have a private character, as they do not usually consist of (public) legislation but of internal guidelines drawn up by migration authorities. Fourthly, au-pair work regulation is permeated by the tension between *public* migration legislation – where the main aim is to exclude labour migration – and a loophole in this legislation for 'cultural exchange', where the relationship between the individuals is regulated in *private* (employment) law. Thus at least four dimensions of the public–private divide in law may be said to be involved in this study.

The chapter deals with state policies concerning au-pair placements in four Nordic countries: Denmark, Finland, Norway and Sweden. Its aim is to analyse how 'au pair' is constructed, and how rights and obligations shaping au pairs as empowered or dependent individuals are distributed according to whether they are constructed as workers or students/family members in these countries. Despite many similarities in legislation between the Nordic countries, there is reason to believe that, because of recent political developments, national policies concerning au-pair work display differences in the various states' notions of gender and domestic work, the privacy of the home, or labour immigration. The Nordic countries have had a common labour market since 1954, but once Denmark, Finland and Sweden, but not Norway, joined the EU differences began to appear. Furthermore, Denmark has opted out of certain provisions of the Maastricht Treaty, implying, among other things, that it will not participate in specific aspects of supranational cooperation within the EU.

Method, sources and scope

The starting-point for the present analysis of the status of au pairs will be the regulation in migration law of residence and work permits in the countries studied. With the exception of Norway, these regulations are very brief, consisting merely of a statement that permits may be granted 'for other special reasons' and so on. The application of these regulations relies on guidelines governing the granting of permits for such 'special reasons' (such as, for example, for au pairs) issued by the migration authorities. These guidelines are the only national documents regulating the au pairs' circumstances, and will thus constitute the material used to analyse their rights and obligations in the various countries. The guidelines for each country, as conveyed to potential applicants for au-pair permits, will also be analysed in the light of social constructionism (Burr 1995). Such an analysis aims to reveal the underlying ideas, values and other premises contained in legal documents.[4] The construction of the au pairs and the families will be analysed in order to convey a concept of the image of au pairs and families created in the various states and of how these images may influence their choice of policies and methods for administration and control.

The regulation of work and residence permits concerns only citizens of countries outside the EU, Iceland, Norway, Lichtenstein and Switzerland, and thus forms part of Fortress Europe.[5] Similar conditions as regards the relationship between the au pairs and the families may, however, be applied to the thousands of au pairs who are citizens of EU countries, as the regulations in migration law have been inspired by the European Agreement on 'au pair' Placement (Strasbourg, 24 November 1969), which, as will be seen, is the basis for all au-pair regulation and culture in Europe. The analysis in this chapter of concrete rights and obligations will only consider the relationship between the au pair and the family – the employment law dimension. A study of rights and obligations versus the state as stipulated in social law and tax law would be most interesting but would require a further, extensive, in-depth study.

The main sources of knowledge for the investigation have been the European Agreement and the appended Explanatory Report, national migration law and employment law, and information and standard contracts for au-pair placements adopted by authorities in Denmark, Finland, Norway and Sweden. The information concerning the migration offices' guidelines is constantly changing; the versions used in this chapter date from January 2010. Numerous contacts with the migration authorities in the four countries have also helped in the investigation, while empirical studies of the status of au pairs in Norway and Denmark, and in particular the works of Marte Bertelsen (2007) and Helle Stenum (2008), have been of great value in understanding the context of au-pair regulation.

The Agreement of the Council of Europe

The central European policy document on au-pair placement is the European Agreement on 'au pair' Placement, concluded by the Council of Europe in 1969 (hereafter the European Agreement or the Agreement).[6] The Agreement has been signed by Belgium, Denmark, France, Greece, Italy, Luxemburg, Norway, Switzerland and Germany. This means that out of the countries in this investigation, Denmark and Norway have signed the Agreement, implying that its provisions are applicable to all au pairs in these two countries. However, the Agreement has also inspired the regulation of residence or work permits for au pairs in Finland and Sweden, who are not signatories.[7] Thus, in these two countries most of its provisions are applicable to au pairs from countries outside the EU applying for au-pair permits. At the same time, au pairs of all nationalities working in Sweden and Finland may be indirectly affected by the Agreement's provisions through the practices of au-pair agencies, the au-pair culture or – not least – competition in the market for au pairs.

The European Agreement was a product of transitional conditions in the 1960s. As described in its Explanatory Report, it was an attempt to settle a problem of 'ever-increasing magnitude', as the number of young people going abroad to improve their knowledge of languages had risen constantly since the end of the Second World War. Although a form au-pair placement had existed for a long time, its nature had changed. Where once it had been arranged on a friendly basis between families known to each other through mutual acquaintances, the au pair had become a unique social phenomenon because of its frequency and the large number of persons involved. It was obvious that the uncontrolled development of such temporary migration could not be allowed to continue, if only in the interests of the parties concerned (Explanatory Report).

From the beginning the regulation of au-pairing was coloured by ambivalence between a family model based on unpaid labour and a worker model based on paid labour. Au pairs were considered to belong to a special category, one with features of both the student category and the worker category, and were therefore and because of their young age considered to be in need of appropriate arrangements and special protection (Preamble of the Agreement). Thus the European Agreement's aim was merely protective and did not take into consideration the need for domestic work in the various countries concerned. There was, however, a strong interest in making a clear distinction from labour migration, which caused disagreements among the signatories regarding the extent of the au pairs' entitlements. As will be shown, some of the provisions are concrete expressions of this interest.

Au-pair placement protected by the Agreement was defined as

> the temporary reception by families, in exchange for certain services, of young foreigners who come to improve their linguistic and possibly professional knowledge as well as their general culture by acquiring a better knowledge of the country where they are received. (Article 2)

It was emphasized in the Explanatory Report that the au-pair placement must be of a 'temporary' nature; its purpose must be cultural; the persons placed must be foreigners; and the placement must be made in families. The Agreement applied to any person placed as an au pair in the territory of any contracting state without discrimination as to that person's nationality (Explanatory Report). In other words, even if the Agreement focused on European exchange, its provisions were also to be applicable to au pairs who were not European citizens.

The cultural purpose is most apparent in the age limits set for au pairs protected by the Agreement, namely from 17 to 30 years of age. It was felt that to have included those over 30 years of age would be to depart from the purpose of the Agreement – to protect young people going abroad to improve their knowledge of languages. As regards gender, the Agreement mentioned 'persons' or 'young foreigners', meaning its scope was young women *and* men. According to Annex II, any contracting party may however declare that it reserves the right 'to consider that the term "person placed au pair" shall apply only to females'.[8] Thus the Agreement does contain exclusionary criteria according to age, but none according to gender, family status or ethnicity.

An au pair's rights

As regards the au pair's rights and obligations in relation to the host family, the similarities to a *work contract* came to the fore in both the content and form of the Agreement's provisions. Thus its delimitation in respect of labour migration was emphasized, and uncertainty over whether the au pair held worker's rights or family/student status permeated the discussions. According to Article 6, the rights and obligations of the au pair and the host family were to be the subject of an agreement in writing between the parties concerned. This provision was discussed at length, some wishing it to be considered as an actual contract of employment, others not being able to accept that for a number of reasons, primarily the strict regulation of the immigration of workers (Explanatory Report).

The rights of the au pair were dealt with in Article 8. Some of these rights clearly related to family member/student status. The au pair was to receive board and lodging from the host family and, where possible, should occupy a separate room. The au pair was to be given 'adequate time to attend language courses as well as for cultural and professional improvement'. This is particularly interesting as the word 'improvement' was used to show that there could be no question of the au pairs pursuing a professional activity or full-length training course. The provision was thus meant to rule out the possibility of clandestine work (Explanatory Report). On the other hand, registering for courses was not made compulsory, with reference to the fact that placements would not necessarily be limited to towns where organized courses were held (Explanatory Report). There was also no mention of the crucial issue of who was to pay for any such courses.

Other rights were more coloured by the notion of the au pair as worker. The au pair was to have at least one full free day per week and was to receive 'a certain sum of money, as pocket money'. The amount of money and the intervals at which it was to be paid were to be determined by agreement between the two parties. The term 'pocket money' was expressly used to prevent the sum paid from being thought a remuneration or wage (Explanatory Report). No guidance was given as to its amount, as it was expected to vary with the customs of the countries and the mutual services rendered.

The obligations of the au pair consisted in rendering the host family services through participation in everyday family life. The time the au pair spent on such services should generally not be more than five hours a day (Article 9). The particular services singled out were housework, cooking and looking after the children, even at night.

The termination of the agreement between the au pair and the family (Article 11) was clearly influenced by the provisions of international employment law.[9] Where the parties had not set a time limit on their agreement, each was entitled to terminate it by giving two weeks' notice. In the event of 'serious misconduct by the other party or if other serious circumstances made such instant termination necessary', either party could terminate the agreement with immediate effect.

Opinions varied among signatories regarding how appropriate benefits should be provided to the au pair in the case of 'sickness, maternity or accident'. Difficulties had arisen because, in the absence of wages, affiliation to a national social security scheme was impossible in the majority of countries. Thus measures taken to distinguish au-pair work from labour migration had an effect on the au pair's social entitlements. Article 10 was a compromise, which aimed to cover *both* situations in countries where the au pairs were eligible for the social security benefits *and* situations where no such scheme was applicable to them. Each contracting party was to list the benefits to which the au pair was entitled in the event of sickness, maternity or accident. If such benefits were not covered by 'national social security legislation or other official schemes' in the receiving country, the host family was to take out private insurance at their own expense.

Denmark

Denmark has signed the European Agreement, and the Agreement's contents are therefore to be applied to all au pairs in Denmark. The national regulation of conditions of au-pair work falls to the Danish Immigration Service. Au pairs from countries outside the EU must have a temporary residence permit according to the Danish Aliens Act s 9c(1), which refers to special grounds for the granting of a residence permit and makes applicants subject to the special eligibility criteria and procedures of the migration authorities. Denmark has seen an increase in applications for residence permits for au pairs since 2000. Before 2006 the number did not reach 2,000 persons, but in 2007 2,207 persons and in 2008 2,939 persons were granted residence permits as au pairs.[10] This phenomenon parallels a general tightening of migration regulations concerning citizens of non-EU countries (Stenum 2008). The au-pair scheme has been much debated. Abusive situations concerning au pairs have been revealed and a special penalty has been introduced under 'indsatsen mod misbrug av au pair-ordningen'.[11]

The official policies of the migration authorities on residence permits for au pairs are presented on the website 'New in Danmark/ Ny i Danmark'.[12] This information is clearly influenced by the rationalities of migration law and has a strong emphasis on exclusion, discipline and repression. The first paragraph explains the aim of au-pair placements, simultaneously defining working more than the stipulated 30 hours as 'working illegally in Denmark'. One does not need to look far before encountering the section entitled 'Consequences of abusing the au-pair scheme', which spells out that all adult members of the host family must declare that they have not been convicted of violence against an au pair in the last ten years, or of illegal employment of an au pair in the last five years, or been registered in a special au-pair register as a result of other abuse of the au-pair scheme (that is, disregarding the limitations regarding an au pair's tasks and duties, maximum work hours, accommodation, minimum allowance, etc.).

A large part of the information from the Immigration Service consists of detailed eligibility criteria for the au-pair permit, relating both to the au pair and to the family. Thus, it is a precondition that the au pair already has 'the necessary linguistic and cultural foundation to receive the full benefit' of her stay in Denmark. The au pair must have completed the equivalent of nine years schooling and have a working knowledge of Danish, Swedish, Norwegian, English or German. She must not be married and must not bring with her children under the age of 18. For receiving families, detailed criteria are defined to the effect that child-care is a condition for granting an au-pair permit – in other words, the host family must comprise at least one parent and one child under the age of 18. In families with shared custody, both parents must meet the conditions for being a host family, as the au pair will follow the children. Some exclusionary criteria relate to citizenship/ethnicity, with the stated aim of introducing the au pair to the Danish language and culture. Normally, at least one parent must be a Danish citizen. However, parents who are EU citizens residing in Denmark under the EU regulations on free movement, or foreign nationals who have lived in Denmark for a long time and have a strong attachment to Denmark, are also accepted as host families.

The special application form for au pairs contains questions on family status, previous stays in Denmark, education and knowledge of languages, number of children in the host family, and a requirement for a weekly work schedule. The applicant has to vouch for the correctness of the information, and consent to information being passed on to local authorities, the host family, intelligence agencies and prosecuting authorities. The applicant is reminded several times that she may be subject to penalties if the information provided is false or incomplete or if she violates the conditions of the residence permit.

The au-pair applicant may be given a permit for a maximum of 18 months, which is longer than the period stated in the European Agreement. In exceptional cases the permit may be extended to a maximum of 24 months. One informative example given of such an exception is if a child in the family has an illness or condition that demands care or has a special connection to the au pair. This exception falls far outside the purposes of the European Agreement and is obviously a criterion based on the need for domestic services. Parental ill-health or disability, however, is said not normally to be a special reason.

The rights and obligations of the au pair and the family are stated in the Immigration Service's Standard Au Pair Contract, which must be attached to the application for a residence permit. As a student the au pair has the right to sufficient time off to take language courses, pursue her cultural and professional interests, and participate in religious events,[13] but there is no requirement for registration for courses or that the au pair actually attends language courses. There are also no provisions regarding who is responsible for paying for courses. It is explicitly stated that the au pair's daily chores are not considered work. The money paid to the au pair is called 'pocket money', set at a minimum of DKK 2,900 per month.

It is also stated, however, that the relationship between the au pair and the host family is regarded as an employer/employee relationship and as such subject to Danish law on holidays and taxation. The information about holidays is not readily accessible, however: according to the application form, the host is obliged to ascertain whether the applicant is covered by the provisions of the Holiday Act (2000) or the Act on Certain Working Conditions in Agriculture (1994) and to inform the applicant in writing whether or not she is entitled to paid holidays. Other stipulations on work concern neither rights nor obligations, but prohibitions. The au pair is not allowed to carry out chores for the host family outside the time limits defined, carry out tasks other than household chores, carry out chores, or work outside the host family's home or take on paid or unpaid work. This message is repeated three times in the Immigration Service's information.

As regards employment protection, both parties have a right to terminate the contract with two weeks' notice or with immediate effect in the case of a serious breach. However, the au pair's right to stay in the country is conditioned by the fact that she is allowed to find a new family who meet the requirements of the Immigration Service, which, of course, might limit her possibilities of terminating the contract.

In the Danish information concerning the au-pair scheme, restrictive migration legislation has encroached on the protection of au pairs. Through detailed eligibility criteria and provisions on punishment, the au pair is largely constructed as an alien trying to sneak into the country, either for economic reasons or in order to join relatives. She is also constructed as a person who may be subject to abuse. The family is likewise largely constructed as either wanting lots of cheap labour or wanting to bring in relatives to Denmark – and as potential criminals.

Some of the eligibility criteria make au-pair placements an institution for (qualified) child-care. The idea of professional and cultural improvement has been allowed to shape the eligibility criteria but not to safeguard the rights of the au pair as a student. There are no rights – except the right to free time in accordance with the Agreement – for the au pair as student. As a worker she has the right to a monthly allowance, limited working hours in accordance with the European Agreement, and the right to holidays, but the existence and the extent of this right is unclear in the information. Finally, either party may terminate the relationship with two weeks' notice, but the au pair is only allowed to stay in the country if, within a short period of time, she can find a new family offering conditions that accord with the requirements of the migration authorities. Thus, if for some reason she needs to stay in the country, she is made strongly dependent on the host family.

Finland

Finland signed the European Agreement in July 1997, but did not ratify it, as the legislation of the country did not comply with the Agreement's requirements.[14] However, the basic content of the European Agreement has inspired Finland's policy regarding residence permits for au pairs, which citizens of countries outside the EU are required to have and which are the subject of this investigation. This permit, a permit 'for other special reasons', according to the Finnish Aliens Act 45 s 1(4), is a 'B permit', meaning that it is considered temporary and may be issued for a period of one year. Whereas other B permits can be extended, the au-pair permit cannot.

Au-pairing in Finland is not publicly supported, but is permitted.[15] No statistics are available on the number of au-pair permits issued in Finland, but the websites of au-pair agencies give the impression that quite a few people in Finland are looking for au pairs.[16] The information published by the Finnish Immigration Service on residence permits for au pairs is based on a definition of au pairs as 'foreign citizens of 17–30 years of age who come to Finland to study or to become acquainted with the Finnish or Swedish language and culture, who live with families, and compensate for their upkeep by means of light housework'.[17] A statement that au pairs are not full-time child minders or home-helps distinguishes them from regular domestic workers.

There is a requirement that, upon arriving in the country, an au pair must possess Finnish or Swedish language skills or have studied Finnish culture, for example, history and politics, and have proof of such (for example school or university certificates). The applicant must also state why he or she wants to enter Finland to learn the language or become acquainted with the culture. Other eligibility criteria relate to the au pair's family status and family relations: it is stated that the au pair must not be a relative of the host family. In addition, au pairs cannot bring children who are minors to Finland. This is a deviation from the provisions for other temporary residence permits.[18]

There is, however, no definition of a host family. Instead it is left to the discretionary power of the Migration Office to decide whether 'other special reasons' prevail; that is, whether it is question of an au-pair contract or a contract for domestic work. In this decision, the emphasis is on the total situation and especially on the nature and amount of work.[19] In its decision, the Migration Office has at its disposal the application form containing detailed information concerning education, family (spouses or cohabitants, small and adult children and parents) and criminal history. The information emphasizes the role of the au pair as a family member. Thus other family members' circumstances serve as a yardstick for the rights and obligations of the au pair. For example, it is set down that the au pair's housing conditions must be equivalent to those of the rest of the family. Likewise, the au pair's work must not exceed the amount of housework or childminding carried out by family members. The information thus conveys an idyllic image of au-pair placements. The au pair is constructed as a student wishing to study the Finnish culture; the family as an egalitarian place, where the members have the same rights and obligations. Thus an au-pair placement is constructed as one that does not require state intervention.

The rights and obligations of the au pair and the family are to be stated in a contract and attached to the application for a residence permit, but there is no standard contract. The status of the au pair as a student is supported by a requirement for clarification of the Finnish or Swedish language courses the au pair will be registered for, the course timetable, and who will be paying for the courses. Their student status is also supported by a requirement for a written clarification of how the day care for the host family's children has been arranged during the au pair's stay in Finland. Au pairs are not considered as workers; their payment is called 'monthly net remuneration' (€ 252), and they do not have any rights or obligations as workers. An au pair does not need a permit for employed persons and labour law is not applicable. There is no state intervention in such issues as the termination of the relationship or rights to paid holidays. This means the required au-pair contract as constructed by the two parties is the only legal basis for the relationship. Being a mutual agreement, the contract can be cancelled by either party. However, the au-pair permit is not tied to one family but rather is issued as a general au-pair permit, meaning the au pair is free to change families without notifying the migration authorities.

To conclude, in Finland au-pair regulation is strongly influenced by the boundaries between private and public, implying an exception from the regulation of the home and the inner life of the family. There is very little state intervention in the relationship between the au pair and the family. In the migration authority's information, the family is constructed as an egalitarian place, where the members have the same rights and obligations. Thus an au-pair placement is constructed as being in no need of state intervention.

The status of the au pair as student is, however, supported by a requirement for registration in language courses and information on who will be paying for the courses. The family also has to show how the day care for the children has been arranged during the au pair's stay. In other words, certain concrete measures have been taken to ensure that the au pair is a student and not a nanny. There is no standard contract for the mutual rights and obligations of the parties – Finland has chosen to have a minimum level of intervention in this relationship.

The rights of the au pair as worker – except for a monthly allowance and limited working hours as in the European Agreement – are entirely the business of the two parties involved. This in turn implies that the au pair does not have a right to any social or employment benefits from the state, and consequently is totally dependent on the family in that respect. On the other hand, the au pair is free to change families without the input of the migration authorities.

Norway

Norway has signed the European Agreement and has legal regulations stating the conditions for granting au-pair permits. The relevant provisions are Section 26 of the Norwegian Aliens Act (Lov 2008-05-15 nr 35) according to which residence permits may be granted for studies and for scientific, religious or cultural purposes etc. and the Aliens Ordinance (FOR 2009-10-15 nr 1286), of which sections 6–25 apply to residence permits for au pairs. Accordingly, a permit may be granted for a total of two years if the contract meets the requirements decided by the Directorate of Immigration. This is elaborated in detail in the circular on residence permits for au pairs issued by the Directorate (RS 2010–102).

Since 2000 Norway has seen an increase in the number of au pairs from countries outside the EU; their number had reached 1,760 by 2007 and 1,980 in 2008.[20] There has been an intense debate concerning au-pair placements.[21] The au-pair rules were amended in October 2007, after the Ministry of Labour initiated a process of regulation. This resulted in improvements to the au pairs' economic circumstances and an updating of the standard au-pair contract, which was also made mandatory. Further, the au pair, the host family and – where applicable – the mediating agency were obliged to sign an information sheet on rights and obligations when signing the contract.[22] A further amendment to the regulations on au pairs came into force on 1 January 2010. The requirement for a work permit was then abolished and a residence permit only was required.

The ambivalence between work and cultural exchange is obvious in the information on residence permits for au pairs from the Norwegian Directorate of Immigration. It is emphasized that the purpose of the stay is cultural exchange, but on the other hand the family is supposed to provide an 'offer of employment' and the au pair is not allowed to work for 'other employers' or to perform 'other work'. The payment was referred to earlier as a wage but is now called 'pocket money' or 'pay' and is NOK 4,000 gross per month. There is no mention of cultural exchange in the information concerning the application procedure. Instead there are references to 'when you start working' and the fact that the au pair 'must not start to work for the family'. There are also restrictions as to the workload allowed. For example, the au pair is prohibited from working for anyone other than her host family, and may not combine her work as an au pair with other work, regardless of whether this is paid or unpaid. She must not work for more than 30 hours a week even in return for extra pay. Thus the au pair is constructed not primarily as a student but as someone intent on working as much as possible or making as much money as possible.

The eligibility criteria set out by the Directorate are detailed, relating to the au pair and the family, and to the relationship between the two. Host families may be married couples, partners or cohabiting couples (regardless of gender) with or without children, or single parents with children. Thus, the definition of family does not make childminding a condition for an au-pair permit. In the case of single parents, the children must live with the host family at least half the time; a measure designed to exclude single persons without children from constituting a host family.[23] Other criteria, relating more to the relationship between the parties, are based on a mixture of ethnicity, language and family ties, and are obviously intended to prevent family reunion and other forms of immigration. Further, a general condition for granting a permit is the probability that the au pair will return to her home country at the end of her stay and that circumstances in her home country indicate that she will be able to do so.

The rights and obligations of the au pair and the family are stated in a standard contract, which has to be attached to the application. The au pair's status as a student and family member is defined by obligations and rights. The au pair is explicitly obliged to live with the host family for the entire period of the contract. The host family on their part must treat the au pair as a member of the family. Concerning the rights, the au pair must be given the opportunity to take part in Norwegian language tuition and leisure activities, and the host family is obliged to pay up to NOK 6,000 a year for language tuition. The school to be attended and the amount paid by the family have to be stated in the standard contract.

As has already been mentioned, the relationship between the au pair and the family is often labelled employment in the information supplied by Norway's immigration authorities. Au pairs' conditions have also been adapted to employment law in several ways and strengthened in relation to the European Agreement. Thus the au pair is 'entitled to a minimum of 48 hours off per week, a free period which should be continuous if possible and never shorter than 24 hours'.[24] Further, an au pair is entitled to a total of 25 days holiday per calendar year.[25] When it comes to employment protection, either party may terminate the contract in writing with at least one month's notice. The au pair is not required to provide grounds for termination, but the host family must have reasonable grounds for dismissing the au pair. If the au pair so requests, the host family has to state the grounds for termination in writing.[26] The right of an au pair to stay in the country after the termination of a contract is dependent on whether she can find another family which meets the requirements of the Directorate, however.[27]

To conclude, the Norwegian regulation of the relationship between the au pair and the family is relatively 'public'. It takes the form of legislation, and the au pair has clear rights, both as a worker and as a student. Simultaneously, the ambivalence between student/family and worker is obvious. In the guidelines of the migration authorities the au pair is constructed not primarily as a student but as somebody striving to work as much as possible. On the other hand, au-pair placements are not constructed as childminding, as they are not limited to families with children. The au pair's position as student is fairly strong, as the family is obliged to pay for courses. As a worker, an au pair has clearly stipulated rights to rest and vacations, stated in numbers of hours and days, and also a fairly high degree of employment protection.

Sweden

Sweden has not signed the European Agreement, one rationale given being that, according to Swedish law, an au pair is considered an employee and subject to protective employment legislation.[28] Although Sweden has not signed the Agreement, it has strongly inspired its policy regarding work permits for au pairs, applicable to citizens of countries outside the EU. The legislation concerned is the Aliens Act (2005:716) chapter 6 s 2:3, stating that a work permit may be granted 'to an alien who is participating in an international exchange'. Au-pair placements have been characterized as international exchange, as they have not been considered open to the labour market.[29] The number of work permits lately granted for au pairs is not large, fluctuating around 200 a year.[30] This might be explained by the fact that domestic workers – au pairs and regular domestic workers – are increasingly available within the EU and they are not required to have permits.[31]

In Sweden, au pairs' conditions of have received attention in the media, and bills have been introduced in parliament concerning the risks of exploitation and the absence of control over au-pair working conditions.[32] These discussions have usually concerned au pairs from the Baltic countries and Poland. There is sometimes confusion about the role and the status of au pairs. Recently it was revealed in the media that an au-pair agency offered jobs on au-pair conditions in Sweden to jobseekers in Sweden. This caused the public employment agency to remove the agency's advertisement from its publications, concluding that the agency was not acting appropriately.[33]

The information from the Swedish Migration Board on work permits for au pairs from countries outside the EU is short and to the point.[34] It consists of a definition and the stated aims of the au-pair visit: an au pair lives with a family and receives payment for light household duties/taking care of children. The aim of the visit is to acquire international experience and to have the opportunity to learn Swedish and become acquainted with Swedish culture. There is also a short list of requirements concerning the au pair and the family, the supporting documents needed, and information about the application procedure. The monthly pay for au-pair work is called a 'salary' (SEK 3,500 gross), which is consistent with the fact that an au pair is considered a worker. However, there is also an element of uncertainty as to the notion of what au pairs are. Recently, in 2009, the information contained a sentence emphasizing that an au pair is something between a student and an employee, but that has now been removed.[35]

Many important issues such as entitlements under employment law and social benefits are not covered, but left to the applicant to investigate. Thus there is no information about the right to terminate the contract or to change conditions or employer. In the Swedish version, but not the English version of the information, reference is made to the Domestic Work Act (1973), which is applicable to the employment relationship. Further, the applicant is informed that, as she will be staying in Sweden for a limited period of time, she will not be entitled to the same social benefits as permanent residents in the country. Therefore she must find out what insurance cover she needs. Expressions such as 'appeal', 'attorney', 'important that you find out' are used, and thus the au pair is constructed as a legally competent, resourceful and well-informed person.

There are not many explicit eligibility criteria on the information page. Apart from the requirements of the European Agreement regarding age and foreign citizenship, the au pair must demonstrate that he or she has a clear interest in or use for Swedish language studies. Recently a new criterion has been added, aimed at excluding labour migration: 'A previous period spent as an au pair in another country immediately prior to the planned stay in Sweden could reduce the chances of being granted a permit.' Even if there are few explicit eligibility criteria, the application form asks detailed and exhaustive questions about the applicant's family members; for example, the number of her children, relatives in Sweden, earlier stays in Sweden, and so on. Based on the information in this application, the Migration Board decides at their discretion whether the person may be expected to meet the criteria of an au-pair placement.[36] The upshot is that there are eligibility criteria, although neither explicit nor exact, as to education and criteria aimed at excluding family ties and labour migration.

A written offer of employment from the host family must be attached to the application for a permit. There is no standard contract, but the requirements for the permit intervene in the parties' freedom of contract. Thus it is a requirement for the work permit that the au pair engages in studies of the Swedish language for 'a large part of a normal 40 hour working week remaining after a maximum of 25 hours of housework'. The applicant needs to enclose a certificate from the relevant school stating how many hours per week she will be studying.[37]

As has already been mentioned, an au pair is subject to employment legislation. The legislation applicable to au-pair work is the Domestic Work Act (1970:943); a special act concerning all kinds of housework performed in the employer's home, for example, childcare, cooking, cleaning and washing. The act contains rules regarding the concluding and termination of the employment agreement, working hours, and working environment that deviate from general employment legislation. However, the au pair's status as a worker and the employment legislation make little difference to their status compared to the entitlements inspired by the European Agreement, as it is a question of legislation applying to employment in private homes. A provision of the Domestic Work Act for continuous rest for 36 hours each week, preferably at weekends, however gives rights that go further than the Agreement.[38] Regarding employment protection, like the European Agreement the Domestic Work Act contains no requirement for reasonable grounds for dismissal to be given, but longer notice is required than that stated in the Agreement – one month for each party – when the duration of the relationship is a maximum of one year.

The actual possibilities for an au pair to terminate the relationship seem dependent on her right to change family. The work permit for au pairs is limited to au-pair work, but the au pair may change employer without permission from the Migration Board and there is no requirement for a renewed application in such cases. This possibility to change employer represents a deviation from general work permits, which are tied to one employer.[39] No information about these crucial possibilities is issued by the Migration Office or appears in the application form, however.

The au pair's worker status also means that regulations on leave, such as the Paid Vacation Act (1977:480), the Parental Leave Act (1995:584), and the Work Environment Act (1977:1160) are in principle applicable. That said, an au pair has no right to a paid holiday, as that right is based on work in the previous year and an au pair only has the right to stay in the country for one year. Inspection of working hours and working environment in private homes, however, does not take place unless there is special reason,[40] which also makes the value of the application of the Work Environment Act questionable.

The Swedish information on the rights and obligations of au pairs is meagre. Expressions such as 'appeal', 'attorney', 'important that you find out' are used and the onus is on the au pair, who is constructed as a legally competent, resourceful and well-informed person. This is perhaps related to the fact that in Sweden au pairs are considered workers. However, despite being considered workers, au pairs' rights as workers are limited, as the applicable employment regulations concern work in private households and is affected by the traditionally low value attached to such work. This implies a right to weekly rest and a month's notice for termination of the relationship but no other employment protection, while for all else the conditions of the Agreement are applicable. The au pairs' rights as students are limited and consist of defined leisure time and some checks to ensure that studies are initiated.

Overview of rights and obligations of au pairs in relation to families

Table 1 gives a rough picture of the rights and obligations of au pairs in relation to their families according to the European Agreement and the regulations of the countries compared. More precise and detailed information has been given under each country.

Table 1: Rights and obligations of au pairs and families in the Nordic countries

	European Agreement	Denmark	Finland	Norway	Sweden
Age of au pair	17–30	17–29	17–30	18–30	18–30
Time limit of stay/permit	12 months, max. 24 months	18 months	12 months	24 months	12 months
Hours worked per week	–	18–30	30	30	25
Hours worked per day	5	3–5 (6 days a week)	5	5	–
Free time per week	One day	One day	One day	48 hours	36 hours
Contract	Written agreement	Standard contract	Own contract	Standard contract	Own contract
Pay	'Pocket money'	DKK 2,900 gross	€ 252 net	NOK 4,000 gross	SEK 3,500 gross
Language course required	Yes	No	Yes	Yes	Yes
Pay for language courses	–	–	–	Family NOK 6,000	–
Right to terminate the relationship	Both parties	Both parties	As per contract	Both, family on reasonable grounds	Both parties
Notice	Two weeks	Two weeks	As per contract	One month	One month

Conclusions

In all four countries compared here, the states have decided to implement the provisions of the European Agreement on 'au pair' Placement only within the regulatory framework of work permits or residence permits. This means there is no other regulation specifically concerning the conditions of au pairs, although the Agreement's aim was primarily protective. Thus, in this sense, the public dimension, and especially the interest in excluding labour migration, may be said to have encroached on private law with its admittedly limited protection for au pairs.

With the exception of Norway, the conditions for au-pair permits are dependent on policy documents on the outskirts of legislation. Thus they rely on the application of guidelines issued by migration authorities themselves, although the European Agreement (signed by Denmark and Norway and inspiring the policies of Finland and Sweden) compels the contracting states to take all possible measures in the form not only of regulations but also of legislation.

The regulation by migration authorities of the conditions for au pairs are often rewritten and reconstituted, primarily with the aim on the part of the authorities of preventing labour immigration and family reunion – the versions used in this chapter are from January 2010, and are already changing. The student concept is then mostly used as an exclusionary criterion, while simultaneously the reality of applications for *work* affects the use of language and the sometimes repressive tone. Thus au-pair placements are constantly localized with new meanings. Concepts such as student and worker and the duration of permits sometimes seem to be changed without regard to the consequences for rights and obligations in areas such as employment and social law.

In my opinion, the guidelines of the migration authorities are an expression of the rationalities of migration law, but not necessarily of the employment and social rights of au pairs as a court dealing with such matters would assess them. For example, such a court would probably often consider an au pair to be a worker because of her subordination in relation to the family and her workload, regardless of how the relationship was labelled earlier. This view would have consequences for her employment and social rights (and possibly also for her right to stay in the country). However, au-pair matters very rarely end up in courts and everyone knows that. This supports the conclusion of Bertelsen (2007) that the host families in their superior position in relation to the au pairs have the power to decide which laws and regulations are applicable in 'their' specific au-pair relationship.

The most obvious differences between the four countries are not in the rights and obligations of au pairs as summarized in Table 1, but in the construction of au pairs in the information concerning permits provided by authorities to applicants and families. There is a huge difference between the four countries in how authorities have chosen to construct information about their au-pair schemes. It ranges from almost repressive to rather friendly and welcoming, and from very detailed to vague and general.

Eligibility criteria for au-pair placements are treated very differently: two countries choosing to list them openly in detail (Denmark and Norway); and two preferring to gather information from application forms on all issues and then using their discretionary powers to decide who is eligible and who is not (Finland and Sweden). The outcome might be quite similar. Some of the criteria mentioned far transcend the criteria put forward by the European Agreement, but may be interpreted as implementing its aims by excluding labour migration and family reunion.

The host family is defined differently in the various countries. Denmark allows only those with children to have au pairs, thus constructing au-pair placements as childminding; Norway allows persons with or without children; Finland and Sweden have no rules regarding the issue. Meanwhile all four countries have some eligibility criteria concerning education. In one country (Denmark) this seems to serve mostly to obtain qualified personnel, while others seem to take the cultural exchange and study purpose more seriously, demanding registration for courses or that the family pays for courses. Norway is the only one of the four that explicitly obliges the family to pay for language courses.

All countries except Finland show ambivalence towards a family model based on unpaid labour and a worker model based on paid labour. Finland constructs the au pair entirely as a family member; Sweden goes furthest in constructing the au pair as a worker. However, the au pair's status as worker and the applicability of employment law does not matter much in relation to the family/employer. This is because it is a question of special regulations for employment in households, which are generally less protective of the employee than other legislation. They are in fact similar in outcome to the provisions of the European Agreement. Norway, however, has introduced a requirement for reasonable grounds for dismissal in their au-pair rules, which means a strengthening of the position of the au pair in relation to the European Agreement and the regulations of the other countries.

When it comes to social rights, the status of worker regularly affords au pairs a better position than that of student/family member, as the social security system is largely based on waged labour. Information about the extent of social benefits is obscure in all countries, however, and the migration authorities do not have such information. A list of rights drawn up by authorities, presupposed in the European Agreement, is non-existent. None of the countries seems to have appointed such public or private bodies as were foreseen in the Agreement, which were to supervise the placement conditions, provide consultation, and settle differences between au pairs and receiving families.

Notes

1 A Norwegian local court has described this development as follows: 'Today most au pairs come from non-Western countries. In these countries many people wish to create a better future in the West. Therefore immigration issues manifest themselves. The au pair scheme is distinct from labour immigration, which is otherwise strictly limited' (Oslo Tingrett, dom 18 February 2008. Saksnr 07-130127TVI–OTIR/08).

2 This protection may be traced in the legislation and case law in many legal areas, and is explicitly stated in a number of international conventions, including Article 8 of the European Convention for the Protection of Human Rights and Fundamental Freedoms (ECHR).

3 See ILO report *Decent Work for Domestic Workers*.

4 Social constructionism permeates, for example, the dissertations on law by Monica Burman 2007; and Eva Nilsson 2007.

5 A term sometimes used to describe the very restrictive immigration regulations of the European Union.

6 Council of Europe; European Treaty Series No. 68.

7 This is obvious from its contents, and has also been confirmed by the migration offices.

8 Annex II, article 18.1. This provision seems to conflict with today's bans on discrimination. None of the four Nordic countries has limited the scope of its provisions for women.

9 See, for example, the recommendation of ILO1963 no 119. The convention was not established until 1982.

10 *Tal og fakta på udlaendningsområdet 2007*, 21. Ministeriet for Flygtinge, <www.nyidanmark.dk>.

11 Folketingets enstämmiga vedtagelse av lagförslag L 198, a parliamentary decision of 28 March 2007 (styrkelse av indsatsen mod misbrug af au pair-ordningen).

12 <http://www.nyidanmark.dk/da-dk/Ophold/au_pair/>, accessed in January 2010. It has subsequently been changed.

13 The right to participate in religious events (supposedly Christian, as they were expected to take place on Sundays) is derived from the Agreement.

14 According to an answer from the Ministry of Internal Affairs, Finland, conveyed by Mirkka Mykkänen, Senior Adviser.

15 See article by Zechner in this volume.

16 See for example <www.findaupair.com> or <www.aupair-world.net>.

17 'Entry into Finland as an au pair', a fact sheet from the Finnish Immigration Service.

18 The Aliens Act 45 § states that when an alien has been granted a temporary residence permit, his or her family members will be granted a temporary residence permit for the same period of time.

19 According to an answer from the Ministry of Internal Affairs, Finland, conveyed by Mirkka Mykkänen, Senior Adviser.

20 *Tall og fakta 2008*, UDI, 12.

21 A number of very interesting articles can be found at <http://www.aupair-norway.org/>. See also Cecilie Öyen, *On equal terms – an evaluation of the Norwegian au pair scheme*, Fafo-rapport 2009, 29.

22 See <http://www.udi.no/Norwegian Directorate-of-Immigration/News/2007/Changes-in-the-au-pair-regulations/>

23 Beate Holter, UDI.

24 Marte Bertelsen (2008) has pointed out that this regulation is unclear. A person who has 48 hours off, for example at the weekend, and works 5 hours a day Monday to Friday, will in fact work 25 hours and not 30 hours, which is the maximum allowed.

25 The wording 'per calendar year' seems to mean that the right to paid holidays for au pairs differs from general regulations on holidays, implying that a person will have to work one whole year before they have the right to a holiday.

26 The meaning of reasonable grounds in au pair work has been discussed

at length in a local court (Oslo Tingrett, dom 18 February 2008. Saksnr 07–130127TVI–OTIR/08).

27 A change of host family is crucial, as this may be the only measure the au pair can take to improve her situation. The interviews in Bertelsen (2008, 80) show that au pairs who changed families were in a better situation after concluding their second contract.

28 Utrikesutskottets betänkande AU2005/06: UU15. According to Susanne Lind of the Migration Office, nobody now employed in the Migration Office knows the reason Sweden has not signed the Agreement; neither is there any legal document that explains why.

29 SOU 1982:49, 105. Today this is far from the case. Au-pair positions are openly advertised by employment agencies on the Internet. The Swedish rules concerning au-pair permits have had clearly ambivalent features since the 1970s (see Calleman 2007, 40–46).

30 More specifically, 196 in 2006, 202 in 2007, 189 in 2008, and 130 in the first eight months of 2009 (information received from Rita Ylikivela, Migration Office).

31 Several thousand au pairs may be working in Sweden. According to the owner of the agency mentioned below, it places 2,000–3,000 au pairs a year in Sweden (mostly foreign women).

32 See for example the Motion to Parliament 2002/03: A270.

33 *Helsingborgs dagblad,* 7 August 2009.

34 <www.migrationsverket.se/info/159.html>.

35 <www.migrationsverket.se/info>, august 2009.

36 As for the family, it may consist of two parents, or a single parent with children, or adults only. It is most unusual that the applicant asks to bring a child, but such an application has once been accepted (Gunilla Wickström, Migration Office).

37 Applicants are regularly registered for language courses, but as these are usually short, for example one month long, there are no checks that au pairs continue the classes after that (Gunilla Wickström, Migration Office).

38 These provisions derogate from the Swedish Working Time Act, as employment in households is exempt from the Directive 2003/88/EG, which has been implemented in the Working Time Act.

39 This exception has been made in order not to force an au pair to remain with a family where the relationship has not worked out well (Gunilla Wickström, Migration Office).

40 Article 15,3 of the Work Environment Ordinance.

References

Literature

Bertelsen, Marte (2007), *Au pair-ordningen i søkelyset. Masteravhandling i rettssosiologi om au pair ordningen i Norge* (Oslo: Institutt for kriminologi og rettssosiologi, Juridisk fakultet, University of Oslo).

Burman, Monica (2007), *Straffrätt och mäns våld mot kvinnor: om straffrättens förmåga att producera jämställdhet* (Dissertation; Uppsala: Iustus förlag).

Burr, Vivien (1995), *An Introduction to Social Constructionism* (London: Routledge).

Calleman, Catharina (2007), *Ett riktigt arbete? Om regleringen av hushållstjänster* (Säter: PANG förlag).

Decent Work for Domestic Workers (International Labour Conference, 99th Session, Report IV(1); Geneva: International Labour Office).

European Agreement on 'Au Pair' Placement, Council of Europe (European Treaty Series No. 68, Strassbourg, 24 November 1969).

Nilsson, Eva (2007), *Barn i rättens gränsland: om barnperspektiv vid prövning om uppehållstillstånd* (Dissertation; Uppsala: Iustus förlag).

Øien, Cecile (2009), 'On equal terms? – an evaluation of the Norwegian au pair scheme' (Fafo rapport 2009, 29; Oslo).

Rotkirch, Anna (2003), 'Vem är rädd för städerskan? Globalisering och kvinnors autonoma migration', *Sociologisk forskning* nr 2/2003, Sveriges sociologförbund, Uppsala.

Stenum, Helle (2008), *Au Pair in Denmark – Cheap Labour or Cultural Exchange* (Copenhagen: FOA).

Primary sources

Motion 2002/03: A270 to the Swedish parliament.

Oslo Tingrett, dom 18 February 2008. Saksnr 07–130127TVI–OTIR/08.

SOU 1982:49 *Invandringspolitiken* (Stockholm: Liber/Allmänna förlaget).

Tal og fakta på udlaendningsområdet (2007), Ministeriet for Flygtinge, <www.nyidanmark.dk>.

Utrikesutskottets betänkande AU2005/06: UU15.

Interviews and e-mail contacts

Susanne Lind, Swedish Migration Office, 14 August 2009.

Beate Holter, UDI, 22 December 2009.

Answer from the Ministry of Internal Affairs, Finland, sent by Mirkka Mykkänen, Senior Adviser, 30 October 2009.

Gunilla Wickström, Swedish Migration Office, 19 February 2010.

Internet sources

<www.aupair-world.net>, accessed on 15 May 2009.

<www.findaupair.com>, accessed on 15 May 2009.

<www.migrationsverket.se/info/159.html>, accessed on 10 December 2009.

<www.nyidanmark.dk/da-dk/Ophold/au_pair/>, accessed on 15 December 2009.

<www.udi.no/templates/Tema.aspx?id=4661>, accessed on 3 May 2008.

<www.udi.no/upload/Rundskriv/2007/RS%202007-020-en.doc>, accessed on 1 December 2007.

<www.udi.no/Norwegian-Directorate-of-Immigration/News/2007/Changes-in-the-au pair-regulations/>, accessed on 20 November 2009.

<www.udi.no/upload/Pub/Aasrapport/2008/UDI_Tall_og_fakta_web_rettet_versjon.pdf>, accessed on 14 August 2009.

CHAPTER 5

Doing gender equality

Cleaners employed in Norwegian middle-class homes[1]

Tove Ingebjørg Fjell

An increasing number of people choose to employ help in the home. Some hire au pairs, who have formal contracts and are paid a small wage to live-in and do both child-care and housework. Others hire cleaners without formally written contracts, who are most often paid cash in hand, who live out, and have limited duties such as cleaning (Calleman 2007, 28; Anderson 2000, 28). In this chapter I will focus on the distribution of household chores in Norwegian homes, particularly the receivers of domestic services, mainly cleaning, and the hiring of a private cleaner. What does the hiring of a private cleaner signify? Is the introduction of a private cleaner detrimental or conducive to gender equality?[2]

The Norwegian national LOGG study (Studies of life span, generation and gender by Statistics Norway) shows a certain cultural shift towards private cleaning becoming more acceptable: from the 1970s to the 1990s there was not much increase in hiring private cleaners, and around 2000 some 6 per cent reported having private cleaners. In 2000, however, 13 per cent reported buying the services of privately hired cleaners (Kitterød 2009). This study does not differentiate between legal and illegal job markets, and it is notoriously difficult to obtain reliable statistics on trends in the latter. What the study does indicate, though, is that it is primarily the level of education and household income that determine whether a private cleaner is hired: most employers of private cleaners are well-off, have higher education, work more than 40 hours per week, have children under school age and own large houses. The scope of assistance provided is only modest.

Outsourcing domestic work has been interpreted as a strategy for well-off, educated families (Kitterød 2009). In this chapter I will look into housework arrangements in the homes of a small group of these highly educated couples; a group which according to scholars tends to be more geared towards gender equality than less well educated couples (see, for example, Kitterød 2003). Normally three different types of relationship are singled out. The first is associated with traditional, complementary, gender-specific ideology and practices, by which women are responsible for family matters, men are care providers who lend a hand, and both parties feel they are doing their bit. The second type is a transitional variety that encompasses traditional elements as well as gender-equality elements and is found among couples who demonstrate a gender-equality orientation and gender-neutral ideology in combination with gender-specific practices. Women in this type of relationship are often dissatisfied, while their male partners tend to agree with the ideals yet are quick to argue that they cannot be implemented in real life. The third type of relationship covers couples whose practical arrangements and gender role ideology are gender-equality oriented and gender neutral (Syltevik 2000, 75–101; see also Martinsson 1997, 82; and Platzer 2007, 107). The norm of gender equality is stronger the higher the couple's education (Kitterød 2005, 13) and some studies show that any gender-equality deficiency in a couple's relationship will be hidden (Bäck-Wicklund & Bergsten 1997, 191–192).

In order to provide answers to questions about housework and private cleaners, I have conducted interviews with a small group of receivers of cleaning services. The informants have varying levels of higher education and many of them hold good positions in academia or business. One of the informants is male, and in age the informants are anything from their late thirties to their early sixties. All informants live in heterosexual relationships with similarly well educated spouses or partners. Most have children living at home. The children of the oldest informant no longer live at home, but she was nevertheless included in the group because she hired her cleaner when the children were small and still makes use of her services.

Eight of the informants have hired their cleaner on the grey market while the other two have done all the relevant official paperwork.[3] I have also followed the recent media debate on the issue of domestic help in order to find out more about how contemporary media present cleaning. I have not conducted interviews with the cleaners, but the cleaners who are employed by the informants in this study are mostly from Eastern European countries and they *live out*; a group that the sociologist Bridget Anderson categorizes as more independent of employers (Anderson 2000, 48). The cleaners are all female, apart from one man who cleans together with his wife.

Less cleaning, more child-rearing

If we listen to the public debate, it is difficult to tell whether we clean our houses or not. Newspapers carry reports that too little housework is being done, which is why children grow up with asthma from all the house dust, while other reports maintain that too much housework saps the energy that women really ought to spend on having sex (*Aftenposten* 2004). We are also told that all the bickering over cleaning leads to divorce, and that a domestic help, by way of a fringe benefit, is a good divorce prevention measure as well as a tool to secure the recruitment of more women to senior positions (Haraldsen & Schjerve 2004; Magnus 2003, Egeberg 2003; see also Sogner & Telste 2005, 162). Furthermore, there are reports of scientific evidence that housework, as opposed to leisure activities, reduces the risk of cancer, particularly breast and uterine cancer (Teimansen 2001; Unanue-Zahl 2004; Friedenreich et al. 2001).

We have long been told that while women have been going out to work, men have failed to demonstrate a matching increase in their housework contribution levels. Time-use surveys show that the time spent on housework has fallen considerably over the last 30 years, and provide answers to some of our questions with regard to division of labour (Kitterød 2002).[4] Two matters may be of particular interest in this respect. First, the infant and toddler phase tends to see men and women slipping into traditional and complementary roles: the man becomes the provider and thus does less housework, while the woman stays at home, possibly with a part-time job, and does most of the housework (Time-use survey 2000b; Kitterød 2003, 15). The two parties have ended up in the so-called gender trap (Nielsen & Rudberg 2006, 338; Maushart 2001, 123). Secondly, the overall distribution of labour between men and women is better balanced if both go out to work. This is not because men do more housework than indicated in the first time-use surveys conducted in the 1970s, but because women do considerably less. There has been a rise in the total number of working hours put in by couples with higher education, because the women have increased their hours of non-domestic employment while the men have never reduced theirs (Vaage 2005a; Vaage 2005b; Kitterød 2003, 15; Kitterød 1998, 189). In Norway, the time spent on house-cleaning and cooking has been almost halved since the 1970s, and households in which the woman works long hours and is well educated will have the least time spent on housework (Kitterød 2005, 48; Kitterød 2003; Grønning & Håndlykken 2006). Norway is thus near the bottom of the European league when it comes to housework – only Sweden is below.

Attitudes towards housework are determined by cultural and historical factors. The same applies to perceptions of good parenting. In the 1950s it was all about having a pleasant, spotless home and clean, well-behaved children. These days it is all about taking part in one's children's development, spending more quality time together, stimulating them, and helping with homework (see Danielsen 2006). Something changes in people's practical arrangements when they have children; these are cultural changes that effectively reduce the time available for housework even further (Wærness 2000, 64; Danielsen 2002). This trend is referred to as 'the fear of falling' (Williams 2000, 35; see also Kitterød 2003, 15, Ehrenreich 1989, 82 ff.), which is a strong wish to raise one's children within a framework of middle-class ideals, to ensure that the kids will stand a better chance of making it out there. For many parents this is a serious challenge, which is reflected in the ever-increasing involvement of families with children in a number of new arenas (see Bäck-Wicklund & Bergsten 1997, 113–114). If a big chunk of time is set aside for spending with the children, which is the *one* big unwaged job in the private sphere, then the consequence will be a reduced number of hours available for housework, which is the *other* big unwaged job in the private sphere.[5]

Few complaints about the cleaner

When reading Barbara Ehrenreich's *Nickel and Dimed. On (Not) Getting By In America* (2001), we learn that Ehrenreich's customers are more than happy to complain about the cleaning not having been done. One of Ehrenreich' customers used to place little mounds of dirt on her Persian carpets in order to see whether they had been properly vacuum-cleaned, and the cleaner was reprimanded when failing to vacuum far enough under the carpet (2001, 93). But complaining is not an important issue in this present study, apart from the informants who have hired their cleaner through lawful channels and who appear to have no second thoughts about complaining if they are unhappy with the work. Sometimes their very reason for hiring their cleaner through an agency that operates above board is to make it easier to voice any concerns. Complaints are never raised with the person who does the cleaning, but with his or her supervisor. However, most of those who have hired a help on the grey labour market find it difficult to complain about their work. Karl has never bothered to complain to the cleaner, even if his parquet floor is 'cracking' from excessive use of water:

> *Karl*: I've met her a couple of times. I've been at home ... I work away from home for long periods at the time ... but on occasion I *have* been at home when she arrived. I've gone downstairs to the computer in the basement then, while she's been getting on with the cleaning. Sounds as if she's tearing down the house ... I'm not actually all that pleased with everything she does. She pulls the furniture along the floor and uses so much water on the parquet flooring that cracks have started to appear in all sorts of places.

Karl has not talked to the cleaner about the fact that he is not all that happy about the work. I ask him why and he explains that at work he is not the kind of person who likes going into miniscule detail:

Karl: My threshold is pretty high. At work, for instance, where I've been supervising quite a large number of people, … Everything's very fast and detailed … So you should be really careful with how you … about the level of detail you go into when passing on instructions. And it's not as if the floor was all that wonderful to start with, anyway. Perhaps I ought to … I don't know if I've told my wife and she in turn may have said something. I don't think you're supposed to use any water at all on parquet floors.

Many report having put a lot of work into finding a cleaner and building up a trusting relationship with her, and those who found their cleaner on the grey market feel that much is at stake if they were to complain. Also, they are uncomfortable with putting their cleaner right or even passing on a message. Ranveig has agreed with her cleaning lady that she should put in two hours of work, but she suspects that only a single hour is spent. In contrast to what was the case in Ehrenreich's study, Ranveig has never told her cleaner *what* to clean. The cleaner receives a set sum every week, and they have agreed that she can do as much as she likes for that amount of money:

Ranveig: Over the five years she's been coming I think I've asked her on two occasions to polish my brass candlesticks before Christmas. Apart from that, she decides what she wants to do herself. I put out all the detergents, and the brushes and sponges and fresh dusters for her every time, and she … I don't know when she arrives and I don't know when she leaves. If I happen to be at home, which is very rare indeed … but if I haven't managed to get off before she arrives, I leave straight away, 'cause I don't want to be checking on her. And I don't want to check up on when she arrives and when she leaves.

Tove: So, perhaps you've never complained about her work either …

Ranveig: Never! In my opinion, she cleans well enough, although it's clearly surface cleaning only. That goes without saying, in a way. You can't possibly clean a house this size in an hour.

Tove: Have you got any idea how long she spends here?

Ranveig: No. We started out with two hours. I think she spends round about an hour here for that amount of money. And I have told her that I won't be paying her any more to get her to do a better job. That's what I feel I can set aside to make my house look clean, even if it's not.

Ranveig feels that her home is not really being cleaned, it only *looks* clean. This is also what Ehrenreich found: the cleaners in her study are not given enough time to actually *clean* a house, but rather to give the impression of clean (Ehrenreich 2001, 83–84). Ranveig suspects her cleaner works for one hour rather than the two they have agreed; nevertheless she has never voiced a complaint, nor is ever going to. She does feel annoyed at the poor cleaning, but she never tells her cleaner for fear of making her feel inferior. She does however write notes to her, but along the lines of 'Have a nice day! Love from Ranveig', with a little heart drawn on the bottom of the note. She is anxious about coming across as 'a snooty upper-class lady with a glamorous job. I'm really asking her to clean up after me, you know … and then I'm not even happy with what she does'. The difference in status between the two women makes it difficult for Ranveig to complain, and even to tell the cleaner what she wants to be cleaned. The anthropologist Marianne Gullestad claims that there is a logic of equality at stake in Norwegian society: one has to regard oneself as equal in order to perceive 'sameness' (Gullestad 2002, 82). Ranveig and her cleaner do in many ways live very different lives, and there is a certain discomfort about one doing the housework for the other one. The real differences between them and the discomfort itself are being undercommunicated in order to establish a notion of 'sameness' and 'friendship' (see Vike 2001, 167–168).

Establishing notions of sameness will not always be considered necessary, though. Gunhild applied for a cleaner by putting up a note in the local supermarket, and an Eastern European woman got in touch and did a trial cleaning session, but this was not a success. Gunhild's feedback was clear and unambiguous:

Gunhild: When I came home, there was a big puddle on the bathroom floor upstairs [laughing]. You see? And it was just left with

a towel in it; she hadn't even bothered to mop it up. ... I felt she
was untrustworthy, that she didn't ... And she was expensive. ...
I phoned her and said ... you get more per hour than I do when
I work as an examiner, and I've got a Ph.D. while you're unskilled
and work for cash in hand without even paying taxes. ... And you've
not made a very good job of it. I can't use you.

Tove: What did she say?

Gunhild: Well, you know ... What could she say? It was true, after
all. We didn't get into a spat or anything. I asked her to return our
keys, but she still hasn't done that, so it's a bit worrying.

Gunhild had not been introduced to the cleaner by friends or acquaintances, she was not at all happy with the work that was carried
out and she had no worries about letting her cleaner know. Gunhild
was the only informant in this study who clearly expressed that she
was able to complain about the cleaner's work. This may have been
because she did not yet know the woman concerned. Others who
made use of grey labour would tend to look the other way regarding
matters that gave rise to irritation or dissatisfaction. Some of the
reason may be the fact that they were indeed involved in the grey
labour market; they saw themselves as conspirators, contributing to
something illegal, and were therefore not in a position to complain.
Informants said that they were uneasy about the illegal side to their
cleaning arrangements. One informant said that on principle she was
against paying her cleaner without reporting it to the tax authorities, and that she wanted to change the arrangement, but that her
cleaner objected. She was worried about loosing her cleaner were
she to push too hard for her to accept legal payment. Furthermore,
the informant felt reassured by the fact that she *knew* her cleaner
and was aware that she felt 'some sort of love' for her house, which
she could not expect were she to go through a cleaning agency with
lots of employees. Another informant had strongly held objections
to a hidden economy and the untidy, chaotic social situations that
it inevitably spawns. Nevertheless, this informant felt that we need
to accept that a society like ours has a bottom stratum of workers,
and that we should not forget the fact that these are ways in which
immigrants have a chance of earning a little extra. This is the situ-

ation for immigrants to Norway, just as it used to be the situation for our own ancestors who emigrated to America, says this informant. In saying so, she makes the same observation as Sogner and Telste, who point out that domestic servants, as we know them, have disappeared from official statistics but have made a comeback in the grey economy (Sogner & Telste 2005, 166; Vik 2003). In other words, the tenor of the informants' argument is that they are opposed to grey market labour *in principle*, but that *in practice*, for various reasons, they see themselves forced to accept the situation, either because the cleaner refuses to work legitimately or because 'this is how society works'.

Reasons for hiring a cleaner

What makes these families take on an extra monthly cleaning cost? Some explain that it was due to extraordinary circumstances: the impending submission of a doctorial thesis put exceptional pressures on family life; a wife was taken ill and the husband decided they should consider hiring domestic help; a wife embarked on a university course and realized she needed to spend all her spare hours poring over her books: 'I realized pretty soon that I was unable to combine it all, four kids and a husband away on business, and then needing to study on top of it all. It was just too much'. Others cite no special trigger for deciding to hire a cleaner, other than a breakdown in the domestic cleaning arrangements. A number of informants, like this one, faced the following problem before they decided to call in the services of a cleaner:

> *Grete*: But even if I worked shifts, then there was the responsibility for the kids on top of everything. And then we tried to divide up the house so that one of us would be responsible for this bit and the other for that. And then *that* didn't work. And then we decided to do it every second time, and then *that* didn't work. And then it all became very unsatisfactory. And we spent an awful lot of energy on it, and there was an awful lot of bickering. We weren't really interested in living like that; just felt it was extremely unsatisfactory. And then of course these things *need* to be done. These are

trivial jobs, they're boring, but we don't feel happy unless they're done. So … my husband decided that since he was so bad at doing his bit, he would prefer us to have a paid cleaner. And of course, it comes out of our joint funds. In that sense we're both paying for it.

The couple have clearly tried to split the chores evenly between them, but with no success. The fact that it is the husband who thinks of hiring a cleaner is rather unusual (see Kitterød 1999, 345). Gunhild, on the other hand, claims to have a husband who does no housework at all. Also, he is not keen on hiring a domestic help:

> *Gunhild*: Well, *I* have always thought that having a cleaner was wonderful, but my husband has been a bit half-hearted, because … He's very positive when it's all done. He does admit that it's really nice to come home to a clean house. But he feels like 'well, surely we could do it ourselves'. That means *I* would be doing it, really. That's much simpler for him, because then there's no big fuss about tidying up once a week to get ready for the cleaner. That's his attitude to it all.
>
> *Tove*: So he's not always been that supportive of it?
>
> *Gunhild*: No, not *at all*. But he has … I should say, when talking about my house and my everyday life … that he has a very demanding job. He works shifts and goes to meetings and I never know when he'll be home. And I can never count on him when it comes to … everyday things like making dinner or cleaning and … I can never count on him being there. And that makes me think I deserve it, because I'm totally on my own with it all and because I've got a demanding job myself and … Not only do I *deserve* it, I *need* it!

The remark that she not only *deserves* but *needs* a cleaner can be seen as a comment on the moral indignation which has often been media-voiced over the use of private cleaners, as people feel everyone should be able to clean up after themselves (see, for example, Kitterød 1998, 189; Skilbrei 2004, 81). Barbara Ehrenreich states in her book that she has never herself hired a cleaner in her house, not even when her children were small and she might have needed one. When she later could afford a cleaner, she 'found the idea repugnant' (2001, 91) and explains that by referring partly to the influence of her own mother's principles that a self-cleaned house was a 'hallmark of womanly virtue' (ibid.) and partly to the fact that cleaning functions as a break in her own sedentary life.

None of the other interviewees in this current study demonstrated any level of sympathy with the indignity of private cleaners. Furthermore, Gunhild's husband is clearly not keen to spend money on a cleaner, and he feels they should be able to do the job themselves, which in her opinion means that *she* would be doing the job. Neither is he particularly happy to comply with the tidying which is required before the cleaning day. Later on, she defends her husband and explains why he never does anything in the home: his job is incredibly important. Just like Gunhild, Annlaug also had to negotiate with her husband about getting a domestic help. He was reluctant about the whole project, the negotiations took a long time, and he felt it was all unnecessary. However, she takes care to emphasize that they have never argued over housework:

> *Annlaug:* Frustrations and discussions. We've never really *squabbled* over who should do it. No. We haven't. … It was really me, who felt this negative atmosphere creeping in, because I kept feeling that something needed doing all the time. It's not as if I've got dust on the brain, it's just that I cannot stand a mess. I'm not able to function properly. … I'm constantly juggling a great number of balls and I'm extremely busy because I'm doing so many things besides my work. I'm not smart enough to say no. So I decided it would be a good idea to do something about it, in a way. Try to … that this could be one of the things that would help make me and our family life function better. I do have a tendency to say yes. At that point I learned how to be better at saying no. But it's all to do with the rhythm of our family life. For none of us has ever had a nine-to-five type of job. None of us. Ever. And we've been travelling a lot, both of us. At the same time and at different times. I spent a lot of time away working, for weeks, and the first thing I did when coming home was to clean the house. For he, as a dad, never touched anything like that when he stayed at home with the kids, see. So … that was the reason why we wanted a cleaner.

Annlaug clearly takes the bulk of the blame for why things turn out the way they do. She explains that her husband's job involves a lot of travelling. But so does *hers*. When he stayed away on business for weeks on end, she took care of the house and the children. But when she stayed away on business for weeks on end, he took care of the children, not the house, which is far from unusual (see Kitterød 1999, 345). Consequently, on returning from a business trip the first thing she had to turn her hand to was cleaning the house.

In the next quote, the couple I interviewed touch on the same set of problems. They have tried to agree on how to divide the chores between them, but none of the arrangements ever worked. Unni tells me that their cleaner is the outcome of 'eight years of housework squabbles':

> *Unni*: It's a bit complicated. For he works away. He comes and goes a bit, while I'm here all the time. And then I get into the rhythm of me being the one who's here. But … it doesn't actually change when he's at home and *can* do his share. 'Yes, I'll do it … tomorrow … I'll do it … I'll do it'. But it never gets done.
>
> *Tove*: Is it because he does it in a way you don't like or doesn't he do it at all?
>
> *Unni*: He doesn't do it at all. … It was a friend of mine who said that … if you want the house to be cleaner than he does, then you'll have to carry that particular load yourself.

Unni's husband, Karl, has a somewhat different view on how they split the chores between themselves. He agrees with his wife that he does less than her, but maintains he was responsible for specific rooms that he used to keep clean before the private cleaner arrived. He is, however, aware that the level of conflict used to be high before the cleaner was employed, not because he never did anything, but because his wife's standards are different from his. In his opinion, the reason for this is found in their different upbringing. He can cope with more dust and grime because he grew up in a home with a working mother, while his wife cannot stand any dust or dirt at all because she grew up with a housewife mother who kept the house sparkling clean at all times.

Balancing the asymmetrical

The group of informants in this study differ from other similar studies in three ways. Earlier studies have shown that relationships that are felt to be unequal at times are presented as being equal. If the division of labour is traditional, with the woman doing most of the housework and the man contributing only to a small extent, this may well be turned into a gender-equality argument; for example: 'We do what we're good at, I'm good at housework and my husband is good at decorating. Overall, we put in the same amount of work'. Relationships that are felt to be unequal become objects of rationalization and are thus described as the preferred state of affairs in order to neutralize job inequality (Skilbrei 2004, 83; Haavind 1984, 83; Maushart 2001, 90; Martinsson 1997, 83). The interviews show that this is rarely the case among informants in this current study.

Furthermore, earlier studies have shown that couples with a strong gender-equality ideology and a traditional, complementary division of labour commonly exaggerate the male partner's domestic contribution. This is done in order to make the ideals (gender equality) match the couple's practices (complementary, traditional division of labour) (Kitterød 2004). In the interviews in this study, there is hardly any exaggeration of the male partner's contribution among the informants. Some of the informants' husbands are commented on in no uncertain terms, ranging from the woman who says her husband has never lifted a finger at home to the woman who calmly states that her husband is basically pretty lazy. However, talking about a partner's lack of contribution in such blunt terms ('he's never lifted a finger') may well be part of a strategy to justify the cost of hiring a cleaner. But to a certain extent the male partner's lack of participation is explained by pointing to his time-consuming job and the fact that he looks after the children. This may be due to the fact that the distribution of domestic chores is a touchy subject because it is associated with a couple's relationship and love (Syltevik 2000). The distribution of domestic chores as an issue may well be more of a taboo and a source of shame than envisaged, because the non-existence of gender equality is considered a breach of the norm. If a couple have strongly held norms of gender equality, the lack of gender equality in the home may be difficult to discuss in ways that protect the partner. Hanne Haavind refers to this as 'women's new burden' (Haavind 1984).[6] Not only will the gender-equality-minded woman be doing most of the housework, she will also need to explain why her husband fails to contribute and will sometimes even have to defend him.

Earlier studies have also shown that women in relationships with a strong gender-equality ideology and a traditional, complementary distribution of domestic chores commonly understate their own contribution in order to make their own practices match their ideals (Kitterød 2004). By talking down one's own efforts it will seem as if one does less than one actually does. This type of under-reporting is seen in statements such as 'I'm not particularly good at cleaning', 'I've never been taught how to clean', or any other statement intended to show off one's domestic incompetence. These may be interpreted as encrypted opposition to housework and a traditional definition of femininity (see Boström 2001). There is *little* under-reporting of women's own contributions in the interviews in this study.

My own study has uncovered something new: the unequal is not presented as equal; there is little over-reporting of the male partner's contribution and little under-reporting of the women's own efforts. Is the group recruited particularly perceptive or are there other factors at work? The most important premise on which the informants base their 'perceptiveness' is the introduction of a third person (the cleaner), who through her presence and work creates the balance that the couples have been unable to create themselves. The non-existence of gender equality is not being reasoned away by over-reporting the male partner's contribution or by making out that the sense of inequality is indeed a *preference*; it is addressed by outsourcing (redefining unpaid, invisible housework as paid, visible work carried out by regular/grey market labour) the gender-specific conflict about cleaning (see Isaksen 2003; Anderson 2000). The cleaner is not introduced primarily to make the house clean, but in order to make the house *look* clean and in order to quell the ever-recurring negotiations and occasional conflicts about who should carry the main responsibility for, delegate and carry out domestic chores. There are few complaints about the cleaners' work, because they represent grey labour and because of uneasiness about status differences, but also because a complaint may well lead to the collapse of the entire arrangement: the cleaner might resign and the couple will need to resume their negotiating process. At first glance it looks as if the introduction of a cleaner is conducive to gender equality because the woman no longer needs to carry out the bulk of the housework. However, the introduction of a cleaner may just as well be detrimental to gender equality in that it puts an end to the house-cleaning discussions. That said, negotiations tend to move away from the actual house-cleaning (who should do the cleaning, you or me?) to focus on the tidying that needs to precede the cleaning (who should tidy up before the cleaner arrives, you or me?), which means that the negotiations continue, albeit in different arenas. This might be the emergence of a future pattern of *outsourcing* gender-specific conflicts, one after the other, made possible with the help from private cleaners.

Notes

1 Much of this chapter has previously been published in Norwegian (Fjell 2006).
2 I include cleaning in the definition of care.
3 As in most qualitative research, the group of informants is small. Starting the project, I planned on interviewing people who had private cleaners, and got in contact with informants through the 'snowball method': I knew someone who had a private cleaner, she put me in contact with others in the same situation, and they put me in contact with others. Five informants live in the Bergen area and were interviewed in their homes or places of work. Five informants live in the Stavanger area and the interviews were conducted by telephone (on telephone interviews in cultural studies, see, for example, Bjørvik 2007). Apart from one, they have all have children living at home. All informants hold good jobs in academia, the oil industry, and so on, and their incomes are fairly good. The interviews were done on a one-to-one basis. All informants have signed a statement of consent and have been anonymized in accordance with NESH 8 and 9. The project has been reported to Norwegian Social Science Data Services (NSD) (NESH 10).
4 Statistics Norway conducted time-use surveys in 1971, 1980, 1990 and 2000/2001. In a time-use survey, a large group of people keep a diary of their own activities and social patterns over a period of two days: housework, care, maintenance activities, buying goods and services, journeys made in connection with housework. The data is collated and the results show men and women's respective input relative to their educational background, place of residence and the like (Kitterød 2002; Time-use survey 2000a; Time-use survey 2000b).

5 It has been suggested that the time squeeze is most commonly felt by the well-educated, and that these are the people who define the debate and make it look as if the time squeeze affects all parents (Yttervik 2005). 'The silent time squeeze' refers to the situation of middle-aged people caring for their sick and elderly parents (Rambøl 2006).

6 Liv Syltevik points out that men also have a 'new burden', because many younger men identify with gender-equality ideology and make an effort to present their relationships as being gender-equal (Syltevik 2000, 77–78).

References

Aftenposten (2004), 'En av fire britiske kvinner: Heller husarbeid enn sex', 8 September, <http://www.aftenposten.no/helse/article866253.ece?service=print>, accessed 28 June 2005.

Anderson, Bridget (2000), *Doing the Dirty Work. The Global Politics of Domestic Labour* (London: Zed Books).

Bäck-Wicklund, Margareta & Bergsten, Birgitta (1997), *Det moderna föräldraskapet. En studie av familj och kön i förändring* (Stockholm: Natur och Kultur).

Bjørvik, Eira (2007), "Jeg sitter i et hus hvor alle vegger vender mot syd'. Telefonintervju som kvalitativ metode i kulturvitenskap', *Tidsskrift for kulturforskning*, 6/3, 37–44.

Boström, Katarzyna Wolanik (2001), 'Försåtlig skjortstrykning och subversiva skratt. Om kön, politik och ett polskt familjeliv', in Britta Lundgren & Lena Martinsson (eds.), *Bestämma, benämna, betvivla. Kulturvetenskapliga perspektiv på kön, sexualitet och politik* (Lund: Studentlitteratur), 61–84.

Calleman, Catharina (2007), *Ett riktigt arbete? – Om regleringen av hushållstjänster* (Säter: Pang).

Danielsen, Hilde (2002), *Husmorhistorier. Norske husmødre om menn, barn og arbeid* (Oslo:Spartacus).

Danielsen, Hilde (2006), *Med barn i byen. Foreldreskap, plass og identitet* (Ph.D. thesis; Bergen: University of Bergen).

Egeberg, Kristoffer (2003), '–Kvinner som vil fram, bør ha hushjelp', *Dagbladet*, 10 March.

Ehrenreich, Barbara (1989), *The Fear of Falling. The Inner Life of the Middle Class* (New York: Pantheon Books).

Ehrenreich, Barbara (2001), *Nickel and Dimed. On (Not) Getting By In America* (New York: Henry Holt and Company).

Fjell, Tove Ingebjørg (2006), 'Outsourcing av vaskevannet – veien til likestilte praksiser?', *Tidsskrift for kulturforskning*, 2, 75–88.

Friedenreich, C. M., et al. (2001), 'Case-Control Study of Lifetime Activity and Breast Cancer Risk', *American Journal of Epidemiology*, 154/4, 336–347.

Grønning, Lars Håkon & Håndlykken, Tora Bakke (2006), 'Vi er på bunn i husarbeid', *Verdens Gang*, 9 March.

Gullestad, Marianne (2002), *Det norske sett med nye øyne. Kritisk analyse av norsk innvandringsdebatt* (Oslo: Universitetsforlaget).

Haraldsen, Stian & Schjerve, Hilde (2004), '–Vaskehjelp kan hindre skilsmisser', *Dagbladet*, 11 March.

Haavind, Hanne (1984), 'Love and Power in Marriage', in Harriet Holter (ed.), *Patriarchy in a Welfare Society* (Oslo: Universitetsforlaget), 136–167.

Isaksen, Lise Widding (2003), 'Omsorgskrise og globalisering', in id. (ed.), *Omsorgens pris. Kjønn, makt og marked i velferdsstaten* (Oslo: Gyldendal Akademisk), 185–197.

Isaksen, Lise Widding, Devi, Sambasivan Uma & Hochschild, Arlie Russel (2008), 'Global Care Crisis. A Problem of Capital, Care Chain, or Commons?', *American Behavioral Scientist*, 52/3, 405–425.

Kitterød, Ragni Hege (1998), 'Kjøp av rengjøringstjenester – større sosial ulikhet blant kvinner?', *Sosiologisk tidsskrift*, 3, 185–208.

Kitterød, Ragni Hege (1999), 'Privat rengjøringshjelp – et gode for mødre eller for hele husholdningen?', *Tidsskrift for samfunnsforskning*, 3, 335–367.

Kitterød, Ragni Hege (2002), 'Fortsatt nedgang i kvinners tid til husarbeid på 1990-tallet'. *Samfunnsspeilet*, 4–5, <http://www.ssb.no/ssp>, accessed 4 April 2002.

Kitterød, Ragni Hege (2003), *Min tid, din tid – vårt ansvar? Endring og variasjon i familiearbeidet. Empiriske analyser og drøfting av begreper og målemetoder* (Ph.D. thesis; Oslo: University of Oslo).

Kitterød, Ragni Hege (2004), 'Hvem gjør mest hjemme? Hva sier mor og hva sier far?', *Samfunnsspeilet*, 6, <http://www.ssb.no/samfunnsspeilet>, accessed 6 June 2004.

Kitterød, Ragni Hege (2005), *Han jobber, hun jobber, de jobber. Arbeidstid blant par av småbarnsforeldre* (Rapport no. 10; Oslo: Statistics Norway).

Kitterød, Ragni Hege (2009), 'Vaskehjelp vanligst i høystatusgrupper', (part of the LOGG study) *Samfunnsspeilet*, 1, <http://www.ssb.no/ssp>, accessed 11 January 2009.

Magnus, Gunnar (2003), 'Vil lokke kvinner til toppjobber', *Aftenposten*, 22 January.

Martinsson, Lena (1997), *Gemensamma liv. Om kön, kärlek och längtan* (Ph.D. thesis; Stockholm: Carlssons).

Maushart, Susan (2001), *Wifework. What Marriage Really Means for Women* (London: Bloomsbury).

Nielsen, Harriet Bjerrum & Rudberg, Monica (2006), *Moderne jenter. Tre generasjoner på vei* (Oslo: Universitetsforlaget).

Platzer, Ellinor (2007), *Från folkhem till karriärhushåll. Den nya husliga arbetsdelningen* (Ph.D. thesis; Lund: Arkiv förlag).

Rambøl, Ingvill Bryn (2006), 'Den tause tidsklemma', *Aftenposten*, A-magasinet, 5 January.

Skilbrei, May-Len (2004), 'Mine, dine og våre saker: likestillingspolitikk for viderekomne', *Kvinneforskning*, 3, 76–92.

Sogner, Sølvi & Telste, Kari (2005), *Ut og søkje teneste. Historia om tenestejentene* (Oslo: Det Norske Samlaget).

Syltevik, Liv Johanne (2000), *Differensierte familieliv. Familiepraksis i Norge på slutten av 1990-tallet* (Rapport no. 2, SEFOS; Bergen: University of Bergen).

Teimansen, Even (2001), 'Husarbeid mot brystkreft', *Dagbladet*, 30 August.

Time-use survey (Tidsbruksundersøkelsen) (2000a), 'Høyt utdannede har oftest vaskehjelp', <www.ssb.no/magasinet/slik_lever_vi/art-2002-05-27-01.html>, accessed on 11 January 2005.

Time-use survey (Tidsbruksundersøkelsen) (2000b), 'Klare kjønnsroller for småbarnsforeldrene', <www.ssb.no/magasinet/slik_lever_vi/art-2002-05-21-01.html>, accessed on 30 March 2006.

Unanue-Zahl, Pål (2004), 'Husarbeid reduserer kreftfaren', *Verdens Gang*, 30 March.

Vik, Sølvi (2003), *Mellom nærleik og avstand. Ei studie av strilejenter i huspost* (Master's thesis; Bergen: University of Bergen).

Vike, Halvard (2001), 'Likhetens kjønn', in Marianne E. Lien, Hilde Lidèn & Halvard Vike (eds.), *Likhetens paradokser. Antropologiske undersøkelser i det moderne Norge* (Oslo: Universitetsforlaget), 145–169.

Vaage, Odd Frank (2005a), *Tid til arbeid. Arbeidstid blant ulike grupper og i ulike tidsperioder, belyst gjennom tidsbruksundersøkelsene 1971–2000* (Report no. 15; Oslo: Statistics Norway).

Vaage, Odd Frank (2005b), 'Mer husarbeid og fritid for kvinner i deltidsjobb', <www.ssb.no/magasinet/slik_lever_vi/art-2005-06-24-01.html>, accessed on 28 June 2005.

Wærness, Kari (2000), *Hvem er hjemme? Essays om hverdagslivets sosiologi* (Bergen: Fagbokforlaget).

Williams, Joan (2000), *Unbending Gender. Why Family and Work Conflict and What to Do About It* (Oxford: Oxford University Press).

Yttervik, Linn (2005), 'Velger barna foran full jobb', *VG Nett*, 4 May.

II
TRANSNATIONAL EXPERIENCE
AND THE LABOUR MARKET

CHAPTER 6

Sex workers' transnational and local motherhood: presence and/or absence?

Hanne Marlene Dahl & Marlene Spanger

Female migrants from economically poor countries increasingly work in better-off countries while leaving children in the sending countries to be cared for by other relatives or paid carers. This downside is often forgotten in the glorious celebration of globalization, which neglects the feminization of migration (Kofman 2003; Yeates 2009), the care drain (Hochschild 2003) and a feminized neo-colonialism (Sarvasy & Longo 2004). The separation of female migrants and their children produces suffering on both sides (Hochschild 2001, 2003), and migration erodes social solidarities in the sending communities (Isaksen, Devi & Hochschild 2008). One of the pragmatic solutions put forward to reduce this injustice is a changed migration policy that would allow these caregivers to bring their children with them:

> For social policy, it raises the issue of what we can do to reduce the hidden injuries of global capital. At the very least, we can call for arrangements by which children and perhaps other caregivers can follow mothers to their new place of work. (Isaksen, Devi & Hochschild 2008, 420)

Granting entry rights to the migrants' children would seem to reduce the suffering of both the children and the separated mother (ibid.). It would acknowledge the interdependence of human relationships

(Tronto 1993) and would be in line with recent developments in feminist theories on care and citizenship (Tronto 2004; Tronto, forthcoming; Longo & Sarvasy 2004) which advocate citizenship rights for migrating workers in relation to care both nationally and globally. EU citizens and migrants from outside the EU married to Danish citizens already have a right to bring their child or children into the country.

Acknowledging the need for rights to give and receive care, we want to relate this policy solution to experiences of single mothers involved in global care chains in Denmark. By focusing upon their experiences, we investigate the different ways of doing motherhood and end with a call for more differentiated policy solutions. Ideally we would like to continue a dialogue on 'thoughtful public answers' to the private costs of a global wage gap – a dialogue that started with the publication of 'Gender, Care work and Globalization: Local problems and transnational solutions in the Norwegian welfare state' by Isaksen (2007). To this dialogue we want to add knowledge of the downside of migration, of how single mothers and their children live in the new country. Bringing a child to a new country is not always an unproblematic solution. A migrant running a sports institute in Denmark attended by many Thai children describes the difficulties these children frequently face:

> Mom leaving for a long time and just takes him [the children]. Take him to here … She got new place, new person. New tradition. Then sometimes … not easy to accept, take time.

We ground our discussion in the stories of two female Thai migrants selling sex and living in Denmark: Khem and Nee. Unlike Isaksen, Devi and Hochschild (2008) our focus is not on their children. The two stories represent the downside of the global care chains where women are positioned as low-skilled workers with limited resources;[1] however, this does not mean that they have no agency, as will be seen.

Khem is the story of the absentee mother, for her two children are being taken care of in Thailand by her grandmother and ex-husband. Nee is the story of the present mother having brought her daughter to live with her in Denmark. We analyse these two stories employing three different lenses: one from the literature on transnational motherhood; another from the theory of global care chains; and a third from the feminist literature on citizenship. The stories told by Khem and Nee reveal that there are no simple solutions to the problems of global care chains. This chapter investigates the different framings of motherhood both in a situation where the children are left behind and in a situation where the child is brought to the new country. Based upon fieldwork, this chapter analyses how single motherhood and caregiving are reorganized within the process of migration constrained by the citizenship rights and obligations of these female migrants. This chapter first introduces our theoretical framework and goes on to describe the Danish migration regime. Then, it outlines the methodology applied and in the next two sections analyses the stories of Khem and Nee. Finally, we conclude and reflect upon issues for further research.

The effect of globalizing processes

Our theoretical position is inspired by theories of transnational motherhood (Parreñas 2001; Sørensen 2002), global care chains (Hochschild 2001; Yeates 2009) and citizenship (Lister 1997; Yuval-Davis 2006). Our approach stresses simultaneously the agency of the female migrants through the different ways of performing motherhood in a given Danish migration regime and the potentially negative effects of global care chains.

A body of migration literature examines how gender identities and family ties are reconstructed in the process of migration regarding new formations of households, families and/or social networks (Basch et al. 1994; Levitt & Schiller 2004; Sørensen 2002; Sørensen & Guarnizo 2007).[2] The concept of transnational motherhood was introduced by Avila & Hondagneu-Sotelo (1997) in relation to female labour migration from economically poor to richer countries. It focused on Latino women who leave children with relatives or local nannies while taking up domestic work in the US. They investigated how meanings of motherhood are constructed and how strategies for mothering have changed in transnational families, stressing that female migrants construct new definitions of good mothering through transformations of practices of mothering in order to stay in contact with their children. Parreñas (2001) refines the concept of transnational motherhood by seeing it as shaped by global socio-economic inequalities, social mobility and financial security, including the perspective of the children left behind. She reminds us that the children 'suffer from emotional costs of geographical distances' (ibid., 375) and that the relationship between mother and child is affected by the paradox that the financial security obtained by migration goes hand in hand with emotional insecurity by the absence of the mother. In particular, Parreñas (2001, 387) suggests that feelings of loss and pain in transnational families are social constructions intensified by notions of ideal Philippine motherhood. In many cases, the responsibility and the caregiving towards the children rely solely on the mother. A new concept of 'Skype mothering' (Lutz & Palenga-Möllenbeck 2009) has emerged, stressing a new way of doing transnational motherhood using new information technology such as Skype telephone calls, SMS's and e-mails. Summing up this literature, it perceives the lives of these female migrants as rather contradictory, complex and as involving agency. Mothering is an ongoing process of doing.

Hochschild has developed the concept of 'global care chains', which are defined as: 'a series of personal links between people across the globe based on paid and unpaid work of caring' (2001, 131). In many ways, the concept of transnational motherhood and global care chains overlap by focusing on how female migration, care work and motherhood are linked together by the dynamics of global processes. The literature on global care chains takes a bottom-up perspective with special attention being given to the negative, exploitative effects of the transfer of care on the macro and micro levels. In her investigations of the migration of carers, Hochschild draws upon motherhood performed by Filipino mothers in the US (2001), and in a later article Isaksen, Devi and Hochschild (2008) apply this approach to Indian mothers working in the Gulf and the children left behind. In both places in the South, the locally prevailing discourse of motherhood as presence produces dissatisfaction and unhappiness amongst the migrating mothers and the children left behind (Hochshild 2001; Isaksen, Devi & Hochschild 2008). The understanding of doing motherhood evident in Hochschild (2001) and Isaksen et al. (2008) highlights the locally produced dominant understandings of motherhood and its complexity. However, they are insufficiently attentive to the agency of transnational mothers in the new context. Here Yeates (2004; 2009) is useful as a supplement enabling us to see female Thai migrant sex workers as carers performing different kinds of motherhood, allowing for their potential agency in a particular migration regime by including both top-down (state) and bottom-up dimensions that affect the process of migration. Moreover, our approach necessitates a discussion of the nature of citizenship.

Broadly speaking, citizenship is membership of a community involving rights and responsibilities. Feminists have reformulated the classical notion of citizenship, de-gendering it (Lister 1997; Lister et al. 2007). Lister (1997) advocates a dynamic and inclusive understanding of citizenship to include care. This cannot only be translated into a right to receive care but must also encompass a right to give care, which is often understood as enabling the carer financially by state transfers (Knijn & Kremer 1997). However, a right for the mother to give care also requires the physical presence of her child, thus introducing social and political rights. People migrate and relate to more than one community, creating a more global, multilayered citizenship (Lister 1997; Yuval-Davis 2006). Relating to a community is in our view identical with belonging to it, which refers to an emotional attachment, a feeling of being 'at home' and 'safe' (Yuval-Davis 2006). Khem and Nee feel at home in various spatial contexts and belong to both the Thai and Danish community. Emotional attachment is a dynamic process, shaping as well as shaped by the prevailing politics of belonging. By 'politics of belonging', Yuval-Davis means the 'specific political projects aimed at constructing belonging in particular ways to particular collectivities that are, at the same time, themselves being constructed by these projects in very particular ways' (2006, 197).

Migration regimes

Lutz (2008, 2) defines a migration regime as 'the organisation and corresponding of cultural codes of social policy and practices', but here only the policies of migration in a broad sense, including policies on human trafficking and family unification, are investigated. This approach fits well with Yeates's (2009) framework for analysing the complexities of global care chains using four dimensions: preconditions (low-skilled/high-skilled); the recruitment of care workers either by formal means (state agencies) or through informal networks (friendship, family or local ties); external regulation (policies, social welfare and citizenship); and the organization of the work (private/public agents within the labour network). Following Yeates, we will briefly introduce how policies about family reunification, prostitution and human trafficking regulate the citizenship of female Thai migrant sex workers in terms of their care obligations and rights towards their children, and go on to briefly describe the organization of the work.

The Thais in this study are low-skilled workers recruited through informal networks consisting of acquaintances, family or local ties. They established contact in Denmark, obtained jobs, and/or were introduced to their future Danish husbands through informal networks. Marrying a Danish male citizen is the only way for them to overcome the strict Danish migration policy on residence permits. All of the migrants who figure in the material have acquired residence permits through such marriages. They have children either from former relationships in Thailand and/or with a Danish man. As in the story of Nee, some of the migrants bring their children to Denmark. In some cases they return to Thailand after staying for a period. Other children remain in Thailand, as in the story of Khem.

Global care chains are not only shaped by the family, forms of recruitment and labour opportunities; migration policies also play a major role. Compared to the other Nordic countries, Denmark has the most restrictive policy on residence permits for non-EU citizens. In 2007, the Danish government stipulated a number of demands and obligations – age, the size of the marital home, the married couple's livelihoods, and language training (Danish Immigration Service 2007, 24) – applying to migrants from a non-EU country who apply for residence permit through marriage.[3] After seven years of marriage with a Danish citizen, it is possible to gain a permanent residence permit. If the marriage breaks down before the seven years are up, the residence permit is automatically suspended and the migrant has to apply for a new permit (New to Denmark 2007). According to the Danish legislation on family reunification, the Thais have a right to bring in any children under the age of 15 from Thailand.[4] When the children are granted a residence permit they have a social right to receive care in the form of public crèches and kindergartens as well as free education. In order to bring their children, a number of obligations need to be met by the migrants and their Danish partners.[5]

According to the Danish government (New to Denmark 2010), the purpose of these social and economic obligations put on the parent and the Danish partner is to protect the interests of the child. The obligations encompass, for example, housing requirements (size of the marital home) and neither the migrant nor the partner is allowed to be on benefits.[6] In the case of the Thai migrant sex workers who one of the authors of this chapter (Spanger) has interviewed, the fathers of the children have been absent in nearly all cases. However in Khem's case, one of her children lives with the father.

This social group of female Thai migrants sell sexual services in massage parlours or bars. Besides selling sex, they hold low-skilled jobs as cleaners, kitchen assistants, masseuses, or factory workers. The turnover of low-skilled temporary jobs among these females is high. Some of them only work in the sex industry, whereas others return to the sex industry having once been employed as cleaners or dishwashers. In particular, private forms of loan systems and long shifts define their sex work, while working evenings and nights characterizes their work in general. This can create problems if the migrants care for the children in Denmark, which is why some of them hire other Thais to take care of their children. Nonetheless, the Thai migrant sex workers Spanger has interviewed give the impression that the massage parlours also function as social meeting-points for the sex workers and their friends; places where they can eat together, watch television and play cards. The border between working life and spare time is blurred, and in many cases such kinds of lifestyle hardly make any allowances for caring for children during the day or at night. Both Khem and Nee sell sex at massage parlours or clinics that also function as a space where they establish social relationships with clients and other female Thais.

The legislation concerning the selling of sex in Denmark is ambiguous, since it is not forbidden for persons over eighteen years old to sell or buy sexual services. Since the 1970s the Danish authorities have perceived sex work as a social problem, and a number of social and health programmes offer counselling and help (Spanger 2008). Regardless of whether they are undocumented or documented migrants in Denmark, all migrants who sell sex are seen as potential victims of human trafficking (Spanger 2008). The Danish penal code § 262a on human trafficking and the government's action plan on combating human trafficking are of great importance for the female Thai migrant sex workers who have been granted temporary residence permits. One of the purposes of the action plan is to implement a repatriation programme and offer health and social counselling to migrant sex workers. Nonetheless, very few migrant sex workers have accepted the repatriation programme. This group of documented migrants are caught between the penal code on human trafficking and the legislation on family reunification, given that the female Thai migrant sex workers are not interested in the repatriation programme and at the same time their residence permit relies solely on their marriage with their Danish husbands. This places them and their children, who live in Denmark, in a vulnerable position.

Methodology

The material produced by study fieldwork consisted of observations and interviews (Hasse 2000; Kvale 1994) with Thai female migrant sex workers in Denmark who have children in their care. The purpose of the fieldwork was to identify how they signify care and motherhood within the process of transnational migration. In order to gain access to this highly sensitive field, Spanger conducted fieldwork via a programme targeted at migrant sex workers. The objective of the programme was to provide information about safe sex, to offer support and counselling about social and health problems, and to mediate contacts with the relevant public authorities such as housing offices and social services. In particular, Spanger joined a social worker in her work with the migrants for a period of four months. By doing so, Spanger had the opportunity to meet the sex workers in different places and later interview some of them about their everyday lives. Conducting participant observations in a field that is often conditioned by stigmatization, prejudices and various social problems, Spanger was not allowed to tape conversations between the social worker and the migrants, and instead she took notes. Consequently, the presentation of the two stories of Khem and Nee are different in terms of form. These case stories are representative of the narratives told by the single-mother informants.

Eighteen in-depth interviews were undertaken, most of them with women working in the sex industry, but also with key figures in the Thai community in Denmark. Inspired by Kvales's (1994) interview technique, a thematically semi-structured guide was used to structure the interviews around issues of migration, motherhood and care. Our analytical strategy consists of questions developed on the basis of five dimensions (citizenship, care, (single) motherhood, transnational links, and agency) derived from our theoretical framework. In particular, and inspired by Dahl (2000), we focus upon meaning and ambiguity concerning the migrants' notions and practices of motherhood.

The story of Khem

Spanger met Khem at her workplace, a traditional massage clinic, where she performs traditional massage and a few sexual services. It was through outreach social work by the programme that Spanger came into contact with Khem. She is 36 years old and migrated to Denmark in 1999. It was through her second husband, an Israeli man who already lived in Denmark, that she became familiar with the country. Today, Khem holds a residence permit in Denmark and she has just separated from her Israeli husband. These days she mostly lives at the massage clinic, since she has no home of her own due to her recent divorce. Khem is a single mother and her two daughters aged 14 and 15 from her first marriage live in Thailand. After she migrated to Denmark both daughters moved to live with their grandmother. At present, one of the daughters lives with their father, a decision made by Khem's mother. Thus, Khem's transnational mothering is defined by a global care chain where her children are cared for by their grandmother and father in Thailand.

> *Khem*: I have my mother and my family and my two daughters that I have to take care of and I decided [to go abroad]. Before, I didn't work with such kinds of job [massage]. I choose Denmark because I like a kind of freedom …
>
> *Marlene*: How did you begin your life in Denmark?
>
> *Khem*: I worked. My [second] husband made a contract so I worked for his company. My husband took care of me and I worked. We had a clothing shop. We did imports–exports. I was lucky because my husband teaches me correct [Danish], told me how it should be done – I was lucky. He is my family.
>
> *Marlene*: How often do you contact your daughters?
>
> *Khem*: I call them every day. I buy these cards [prepaid mobile phone cards]. I call my mother. I have her phone number and my daughter's number. And then I call my other daughter in Bangkok.
>
> *Marlene*: What do you talk about when you talk with your daughters?
>
> *Khem*: About her life … if she has any problems then we take care of it together. My mother she is little bit difficult because she is just like old people towards the child. I tell my mother that she shouldn't yell or scream at her, but instead she has to listen and talk to my daughter's teacher if something happen. I tell her that she has to listen to what she [her daughter] says and what the teacher says. And then I ask my child what is going on. I try to explain so she [the grandmother] understands. If they hit my child I get sad and cry and the child cries, too.
>
> *Marlene*: Have you considered bringing your children to Denmark?
>
> *Khem*: Of course! But [sighs heavily] … some families [meaning other female Thai migrants] here in the country are lucky because their husbands accept that they have the child here. But my hus-

band doesn't want ... it is not because he doesn't want to accept them. But he told me that it is better for Thais [probably meaning the children] to stay in their country. I think he is selfish because I want my child close to me. My husband, I don't think he accepts it and he talks in another way because he has two sons. ... they are adults now 30 and 27 years old.

The way she does transnational motherhood has changed during the migration process determined by her former work in her ex-husband's company. Khem migrated as a single mother leaving her children behind. She re-married – an Israeli man residing in Denmark – and visits Thailand and her daughters quite frequently due to the nature of her job. Since she divorced him, she can no longer afford regular trips to Thailand. Thus, her possibilities to exercise face-to-face motherhood are reduced, so she performs transnational motherhood by non-local practices in a form of Skype-motherhood. Through the daily telephone contacts Khem tries to get a solid knowledge of their daily lives and any troubles, and discusses solutions with them.

> *Khem*: ... my husband, he doesn't want to ... it is very hard to ask: can you send money to my children? Can you send money to my mother? Can you send money for my children's schooling? ... he says 'no' ... Since I went abroad seven years ago the last time I was home was three years ago.
>
> *Marlene*: But before?
>
> *Khem*: Every second week together with my husband I went to Thailand. I was helping him buy clothes. Every time I was in Thailand I booked a hotel room for my daughter and my mother. Every day we stayed over together.

Sending remittances has caused problems between Khem and her husband, which is not unusual in marriages between Thai women and Danish men who find it difficult to understand that their wives have financial obligations towards their families in Thailand. As in Khem's case, the migrant often disagrees with their spouse regarding the amount of financial remittances. This new form of mothering, Skype-mothering, allows Khem to understand herself as a caring mother and inscribe herself in a discourse of motherhood that stresses emotional closeness. She is, in our understanding, an absent though emotionally present mother, she shares feelings with her children and discusses their problems on the phone, and is in this sense present as a mother. She obviously misses them, but she has not brought them to Denmark for a variety of reasons. When still married, her Israeli husband opposed the idea, and her rights to bring the children to Denmark relied on his consent given that both Khem and her children were dependant on him with regard to housing and the family finances. Both Khem and he would have had obligations towards the children. After she has been granted a permanent residence permit, she is independent of her ex-husband and his consent. However, Khem would have trouble meeting the social and financial obligations related to the children because of her long working hours, and after the divorce she has not had her own apartment to be her children's family home. Thus, she would have difficulty caring for her children in Denmark in the way the Danish authorities demand.

Khem's notion of mothering is defined by financial responsibility, and emotional and social presence regarding the form of upbringing of the children. Being a caring transnational mother, she experiences the clash between two different ideals of care: the traditional one performed by her mother; and her ideal of care as based on dialogue and trust. She is ambiguous, for though she accepts the traditional motherhood position by letting her mother take one important decision on her behalf concerning where one of her daughters will live, the fact that she interferes in how her mother brings up the children indicates that she takes an active part in how her children should be educated in Thailand. Despite that, she misses being with her children, she stresses that living in Denmark and being her own woman has given her a kind of independence for structuring her working life (she is the owner of the massage clinic) and her leisure time. Thus Khem's brand of transnational mothering is a complex and contrasting construction determined by loss, some financial security, and independence. We suggest that the complexity is also a result of the constraints of the migration regime. The combination of Khem's low-skilled position in the labour market, her difficulties in caring for her children due to her working schedule, and her former Israeli husband's disapproval regarding bringing the children to Denmark constitute a very difficult situation. Khem is a physically absent but emotionally present Skype-mother. She inscribes herself in contradictory ideas of motherhood though stressing the modern, dialogical and freedom-oriented form of motherhood determined by her transnational migration. Care is performed in various ways – not face to face – but through seeing and taking responsibility for needs for care, to use Tronto's (1993) terminology. Khem does motherhood in a different way to Nee, who is the physically present but emotionally absent mother, as we will see.

The story of Nee

Spanger followed Nee, and sometimes her daughter Sank, through the programme, which involved weekly contact with the social worker attached to the programme. This meant that Spanger met her, and sometimes the daughter, in different situations and settings. Nee is 35 years old and arrived in Denmark in 2001. A short time after her arrival Nee met a Danish man whom she married. The contact was established through her sister, who already lived in Denmark. Having one daughter, Sank, from a former relationship in Thailand, Nee was a single mother. Her aunt and uncle and to an extent her ex-mother-in-law took care of Sank after Nee went abroad. In 2004 Nee brought her daughter to Denmark when she was 12 years old. In 2005 she filed for a divorce from her Danish husband and applied for a residence permit. After Nee left her Danish ex-husband in 2005 she, as a single mother, acquired a rented flat for herself and Sank from social services. Shortly after, Nee met a new Danish man.

> *Social worker*: Why did you go to Denmark?
>
> *Nee*: My older sister, who lived in Denmark offered me a job as babysitter. In reality, I could help cleaning.
>
> Nee continues by saying she missed her daughter and wanted to bring her to Denmark. At the same time, Nee stresses that she did not want to bring her daughter the first time round. Every time

she had to leave her daughter after a visit in Thailand her daughter wouldn't let her go. In addition, her ex-mother-in-law did not want to take care of Sank any more. During the three years Nee lived in Denmark and Sank in Thailand, Nee and her new Danish husband visited her daughter once a year.

Bringing Sank to Denmark has not been unproblematic for Nee, or indeed for Sank. Living in Denmark, where Nee works during the day as a kitchen assistant, and sometimes keeps her older sister company at her massage parlour at night, leaves hardly any time for taking care of her daughter. Besides, Nee has a new boyfriend with whom she often stays overnight. This means that Sank is alone all night and in the mornings. Every afternoon Nee sees Sank and gives her some money for food. Such a turbulent life has caused a troublesome relationship between Nee and Sank. Quite often, Sank plays truant from school together with another Thai girl, who is in a similar situation.

The social worker knows that Nee has a new boyfriend with whom she often stays overnight. In an insistent voice, the social worker underscores to Nee that it is important she is at home in the morning, afternoon and evening so Sank is not alone. Likewise, the social worker tells Nee that it is important that they eat together, that she talks to her daughter, does things together with her, holds her and gives her a hug. Nee does not say anything, she just nods. The social worker continues, asking: 'Why do you choose living with your boyfriend rather than living with your daughter? You can't just chuck her over!' Nee's only answer is 'Sank cannot change. She looks like her father too much. She does not behave as I tell her to and she pull faces in front of me'. Nee emphasizes to me and the social worker that she just wants her daughter to go to school and get an education so she can take care of herself. Nee continues: 'It is like that I can't focus on the job when I have problems with Sank, when she doesn't listen to me.' At the same time Nee says that she cannot afford to take care of her daughter. This reply is not acceptable to the social worker, who says: 'You need to have close contact with your child and you are obliged to pay maintenance for your child.

There is no security or love in that kind of institution [24-hour care centre].' Nee is considering sending Sank back to Thailand to her father. Her younger sister suggested that the state could take responsibility for Sank. To the social worker, Nee stresses that she did a lot for Sank when she brought her to Denmark. She repeats this several times during the meeting.

Nee's story reveals some of the complications that arise when the migrants bring their children to Denmark. Nee's transnational migration process is based on informal networks consisting of her sisters already living in Denmark. They helped her settle down in Denmark, find a job and make contact with her former Danish husband. Marrying a Danish man, Nee solved the housing problem for herself and her daughter until she filed for a divorce. The global care chain involves her mother caring for her daughter in Thailand. This care chain changed when Nee brought her daughter to Denmark, which was possibly due to the Danish migration policy on family reunification.

After Nee brought Sank to Denmark, her motherhood changed from one of transnational motherhood to local motherhood; she is no longer part of a global care chain with her child, although she could still be part of a global care chain with regard to her parents. At the point Nee applied for a residence permit for Sank, she depended on the consent of her former Danish husband with regard to their housing and finances, which placed her in a vulnerable position. Nee no longer depends on her Danish ex-husband for her social rights; she is able to receive various social benefits enabling her to meet her financial and social obligations to Sank. However, according to the Danish social authorities, Nee has trouble meeting emotional and social obligations towards Sank. In particular, Nee's story reflects a cultural clash of different ways of doing motherhood. Unlike Khem, Nee, having brought her child to Denmark, is the physically present mother, but she is emotionally absent. Nee is confronted by the dominating discourse of motherhood within social work in Denmark that constructs motherhood as a female subject who is emotionally present, takes an active part in the everyday life of the children and is generally involved. The social worker explains to Nee how she should behave as a (good) mother, which disciplines Nee to a particular ideal of the good mother. This discourse of motherhood is quite different from Nee's way of doing motherhood, stressing facilitative aspects such as housing, food and access to education.

During the process from transnational motherhood to local motherhood, her motherhood changes from a Skype-motherhood to a local, physically present motherhood. Despite the change of motherhood, emotional insecurity and financial security are still characteristic of Nee's situation – just in another form. Placing high expectations on their children, the female Thai migrant sex workers' lives sometimes make it difficult for them to take care of their children, as in the case of both Nee and Khem. Nee expects a kind of gratitude from Sank, given that her daughter has the opportunity to go to school and get an education. In practice, however, there is no space for Sank in Nee's everyday life in Denmark. Being a low-skilled migrant, Nee finds selling sex an attractive alternative to jobs as a cleaner or kitchen assistant. Nee works late at a massage parlour or helps her sister there. Consequently, her working life conflicts with her caring for Sank, despite her rights to bring Sank to Denmark. Nee brought her daughter to Denmark, but her physical presence has not elicited emotional care, and thus emotional insecurity and financial security still characterize her motherhood. Frustration dominates their relationship.

Conclusion

When female migrants bring their children to the receiving country – in this case Denmark – the care chain involving the children disappears. Other care chains relating to parents or parents-in-law might still exist, but they have not been investigated in this study. Despite representing the downside of a global care chain and life in an unequal, globalized world, Khem's and Nee's agency are manifested in their Skype- and local motherhoods. Organizing the ongoing contact with their children through transnational communication, filing for divorce and organizing their own lives reflects their agency. They have both obtained some sort of financial security for themselves and their children. Khem performs emotional presence and physical absence through Skype-motherhood, whereas Nee is emotionally absent and largely physically absent, despite the geographical proximity of her daughter. Khem and Nee do motherhood in different ways. Also at play is the confrontation between Nee's understanding of a good mother and another one represented by the Danish social worker.

How a child responds to a new country depends upon the child's life so far, its relationship with other caregivers, its reactions to change and the motherhood performed. For this group of female migrants, bringing children into the receiving country also depends on two other crucial factors: housing conditions and the consent of their new husbands, as shown in a study by Sørensen and Guarnizo (2007). Due to this complexity, policy solutions are not simple. There is a need for more differentiated policy instruments that go beyond stating rights to offering concrete help to perform motherhood under their specific conditions of work – help where the disciplining effects are minimized by not uncritically reproducing naturalized discourses of motherhood.

These two stories prompt us to reflect on the relationship between rights and obligations. We have not questioned the necessity of a right to bring the migrants' children to the new country. Instead it is our intention to question the often naturalized relationship between rights and obligations inherent in the two stories. Rights are often codifications of obligations such as expectations concerning migrating mothers. The different ways of doing motherhood seem to be at odds with traditional and local understandings of good motherhood as physical presence, which is why policy solutions should be wary of reproducing or facilitating one form of doing motherhood over another.

Notes

1 In contrast to Khem and Nee, the upside of globalization consists of female professionals working in Europe as doctors or nurses (Isaksen 2007; Yeates 2009).

2 Even if it is only one person who goes abroad, the decision affects the remaining family members because of the redistribution of the migrant's domestic duties, child rearing, care, etc. (Levitt & Schiller 2004, 1016). Expenses related to migration and settlement in the receiving society are often met by the family from the same local community in the sending country. Thus migration becomes a family strategy.

3 See Law on foreigners §§ 7–9.

4 However, granting residence permits for their children depends on the connection between the parents and the children, and is governed by the length
of separation and the child's belonging to the sending society. Each application
is processed individually.

5 None of the interviewees had children over fifteen years old when they applied
for residence permits for their children.

6 In addition, the Danish authorities also 'consider whether the child is vulnerable to serious social problems in Denmark by identifying whether the family
in Denmark has social problems' (New to Denmark 2010), for 'if one of the
child's parents continues to reside in the country of origin … and if the application for family reunification is submitted more than two years after the
parent residing in Denmark meets the requirements for family reunification
with a child, a special attachment requirement applies. This requirement
stipulates that a residence permit will only be granted if the child has … an
attachment to Denmark sufficient to form the basis for successful integration
in Denmark' (ibid.). This means that the other parent, who lives in the sending
society, plays a central role in determining the rights of the migrant to bring
the children.

References

Avila, Ernestine & Hondagneu-Sotelo, Pierrette (1997), 'I'm here, but I'm there:
The Meanings of Latina Transnational Motherhood', *Gender & Society*, 11(5),
548–571.

Basch, Linda, Schiller, Nina Glick & Blanc, Cristina Szanton (1994), *Nations
Unbound. Transnational Projects, Postcolonial Predicaments, and Deterritorialized
Nation States* (Luxembourg: Gordon & Breach Publishers).

Dahl, Hanne Marlene (2000), *Fra kitler til eget tøj – Diskurser om professionalisme,
omsorg og køn* (Århus: Politica).

Danish Immigration Service (Udlændingeservice) (2007), '*Tal og fakta på udlændingeområdet 2006*', Ministeriet for flygtninge, Indvandrere og Integration,
<www.nyidanmark.dk/da-dk/ophold/familiesammenfoering/aegtefaeller/>,
accessed on 20 July 2009.

Hasse, Cathrine (2000), 'Overvejelser om positioneret deltager-observation. Sexede
astronomer og kønnede læreprocesser', *Kvinder, Køn & Forskning*, 9(4), 27–39.

Hochschild, Arlie (2001), 'Global Care Chains and Emotional Surplus Value',
in Will Hutton & Anthony Giddens (eds.), *On the Edge. Living with Global
Capitalism* (London: Vintage).

Hochschild, Arlie (2003), 'Love and Gold', in Barbara Ehrenreich & Arlie Russell
Hochschild (eds.), *Global Woman: Nannies, Maids and Sex Workers in the New
Economy* (London: Granta Books).

Isaksen, Lise Widding; Devi, Sambasivan Uma & Hochschild, Arlie Russell
(2008), 'Global Care Crisis: A Problem of Capital, Care Chain, or Commons?',
American Behavioral Scientist, 52(3), 405–425.

Isaksen, Lise Widding (2007), 'Gender, Care Work and Globalization: Local Problems and Transnational Solutions in the Norwegian Welfare State', in M. G. Cohen & Janine Brodie (eds.), *Remapping Gender in the New Global Order* (New York: Routledge).

Knijn, Trudie & Kremer, Monique (1997), 'Gender and the Caring Dimension of Welfare States: Towards Inclusive Citizenship', *Social Politics*, 4(3), 328–360.

Kofman, Eleonore (2003), 'Women Migrants in the European Union', paper presented at a conference jointly organized by the European Commission and OECD, The Economic and Social Aspects of Migration, Brussels, 21–22 January.

Kvale, Steinar (1994), *InterView. En introduktion til det kvalitative interviews* (Copenhagen: Hans Reitzels Forlag).

Lister, Ruth (1997), *Citizenship: Feminist Perspectives* (London: Macmillan).

Lister, Ruth et al. (2007), *Gendering Citizenship in Western Europe – New Challenges for Citizenship Research in a Cross-national Context* (Bristol: Policy Press).

Levitt, Peggy & Schiller, Nina Glick (2004), 'Conceptualizing Simultaneity: A Transnational Social Field Perspective on Society', *International Migration Review*, 38, 1002–1103.

Lutz, Helma (2008), 'Introduction: Migrant Domestic Workers in Europe', in Helma Lutz (ed.), *Migration and Domestic Work: A European Perspective on a Global Theme* (Aldershot: Ashgate).

Lutz, Helma & Ewa Palenga-Möllenbeck (2009), 'The Care Chain Concept Under Scrutinity – Female Ukrainian/Polish Care Migrants and Their Families Left Behind', paper presented at the conference 'Care and Migration', Frankfurt, 22–23 April.

New to Denmark 2007, 'Ægtefæller, registrerede partnere og faste samlevere', the Ministry for Refugee, Immigration and Integration Affairs, <http://www.nyidanmark.dk/da-dk/Ophold/familiesammenfoering/aegtefaeller/aegtefaeller.htm>, accessed on 8 July 2010.

New to Denmark 2010, 'Children under the age of 15', the Ministry for Refugee, Immigration and Integration Affairs, <http://www.nyidanmark.dk/en-us/coming_to_dk/familyreunification/children.htm>, accessed on 11 March 2010.

Parreñas, Rhacel (2001), 'Mothering from a Distance: Emotions, Gender, and Intergenerational Relations in Filipino Transnational Families', *Feminist Studies*, 27(2), 361–390.

Sarvasy, Wendy & Longo, Patrizia (2004), 'The Globalization of Care – Kant's World Citizenship and Filipina Migrant Domestic Workers', *International Feminist Journal of Politics*, 6(3), 392–415.

Sørensen, Ninna Nyberg (2002), 'Transnationaliseringen af husmoderlige pligter', *Kvinder, Køn & Forskning*, 11(2), 9–19.

Sørensen, Ninna Nyberg & Guarnizo, Luís E. (2007), 'Transnational Family. Life Across the Atlantic. The Experience of Colombian and Dominican Migrants in Europe', in Ninna Nyberg Sørensen (ed.), *Living Across Worlds: Diaspora, Development and Transnational Engagement* (Geneva: IOM).

Spanger, Marlene (2008), 'Socialpolitiske tiltag og feministisk gennemslagskraft? Trafficking som policyfelt i Danmark', in Charlotta Holmström & May-Len

Skilbrei (eds.), *Prostitution i Norden* (TemaNord nr. 2008, 604; Copenhagen: Nordisk Ministerråd).

Tronto, Joan (1993), *Moral Boundaries – A Political Argument for an Ethic of Care* (New York: Routledge).

Tronto, Joan (2004), 'Care as the Work of Citizens: A Modest Proposal', in Kari Wærness (ed.), *Dialogue on Care* (Bergen: University of Bergen).

Tronto, Joan (forthcoming), 'Privatizing Neo-colonialism: Migrant Domestic Care Workers, Partial Citizenship and Responsibility', in Hanne Marlene Dahl, Marja Keränen & Anne Kovalainen (eds.), *Europeanization, Care and Gender – Global Complexities* (publisher pending).

Yeates, Nicola (2004), 'Global Care Chains. Critical Reflections and Lines of Enquiry', *International Feminist Journal of Politics*, 6(3), 369–391.

Yeates, Nicola (2009), *Globalizing Care Economies and Migrant Workers* (Basingstoke: Palgrave Macmillan).

Yuval-Davis, Nira (2006), 'Belonging and the Politics of Belonging', *Patterns of Prejudice*, 40(3), 197–214.

CHAPTER 7

Transnational care

The social dimensions of international nurse recruitment

Lise Widding Isaksen

When a group of eight Latvian nurses arrived in a small rural community in Norway in 2002, the local newspaper questioned a widely held public belief that international nurse recruitment was a win-win situation where Latvian nurses in need of work and Norwegian nursing homes in need of skilled staff formed a perfect match. Local grandparents got sufficient and good care by professional nurses, and the quality of care and human dignity in nursing homes was maintained. As an extra bonus, nurses from poorer countries had the chance of a better life and the transfer of care was seen as a kind of development aid. Compared to Latvian wages, Norwegian salaries were far better and the journalist wrote: 'they [the wages] are something to write home about. Maybe even some of it can be sent home' (Eliasson 2002). According to the newspaper, Latvian nurses filled the jobs Norwegian men and women were less willing to take. Even if social norms and public morals demand high quality care for the sick and elderly, the journalist argued that the real problem in the welfare state was a lack of willingness to pay nurses a decent wage (Eliasson 2002). The driving forces behind the nurses' arrival were understood as a combination of emigration strategies in Latvian households and a global solution of a Norwegian care deficit.

The newspaper defined the strongest pull factors in the welfare state's active recruitment, and agreed with the Norwegian nurses' trade union that nurses actually want to work in the public healthcare services, but poor wages, disgraceful working conditions and heavy shifts were tiring people out. Nurses would have returned to the profession if wages and working conditions were better, the newspaper wrote, and international labour recruitment as such could not solve local problems in the long run. The active international nurse recruitment that became apparent in the beginning of this millennium was regarded a short-term quick fix.

Less attention was paid to the social and cultural consequences of international nurse migration. Here I will explore how the recruitment practices paved the way for an emergence of transnational spaces of care in which migrant families exchanged economic, social and emotional remittances, and care providers and care recipients were connected to each other. The news about the Latvian immigration left me curious about the realities behind the 'win–win' definition. In what follows I present a research project based on interviews with the Latvian nurses and the families they left behind. The eight nurses were interviewed in Norway in 2004 and their families in Latvia in 2005. All in all the empirical data includes 27 interviews with the migrants and their families in Latvia.

The analysis examines how overseas recruitment and the Latvian households' internationalization strategies opened the way for transnational spaces of care encompassing those who move and those who stay behind and their ways of staying connected to each other. The cross-border spaces I discuss in this context are oriented towards institutional and informal exchanges of paid and unpaid care and focus particularly on gender and welfare. In general, transnational spaces are defined as 'domains of cross border social relations' (Faist 2000). Here the cross-border relationships will be understood as gender-specific care relations. Transnational spaces of care stem from a combination of skilled and unskilled international care migration and the institutional arrangements that initiate mobility between nations and the families living with these arrangements.

Theoretically, transnational spaces of care are of interest because they challenge traditional understandings of the family and the welfare state as nation-state-specific social institutions. In the public discourse, new combinations of migration and care are primarily understood as a care transfer from one nation-state to another. The

Norwegian welfare state sees care workers as a resource that can be imported and used to fill vacancies in the healthcare services to secure quality care for the elderly. The idea that foreign nurses themselves might have to leave their own parents and grandparents behind is not a public issue. Neither is the idea that import of care workers can expand the national space and transform cultural ideas of family life.

The aim of this analysis is to explore the hypothesis that nurse migration transforms social institutions and creates transnational spaces of care. As theoretical tools I will use perspectives from the theories of global care chains (Ehrenreich & Hochschild 2002), and since this analysis deals especially with skilled nurses, I will also draw on insights from the global nurse care chain perspective (Yeates 2009). When skilled nurses migrate they are participating in 'global nurse care chains' (Yeates 2009). These care chains link together a nursing home or hospital in the host country, the nurses who move along these chains, and the nursing institutions in the home country. Recruitment services, state immigration regulations, nursing licensing authorities and trade union bodies can also be involved in the chains.

The unit of analysis here is not spatially fixed to one national location. It includes multiple locations, and the analysis will illuminate a development of global care chains in the Nordic regions and the social, economic and political contexts in which transnational relations are embedded. To examine how care chains are subjectively experienced, a case-study of one particular family and their cross-border relationships between Latvia, the Ukraine, Norway, Spain and Israel will be presented.

Global care chains

In the literature, families living in different countries are defined as 'transnational families', pointing to the fact that in spite of long distances between them, migrants may still see themselves as a collective unity and share responsibility for the family's welfare (Bryceson & Vuorela 2002). In a transnational family, one or both parents or adult children may be producing income abroad while other family members carry out the function of reproduction, socialization, and consumption in the country of origin (Parreñas 2001).

The core concept 'global care chains' refers to 'a series of personal links between people across the globe based on the paid and un-paid work of caring' (Hochschild 2000, 131). Hitherto, research on global care chains has mainly focused on mothers and their children left behind (Parreñas 2001, 2005; Isaksen 2006; Isaksen, Devi & Hochschild 2008), or on how fathers and grandmothers contribute to global care chains (Lutz 2009). Less attention has been paid to elderly parents and other family members' experiences. This research will expand this knowledge and show how adult and married daughters can be important participants in the making of global care chains and transnational spaces of care.

The archetypal global care chain involves mothers who migrate from poorer to richer countries to take care of children in middle-class families, leaving their own children behind in the care of their family. The transfer of care work is mainly related to 'motherly' labour, and international migration is driven by women with dependent children in wealthy countries. They have entered the paid labour market and solve their family–work balance problems by 'outsourcing' domestic work to paid nannies and housemaids. At the end of the chain the value of the labour decreases, and often it becomes unpaid work for female members of the family. Similarly, the global care chain perspective mainly focuses on care work in private households and families. Yeates (2009) has later included professional women with roles and identities other than mothers to bring more attention to skilled workers' agency, migration strategies and acts of solidarity, support and resistance.

The care deficit

Norway has still not succeeded in solving the problems of gen-der equality in the division of labour in families. Even if greater numbers of young fathers participate in the social and emotional care of children, it is mainly women who bear the responsibility for practical housework and care work at the same time as they pursue full-time careers (Lorentsen & Lappegård 2009). 'Absent fathers' still constitute an important problem in the everyday lives of families with small children. When it comes to family care for elderly parents, the problem is related to 'absentee sons'. Eldercare is usually organized by the welfare state, and even if family care still is the normative ideal it has become more complicated for adult daughters and sons to combine work with care for elderly parents. Only 13 per cent of families say that they are willing to have an elderly dependent parent living in their households. More so than men, middle-aged women reduce their participation in the labour market to care for old mothers and fathers. About two-thirds of the elderly who need round-the-clock care live in nursing homes or in public housing projects for elderly. The rest are taken care of by their families. This means that about 200,000 people in their fifties and sixties combine family care for elderly parents with paid work (Veenstra et al. 2009). The gap between the demand and supply of public care services is increasing, and many families are over-burdened by care responsibilities.

The care deficit is not only related to women's integration in paid employment and to demographic changes, but also to changes in the labour market itself. Strategies to increase the number of nursing students and attract more nurses to public health care services have failed. Too few people want a career as a nurse, and a significant number have left the profession because of unfavourable employer policies. International nurse recruitment is a response to the needs of the labour market and an expression of the fact that the state is responsible for the supply of professional and institutional eldercare. The Norwegian government organized in 1997 one of the first projects to recruit nurses from abroad, Aetat's Health Recruitment (Savides 2005).

The aim with Aetat Health Recruitment was to fill vacancies. The project was led by employers from hospitals and nursing homes, the migration authorities and the nurses' trade union. The state played a crucial role in defining the migration terms. The Aetat project recruited nurses from Finland, Poland and former East Germany, offering a 'package deal': free Norwegian courses in their home country, paid travel expenses and help in finding housing in Norway. Aetat had quite a gender-conservative attitude towards nurses, and

saw husbands and families as 'competitors' to the employer, thinking that families drained energy from the nurses and reduced their
flexibility and availability for the employer. The agency preferred
to recruit single nurses, based on the idea that single women were
more dedicated to their work (Savides 2005). The Polish, Finnish
and German nurses were given work permits for a year at a time, in
accordance with the political regulation of the immigration of skilled
workers. After three years the nurses could apply for a permanent
work and residence permit. Nurses had to sign a three-year contract,
mainly in the eldercare sector, and if the contract was broken, all
reimbursed expenses had to be paid back. The same terms were
offered to the Latvian nurses in 2002. An important difference in
migration terms, however, was that Latvians were encouraged to
bring spouses and children.

In order to work in Norway as a skilled immigrant, nurses have to
get an authorization from the Norwegian Public Office for Health
Care Professionals (SAFH). Today all nurses from EU countries
automatically have their diplomas accepted. But if the SAFH finds
the health care workers' linguistic skills insufficient they can give
nurses a temporary 'licence' to work as nurse. This licence is issued
three months at a time, and a licensed nurse has to work under
the supervision of a registered nurse. According to the Norwegian
Law for Health Professionals § 48, SAFH can demand particular
exams, more education and/or more extended practical skills until
the 'necessary level of knowledge is reached' before a licence can be
turned into full authorization.

Even if foreign nurses have authorizations and a master's degree,
individual nurses benefit differently from their diplomas. Ouali
(2009) found that nursing diplomas conjure up a number of images, and local health regimes redefine the meanings of the diplomas
in ways that create images of skilled workers as unskilled if their
knowledge of the local language is defined as insufficient. In Norway,
nursing home managers saw Polish nurses as a stable, hard-working
workforce using less of their welfare rights than Norwegians. They
were more willing to work overtime, at weekends and during religious holidays (Riemsdijk 2006). They got a reputation for having
a better work ethic and being less demanding than 'native' nurses.

Nursing nowadays is a gender-diversified profession, and gender plays an active role in the construction of ethnic hierarchies. Savides's (2005) study of the Aetat project examined male and female nurses' experiences as migrants in the workplace. She found that employers saw German nurses as 'more like us' while Polish nurses were seen as 'strangers'. Above all, male German nurses were preferred, particularly among hospital employers, since they were seen as easier to integrate than female Polish nurses. Male German nurses climbed the professional career ladders more quickly than Polish nurses, who tended to remain in bedside care in public nursing homes. Many did not get a full authorization and worked for longer periods 'on licence' than the Germans. They therefore earned less than Norwegian and German nurses. As Ouali (2009) found in Belgium, migrant nurses in Norway were also seen as 'warmer' and more 'natural' than the Norwegians, but not 'better skilled' or 'more professional' (Savides 2005). Migrant nurses' professional skills were essentialized and used to create an image of skilled workers as unskilled.

Even if the politics of the diploma can initiate discriminatory practices in the workplace, getting a reputation for being willing to work hard and take on double shifts can also give benefits. Savides (2005) found that nurses periodically preferred to work long shifts in order to get free a week or two to look after elderly or sick parents in Poland or Germany. Today nurses from Poland and Germany have got better work opportunities at home or in other countries, and the Baltic countries have become a more important recruitment area.

The Latvian context

Latvia is a small country with only 2.3 million inhabitants (2007). The nation got its independence from the Soviet Union in August 1991, and has since taken its period of national independence in 1918–1940 as a model for the creation of a 'normal' and 'Latvian' society (Stukuls 1999). The recreation of a pre-war Republic of Latvia is extremely problematic, however, because the politics of 'regaining normality' is confronted with a dramatically changed society (Novikova 1998).

In 1992 the Latvian government introduced new laws to regulate

Latvian citizenship. All those able to prove they are related to people living in Latvia on 17 June 1940 or earlier are considered Latvian citizens. People who arrived in Latvia after 1940 are not automatically granted citizenship. The new law divided the Latvian population into three different categories: Latvian citizens; non-citizens who had a right to stay in Latvia as 'permanent residents'; and stateless persons (Muzergues 2004; Petersone 2006). More than two-thirds of the Russians were classified as 'non-citizens', but could become citizens if they passed a naturalization test. Latvians have blue passports; permanent residents have violet passports.

Russians unable to speak Latvian fluently lost jobs in local public administration. In 1991 there were 700,000 residents of the former Soviet workforce in Latvia (Indians 2007). Most Latvians (99.2 per cent) have full citizenship compared to a minority of the Russians (37 per cent). Russians are now the largest minority group (Latvian Human Development Report 1997, Riga). The Russian minorities also include people from Belarus and the Ukraine. Social integration processes have been complicated, and the ethnic hostility and violence has grown. The Russian-speaking population has experienced downward social mobility. They are considered to be 'losers' because of their inability to speak Latvian, and due to the demand that new jobholders speak Latvian fluently many Russians remain unemployed. They are stigmatized as 'strangers' and 'occupants' associated with military brutality and Stalin's deportations of more than 100,000 Latvians to Siberia (Stukuls 1997). Russian women in particular are made into the Other: Novikova (1998) writes that Russian women in Latvia have internalized a picture of themselves as 'the other'.

After the Soviet occupation of Latvia in 1941 the Latvian population gradually lost their social status and say on the development of their own country, while Russians achieved higher social status than Latvians. During the Soviet period the Latvian language had a low social status while the Russian language was associated with civilization, development, urbanization, modernity and power (Petersone 2006). The Latvian government has now introduced a new school reform and Latvian is the public language in all schools.

The Latvian welfare state is dominated by a gender-conservative ideology. A survey of European men's use of time on housework concluded that Norwegian and Swedish men spend most time on housework than men elsewhere in Europe. Spanish and Italian men do not contribute much; but at the bottom were Latvian men, who contribute less than all other men in Europe (Rydenstam & Caage 2007). However, recent qualitative research in Latvia has shown that young fathers participate more in child-care, but paradoxically they do not rate child-care when asked to talk about their significant everyday activities (Putnina 2006). In general women have double burdens as wage-earners and as mothers and wives. Housework and care for the elderly, the sick and children are female duties. Younger women expect help and support from their husbands, but most masculine local cultures are gender-traditional, conservative and rigid (Grants 1998).

Eurostat data for the period 1998–2004 shows that the gender gap is now decreasing in the Latvian middle class. Latvian women are on average better educated than men. Women are more likely to return to education, they stay longer in the jobs, and their total work experience is greater than men's. In general, well-educated women tend to earn less than their male counterparts. The gender gap in income levels is first of all related to traditional gender segregation in the labour market. In Latvia, as in many other countries, education, health care and social care are female-dominated sectors (Tranpenciere 2006).

Latvian women have for decades lived with an active welfare state. They have had access to employment and education, social services, maternity benefits and protective labour legislation. Novikova (1998) finds that even if reproductive rights such as maternity leave do still exist, the younger generation of women are afraid to use them to the full because they risk losing their jobs if they are absent from the workplace too long, or they cannot afford to take maternity leave because the maternity allowance is miserably low compared to their normal salary. Besides, there are few pre-school networks or acceptable public day care centres. The author concludes that there is a gap between a public, equal-rights culture and a private conservative gender ideology. Contemporary Latvian women are very conscious of the fact that motherhood is a symbolic priority for the process of national unification. The stereotype of a strong mother–worker, maintaining and addressing the constructed values of the 'golden age' when families had good and caring mothers, has become essential for national political ideologies. One expression of this trend is the glorification of motherhood and the sacrifice of mothers' self-interests to the best of the family as a group. In popular culture and in the section of the national press that targets the Latvian-speaking population, women as creators of domestic spaces are glorified. Novikova (1998) claims that Latvian women are witnessing a re-channelling of energy away from public professionalism towards the art of home-making. Contemporary Latvia idealizes the family and lauds maternal duty. Even so, the fertility rate has fallen dramatically. According to the UN Economic Commission for Europe, Latvian women had the lowest fertility rate in Europe, at 1.09 child per women in 2000 (UN Economic Commission for Europe 2008).

Medical cultures

Earlier in Latvian women's migration history, women, as migrant workers for instance in Great Britain in the early 1950s, have contributed to receiver countries' public health care as hospital workers and as domestic workers in private homes (Mc Dowell 2005). Similarly, in Canada female Latvian migrant workers found jobs as housekeepers, factory workers and hospital orderlies after the Second World War (Mietizis & Dreifelds 1998). The women were war refugees from Latvia and were mainly recruited from refugee camps in Germany.

In our own times women leave Latvia for different reasons. According to studies of the medical culture in Latvian health care, the services are strictly hierarchical, and ethnicity and class-consciousness are firmly integrated in the occupational ladder. Doctors openly express degrading attitudes towards nurses in general, but in particular towards Russian nurses. Nurses are ranked according to their kind of knowledge so that a specialist nurse ranks higher than a general nurse. Studies of nurses' working conditions and education system conclude that it became even less attractive to work as a nurse in Latvia after independence (Sandin & Walldahl 1995). Female emigration among nurses from the Russian minority can be understood as an export of gender and ethnicity conflicts.

Six of the eight Latvian nurses who came to Norway belonged to the Russian minority, while six were married and brought their husbands and children. All of them had worked as specialist hospital nurses, but filled vacancies as general nurses in the Norwegian nursing homes. Their education was authorized by the SAFH and gave access to same the pay grades and social rights enjoyed by other nurses in Norway.

These political and socio-economic dimensions were combined with the social and cultural tools individual nurses brought with them and that guided their new lives. In the following case-study of Zofia (fictive name) and her family I will discuss some complexities the migrants' families experience when transforming their social life from one suited to a single nation-state to one that includes other states. This case is typical in the sense that it includes the central aspects of the 27 interviews in general.

The making of a transnational space of care

Zofia was born in the Ukraine in 1974 and arrived with her family in Latvia in 1976. Her grandmother still lives in the Ukraine and both her parents are Ukrainian. She grew up in Latvia together with her older sister and two younger siblings. When we met in 2004 she was married to Joseph, their daughter Ada was eight years old, and they were expecting a new baby. Before she signed her contract to work in the nursing home, the employer offered her the chance to 'try Norway' for three months. They liked it and she, her husband and daughter decided to stay for a three-year period. Their reasons were economic and social: 'nurses are better paid in Norway and we wanted a better life,' she said.

Her mother's inability to speak Latvian had lost her her job as a skilled factory worker and she had to work as a low-paid caretaker in the public housing project where they lived. Her father was a retired fisherman, and in his words his pension had dwindled to 'a joke'. The brother went to the Ukraine to look for better opportunities and her younger sister prepared to migrate by training as a nurse with a view to joining her sister in Norway later. Since none of the members of Zofia's family had lived in Latvia in 1940, they lost their citizenship and became non-citizens after independence in 1991. They found themselves in a difficult situation as part of a Russian minority. Loss of jobs and pensions led to economic problems and reduced their social status.

Zofia was aware of this situation and remained oriented towards her family and culture of care back home. In Norway she worked as a night-shift nurse and she was usually home when Ada got home from school, for she did not want her daughter to participate in the local after-school programme. She said:

> In Latvia children go home after school. They learn to be independent … I work night shifts so I spend a great deal of time at home … My daughter comes home after school. … In Latvia as children we looked after ourselves … there were neighbours looking after us … or grandparents if they were retired or out of work … but since there are many single mothers in Latvia, children mostly looked after themselves.

As a child, Zofia herself received after-school care from neighbours and grandparents in the neighbourhood. As a contrast to most Norwegian families, who send their children to after-school programmes, she prefers family care for her daughter, thinking that this is what normally is done in her home country. She also observes that public care services for the elderly are different than she originally thought:

> In Latvia we do not have nursing homes like here in Norway. Many people think that if you're 'a good child' you take care of your elderly mother and father. But if you do not like them, you send them away. … That's how I thought in the beginning, but now I think that it's better for old people here in Norway because there is someone to look after them and give them food and care … so if you [women] work and the husband, too, and the parents are home alone … then it is difficult to look after them … here in Norway people can come to the nursing home and visit and families

take their mothers and fathers home at the weekend ... so I see it in a different way now.

Zofia experiences the local culture of eldercare as a mix of public care and family care. She changes her mind and accepts that nursing-home patients are institutionalized not because they are abandoned by their families, but because they are a part of another aspect of the work–family balance for working adult children.

The workplace integrates Zofia as a social citizen in the community. Her work is not only economically rewarding. She also receives human gratitude. She describes her patients by using a medical gaze, and says: 'Most of them are senile and do not remember anything from the one moment to the next.' Then she tells with great pleasure: 'Once I had a patient ... she was an old woman ... her daughter told me that she wanted me to visit her at home because she had bought a nice present for me. ... I also have another patient ... she always looks forward to seeing me.' The care connects her to family members in the wider community. Non-material pay-offs such as positive responses, social recognition and gratitude from patients and family members express meaningful aspects of her work.

The job gives her access to full social citizenship:

> Here [in Norway] there is more security when you're sick. You can get part-time sick leave for instance. We do not have this security in Latvia. If you do not have a job here in Norway you can get unemployment benefits. This is not available in Latvia.

Zofia made a room for intimacy in the virtual space where the Russian language and identity could be maintained. In Latvia, Russian has become a politicized language attached to the 'othered' Russian minority (Novikova 1998). Despite the low status Russian has in Latvia, Zofia decided to teach Ada Russian because she believed that 'with Russian you can get further'. She also taught Ada maths and natural sciences. With support from local public services such as the library it was easy for her to maintain her Russian identity:

I like to read books and prefer Russian literature. Home in Latvia
I learned Ukrainian, but also Russian and Latvian in school. Now
I have learned Norwegian. It is easy to find Russian literature here
in the community. The library orders it for us. We fill in a form and
they order the books for us. We read local Latvian newspapers online.
We have access to Russian TV by satellite dish and at the weekends
we watch Russian TV because they have better programmes than
the Norwegian channels. My daughter watches Russian cartoons.

New communication technology was used to keep in touch with
family and friends in the Ukraine, Latvia, Spain and the Middle East:

> I have huge telephone bills. I'm used to having many people around
> me. In Latvia family and friends visit me all the time and I have
> an active social life. Here in Norway I socialize most with other
> Latvians. But since most of them live in other villages, we don't see
> one another very often. It's miles and miles between me and the
> others … it is not very often we see each other.

> I call home nearly every day … I have downloaded a free phone
> programme … I send a lot of text messages, e-mails and we talk on
> the mobile. Sometimes we write letters to one another.

> I miss my two best friends … like me they have two college educa-
> tions … as nurses and bioengineers … one works in Spain and the
> other in Israel … we can chat for couple of hours online … With
> another friend I exchange text messages because she is not online.

Virtual intimacy can satisfy some needs, but in the long run Zofia
wanted to spend more face time with her family:

> I have decided to stay in Norway for five years. After my contract
> here in the nursing home ends I want to move closer to Oslo to find
> a job where I can use more of my skills … I am also educated as a
> bioengineer … it depends on developments in Latvia … I want to
> be closer to my family and from the eastern parts of Norway it is
> cheaper and easier to go home … we need not wait for hours for
> the bus to take us over the mountains.

She had a strategy for career development and social advancement. She imagined her future family life as an urban middle-class dual earner:

> I have applied to have my bioengineer education accepted here in Norway. If we move closer to Oslo it will be easier for me to find a job as a bioengineer ... and my husband works now as a construction worker, but trained as a chemical engineer. His education is accepted by the EU ... and he prefers to work as an engineer.

The family left behind

She felt her ties to Latvia had changed:

> To begin with I was so happy and felt so full of energy when I went home to Latvia to visit, but now ... I've changed ... Latvia has changed ... still ... I must see *everyone* ... family and friends ... when I go home ... I'm so exhausted afterwards ... but ... I just want to see them ... all of them.

Hers had been a modern and socialist dual-earner family, cushioned by a socialist welfare state. Now her father's pension is according to him 'a joke', and when I asked how the family survived economically, Zofia said:

> I help them ... I send money every month ... not a fixed amount of money ... but last month I sent a rather generous sum to my mother's account ... she knows that if she needs money, she can take it out of her account.

Zofia kept the issue of providing female when sending money to her mother and not her father. In the interview with her father he said:

> We are a happy family ... but nowadays I must say we are financially poor ... but still ... in the evenings we're usually between 10 and 12 people at the table ... friends, family and neighbours ... so we are rich because we are a good family ... many children and grandchildren.

Zofia's remittances helped put food on the table, and the housework done to prepare the meals and clean-up afterwards were done by the women of the family. The invisibility of the money and the work behind this hospitality might be an expression of a general social invisibility of housework and consumption.

There were some tensions between the family members. The eldest daughter did not agree with their father's description of the 'happy family', and said:

> We have a lousy life … and when Zofia comes home we go to Riga and welcome her at the airport … when she leaves … all of us cry.

Neither did the younger sister Mira agree with their father's definition. The economic hardships had made her change education plans:

> Originally I wanted to be a web designer or have a maritime education, but Zofia advised me to go in for nursing and look for a job in Norway … so now I'm a student at the school of nursing.

The mother had lost her previous job. In Norway Zofia told me that her mother worked as a caretaker, but the mother herself said she was a 'street *babushka*'. She swept the streets and cleared the snow away in the winter. A feeling of social humiliation came with the loss of her job as a skilled factory worker and a degraded social status as a minority woman cleaning the streets. The pain was evident in her face when she talked about her situation. She said:

> These are difficult times … to begin with it was terrible to clean the streets … I felt so ashamed … but now I've got used to it … my husband helps me when the snow is too wet and heavy … he's very helpful.

She looked after the eldest daughters' children after school and enjoyed taking care of the younger grandchildren too. When Zofia's father was asked if he helped his wife look after their grandchildren, he hesitated and said reluctantly: 'I care for them and help my wife, but it makes me feel like a 'mother with a moustache'.' But even if the combination of care and masculinity gave him a feeling of a hybrid gender identity, he supported his wife and was a caring grandfather.

In this case-study we see how transnational spaces of care connect paid and unpaid care providers and care receivers across borders. Zofia's remittances gave her parents a chance to provide unpaid care that helped with her two sisters' family–work balances. Her parents and sisters could continue to respect local cultures of care. In Norway, Zofia's skilled care work supported the 'native' Norwegian women's family–work balances. Working night shifts in the nursing home gave her an opportunity to look after the daughter herself and not send her to the public child-care like local families in general do. In this way she remained oriented towards Latvian cultures of family care. As a paid care provider in the local community she also is connected to her patients' families. The care receivers appreciate her professional care and express their gratitude in responses to Zofia from their family members. The circulation of paid and unpaid care not only includes 'personal links between people across the globe based on the paid and unpaid work of caring' as Hochschild (2000, 131) defines the global care chains: here a transnational space of care includes the global nurse care chains (Yeates 2009), the Norwegian welfare state's strategies to secure professional care in public institutions, and the particular public–private mix of professional and family care one finds in local civil society.

Discussion

Is international nurse recruitment a 'win–win' situation? According to Hochschild's theory (2000), families in affluent countries are the winners in the care chains. The Norwegian welfare state offers care for elderly parents and supports 'native' women's integration in the labour market. Some even gain emotional surplus value by the personal recognition Zofia gives her patients. But care chains also work in the opposite direction – from the receiver country to the sender country – and non-market productions of care are created in the left-behind family. Here the family in Latvia gives emotional and social support, and strengthens Zofia's feelings of belonging and inclusion back home as well as in Norway.

At the farthest extent of a global care chain, Hochschild (2000) claims that the value of the care labour decreases and becomes unpaid work for female family members. This study finds that the gratitude Zofia receives from home is not only a private and individual value. Personal recognition and positive attention create subjective welfare and energy, which in turn benefit Norwegian patients. Seen in this perspective the welfare state benefits from the gratitude and care that circulate across borders. Latvian women's unpaid care is 'drained' and becomes an invisible part of the production of welfare in Norway. By looking at global nurse care chains, the spotlight is thrown on skilled workers' acts of solidarity, agency, resistance and support. Zofia's support of her sisters' integration into paid work expresses solidarity. As a professional woman she makes plans for future career development and social advancement for herself and her younger sister. Her openly expressed preference for Russian literature, movies and language is a resistance to the degradation of Russian in Latvia.

In this case-study, men had a marginal role in the flow of care and support across borders. The ties between the women in the family express gender differences in power and status. Men did not have roles as the most important breadwinners. However, Zofia's father had become more important as an unpaid caregiver. Equally, the story illustrates how Zofia remained oriented towards the gender-specific social contract in her home country. On the one hand she participated in the international movement of women seeking better opportunities for career development abroad; on the other she continued to observe the moral economy of kin. Her support of her parents showed that she considered herself to be 'a good daughter' and a 'good woman', willing to sacrifice her own interests for the best of the family as a group.

Migration from Latvia to Norway is a move from one welfare state to another. The Latvian welfare state is part of a nation-building process, and for the moment is gender-conservative and centred on 'family values'. The mother and housewife is the pillar of the nation. In Norway care is no longer seen as a 'natural' job for women. Care deficits are defined as a public and political responsibility, gender equality is high on the political agenda, and even if gender and ethnic hierarchies have developed in welfare institutions, Russian ethnicity is not the tense political issue it is in Latvia.

Still, it must be said that nurses in both countries define their working conditions as hard and poorly paid compared to other groups with similar levels of education. Zofia's work as a night-shift nurse fits into a more general pattern where migrant nurses experience occupational segregation in eldercare and where the most unpopular shifts are given to the migrants (Riemsdijk 2006).

International nurse recruitment is more than a question of a care transfer from one nation to another. It transforms families and communities, and turns national health services into global workplaces. In this case Norway's recruitment of Latvian nurses was seen as a short-term quick fix. However, Norway plans to increase the international recruitment of skilled and unskilled care workers. Today, every third care worker employed in public eldercare in Oslo comes from a non-Western country (Høst & Homme 2008). Transnational spaces of care will probably continue to challenge established ideas and meanings of the institution of the family and nation-state borders in the years to come.

References

Bryceson, Deborah & Vuorela, Ulla (eds.) (2002), *The Transnational Family. New European Frontiers and Global Networks* (Oxford: Berg).

Eliasson, Tonje (2002), 'Å plastre en verkebyll' [To Bandage a Wound], *Næravisa*, 14 March. Volda, Norway.

Faist, Thomas (2000), 'Transnationalization in international migration: Implications for the studies of citizenship and culture', *Ethnic and Racial Studies*, 23/2, 189–222.

Grants, Janis (1998), *Gender Role Perceptions in Latvian Women Across Different Socio-Cultural Contexts* (Ph.D. Dissertation; Riga: University of Latvia).

Hochschild, Arlie R. (2000), 'Global care chains and emotional surplus value', in W. Hutton & A. Giddens (eds.), *On The Edge: Living with Global Capitalism* (London: Jonathan Cape).

Homme, Anne & Høst, Håkon (2009), *Hvem pleier de gamle i Oslo? (Who Takes Care of the Elderly in Oslo?)* (Research Report; Bergen: Rokkan Research Centre).

Indians, Ivar (2007), *Workforce Deficits and Labour Policy in Latvia* (Riga: F. Ebert Stiftung, Riga Office).

Isaksen, Lise W. (2006), 'Tilpasning til tomme rom. Globale omsorgskjeders relasjonsøkologi' [Adjustment to Empty Spaces. The Ecology of the Global

Care Chains], *Tidsskrift for kjønnsforskning* (Kilden Informasjonssenter, Oslo), 1–2, 20–35.

Isaksen, Lise W., Devi, U. & Hochschild, A.R. (2008), 'Global Care Crisis: A Problem of Capital, Care Chain or Commons?', *American Behavioral Scientist*, 52/ 3, 405–426.

Latvian Human Development Report (1997) (Riga: United Nations Development Programme).

Lorentzen, Marit & Lappegård, Trude (2009), *Likestilling og deling av omsorgsoppgaver for barn* [Gender Equality and How Care for Children is Shared] (2009/42; Oslo: Statistics Norway).

Lutz, Helma (2009), 'Care Workers, Care Drain and Care Chains – Reflections on Central Perceptions in the Debate about Care and Migration', paper presented at the ESF Workshop, *A Caring Europe? Care, Migration and Gender*, Open University, Milton Keynes, 12–13 November.

McDowell, Linda (2005), *The Forgotten Voices of Latvian Migrant 'Volunteer' Workers* (Los Angeles: University of California Press).

Miezitis, Solveiga & Dreifelds, Janis (1998), 'Muliticultural Canada: Latvia', <www.Multiculturalcanada.ca/ecp.content/latvians.html>, accessed on 19 May 2010.

Muzergues, Thibault (2004), 'Russia and the nation-building process in Latvia', Sens Public Library online, <http//www.sens-public.org/php37, accessed on 19 May 2008.

Norsk Samfunnsvitenskapelig datatjeneste, NSD NYTT, 1 (2005) (University of Bergen).

Novikova, Irina (1998), 'Women in Latvia Today. Changes and Experiences', *Canadian Women Studies*, 16/1, 27–31.

Ouali, Nouria (2009), 'Migrant Nurses in Brussels' Public Hospitals', paper presented at the ESF Workshop *A Caring Europe? Care, Migration and Gender*, Open University, Milton Keynes, 12–13 November.

Parreñas, Rachel (2001), *The Servants of Globalization* (Stanford: Stanford University Press).

Parreñas, Rachel (2005), *The Children of Global Migration: Transnational Families and Gendered Woes* (Stanford: Stanford University Press).

Petersone, Ilze (2006), 'Russeres situasjon i Latvia etter Sovjetunionens fall' [The Russians' Situation in Latvia after the Fall of the Soviet Union] (Master's thesis; Oslo: Department for Social Anthropology, University of Oslo).

Putnina, Anna (2006), 'Gender and Citizenship in a Multicultural Context: Latvia' (QUING Budapest Team; Budapest: Central European University).

Riemsdijk, Micheline (2006), *Rekruttering av polske sykepleiere til Norge* [Recruitment of Polish Nurses to Norway] (Report 27, Oslo: FAFO).

Sandin, Ingrid & Walldahl, Elvi (1995), *The Latvian Nurses' Education and Profession in a Changing Society* (Gothenburg: Institute for Health Pedagogics, University of Gothenburg).

Savides, Susan (2005), '"Omsorg fra Øst til (helse) i Vest." Polske og tyske sykepleieres beretninger om omsorg og fellesskap' [Polish and German Nurses'

Narratives on Care and Belonging] (Master's thesis; Bergen: Department of Sociology, University of Bergen).

Stukuls, Diana (1999), 'Body of the Nation: Mothering, Prostitution and Women's Place in Post Communist Latvia', *Slavic Review*, 58/3, 537–558.

Rydenstam, Klas & Vaage, Odd Frank (2007), 'Time Use in European Countries: Men's Participation in Household Work', paper presented at the International Association of Time Use Researchers, Washington D.C., October 2007.

Tranpenciere, Ilze (2006), *The Gender Pay Gap in Latvia* (Institute of Philosophy and Sociology, University of Latvia, Riga).

UN Economic Commission for Europe, <www.ce-review.org/oo/18/latvianews. html>, s.v. 'Central Europe Review', accessed on 19 May 2008.

Veenstra, Marijke et al. (2009), *Helse, helseadferd og livsløp* [Health, health behaviour and the life course] (Report nr. 3/09; Oslo: NOVA).

Yeates, Nicola (2009), *Globalizing Care Economies and Migrant Workers: Explorations in Global Care Chains* (London: Palgrave, Macmillan).

Zontini, Elisabetta (2004), 'Italian families and social capital: Rituals and the provision of care in British–Italian transnational families' (ESRC Working Paper, 6; London: South Bank University).

CHAPTER 8

Care work and migration politics in Sweden

Ellinor Platzer

The care regime in Sweden is nothing if not a 'Nordic social care regime', characterized as it is by state commitment to public care for children and elderly people (Williams & Gavanas 2008). Beginning particularly in the 1930s, a number of reforms and measures have been introduced to help families create a balance between waged work, domestic work and family life (Platzer 2007). Examples of such reforms are pre-school institutions, parental leave, and tax-deductible domestic services. These reforms and others reflect power relationships and institutional values. For example, the balance is normally disturbed when women start professional careers or return to work after parental leave; yet in contrast to women's paid work, men's work does not have that effect on the family because it is looked on as a constant (Ahrne & Roman 1997).

A supply of workers is necessary in terms of helping middle-class families to find a balance in life. Moreover, there are very firm notions about which categories that are best suited for care and other personal services. Except for some variations in time and place, women in low social positions are generally looked on as good choices for this kind of work (Anderson 2000; Platzer 2002). In the Nordic countries, these workers used to be recruited from rural areas, but because of sweeping urbanization and the extended global division of labour, most care workers are now found in parts of the world far away from Northern Europe. This phenomenon is an effect of global capitalism and creates what Arlie Hochschild (2000) calls 'global care chains' – a series of personal links between people across the globe based on care work, paid or unpaid. Typically, global care chains start in a poor country and end up in a rich one. The workers care for their employers' homes, children and the elderly in both the domestic service sector and formal institutions. The share of migrants in the Swedish service sector is large. Hochschild (2000) discusses this in terms of 'surplus value', which she argues is useful when analysing what rich countries gain from wholesale migration in the care sector. The theory of surplus value is used in this text in the sense that in order to uphold daily welfare in families, and also to contribute to the welfare society as a whole, migrant women replace native women as care workers.

One aim with this chapter is to describe different categories of migrant care workers in Sweden. Another is to study the process over time by which migrant workers replace Swedish women as care workers, both unpaid and paid. To do so, I will consider how social and economic factors have brought changes in how society organizes care work, and how new needs have been met by adjusted migration policies.

Care workers in Sweden

Currently, there are a number of common categories of migrant care workers in Sweden. By far the most numerous migrants are those who have residence permits, and are working in Sweden on the black market, taking care of the cleaning and laundry in private households. They have some security because of their citizenship, but because their employers do not pay any taxes, the workers are not registered as employees and have therefore no right to health, parental, or unemployment insurance, and are not covered by Sweden's labour laws. The *second* category, migrants with residence permits in Sweden, work on the regular labour market, often as entry-grade nurses in institutional care. Although they are covered by the labour laws, they belong to a low-status group in the labour market. Migrants with a residence permit in another country who are working as domestic servants in Sweden, is a *third* category. The scheme of tax-deductible domestic services permits companies from other countries to operate in the Swedish domestic service sector. These migrants work in Sweden legally but under very different conditions to Swedish workers in general. A *fourth* category is young women from, for instance, Eastern Europe who are in Sweden as au pairs. They live in a family for a year at a time. The formal rules state that this arrangement is a cultural exchange and therefore au pairs do not have to apply for a work permit. They have no employment or citizen's rights whatsoever. Despite that, a lot of au pairs make a significant contribution when helping their host family with child-care and cleaning. Meanwhile, the expansion of the EU, combined with its principles of the free movement of labour, have made it easier for families to legally employ nannies without having to follow the same rules or pay the same wages as for Swedish employees. This *fifth* category is likely to replace the au-pair system to some extent. The *sixth* category exists especially in the largest cities and consists of domestic care workers either on tourist visas or without any papers at all. It is not unusual for their transport, entry into the country, and contact with employers to be organized by someone else. These domestic care workers normally work under very poor conditions and without any security at all. The *seventh* and last category is the growing number of so-called mail-order brides who come to Sweden particularly from Russia and countries in Asia and Latin America. It is relatively easy for these women to get Swedish residence permits, not only because of family ties but also because the immigration office views them as needed in the labour market. It is a requirement of the migration law that they have to stay for at least two years in Sweden before they can get a permanent residence permit. Until that time has passed, they barely have any rights at all (Broman, Flodin & Platzer 2008; Elmhorn 2008; Khosravi 2006; Nilsson 2005; Platzer 2002; Roks rapport 2009; Williams & Gavanas 2008).

The post-war period

For Swedish women, an important step away from their traditional position came when the labour market's need for well-educated women increased in the 1930s. Women's discontent with the traditional gender division of labour eventually resulted in a growing acceptance of women working outside their homes. The demand for domestic services increased, especially from economically well-off households in the cities. During this period, the supply of migrant workers was very small. Instead, women working as maids came mainly from rural areas and were considered suitable as maids because of their subordinate manner (Moberg 1978). They normally worked full-time under poor conditions and lived in their employers' homes. Because of a growing number of other employment alternatives, a lack of domestic workers was soon a fact. The situation for the middle classes became problematic. A serious decrease in the fertility rate was interpreted as discontent among middle-class women, and because of this the issue of domestic services became important. A number of public solutions were discussed.

After the Second World War, the phenomenon of middle-class women working full-time was generally accepted. Families with two breadwinners still had a need for domestic workers. Because of the great lack of domestic workers, the state made it possible to recruit workers from other countries. During and after the Second World War, many refugees from, for example, Poland, Germany and the Baltic states were offered entry to Sweden. There were definitely humanitarian reasons for welcoming the refugees to Sweden, but the demand for labour did speed things up and contributed to the warmth of the welcome. According to the historian Lars Olsson (1995), it was striking how efficient the official labour agents were, and how quickly they moved to get survivors from Nazi concentration camps and bring them to Sweden to work. General work permits were issued for sectors in which refugees could easily be placed. This was particularly true within the sectors of farm work and domestic work, and therefore men and women who fled to Sweden were directed to these sectors. If they did not accept the work it became more difficult for them to get any permits at all (Olsson 1995).

Catharina Calleman (2007), like Olsson, describes how changes in migration policies during and after the Second World War became a way to recruit labour for the domestic-service sector, among others. At the end of the war, over 30,000 refugees from the Baltic states and over 100,000 refugees from the Nordic countries fled to Sweden. The solution to the lack of domestic workers in Sweden became migrant labour. After the war, domestic workers were recruited especially from Germany, Finland and Norway (Calleman 2006).

The recruitment of foreign domestic workers became less important as homes became more modernized and domestic appliances reduced the amount of human effort in domestic work. From the mid-1950s a new category of domestic workers was introduced – home assistants – who worked part-time in other people's homes but had their own families and their own homes. According to Calleman (2007) there were still a rather large number of foreign citizens within the category of domestic work, though: between the years 1950 and 1958, on an annual basis 8,000–10,000 were reported to the migration authorities. The majority came from Germany, Finland, Denmark and Norway. The share of women in the migration labour force that arrived in Sweden during the post-war period was 55 per cent. During this period a new migration principle was introduced: the labour unions were given the right to control every first-time application for a work permit. Because employment in the domestic-service sector, and also the peat industry, did not call for a work permit, the employment conditions in these sectors were not the subject of control.

Welfare expands

During the 1960s and 1970s, young women in certain forms of education had to work in private homes for a period of time to get job experience. That became a popular alternative for two-breadwinner families in need of nannies. These arrangements were not very long-lasting, however, and were replaced by an expansion of public childcare. Care of the elderly, organized collectively, was also introduced at the time. The professionalization of women's traditional work was now comprehensive, while working-class women had now extended their waged work thanks to the growing public sector that for many was the employer of choice (Florin 1999). Comparatively high taxes made these reforms possible and had numerous consequences, such as making the purchase of many domestic and home-related services quite costly, resulting in a large increase in the tasks people performed themselves as unpaid work.

Considering this change it was not surprising that, from 1965 on, the labour organizations in Sweden began to object to labour migration. One argument was that jobs should be reserved for domestic labour, such as married women, older people and the disabled (Calleman 2007). Another was that immigrants in general were being exploited by employers and solely recruited to low-wage sectors in Sweden (Frank 2005; Schierup, Paulson & Ålund 1993) and therefore the arrangement was not considered to be a good one.

In 1967, new regulations, for instance on how to apply for work permits before entering the country and migrants' entitlement to the same wages as Swedish workers, were issued. The effect was an improvement of the working conditions for migrant labour but also a reduction in their number. This became a strategy for Swedish labour organizations to keep general wages, working conditions and working hours steady at a certain level. It is important to underline that this was possible because the need for migrant workers was low at the time. Demand had also decreased, and in 1972 the requirement for work permits for domestic servants was reintroduced. In the early 1980s, the National Swedish Labour Market Board (AMS) decided that applications for work permits in the domestic-service sector were no longer going to be accepted. At the same time, authority over au-pair regulation was delegated from AMS to the Swedish Migration Board. In 1985, AMS stated that labour migration should only be allowed when the demand could not be met by Swedish labour (Calleman 2007).

Gender equality

From the mid-1980s, women's full-time work increased but the gender division of labour in households remained unchanged. From 1990–2000 the birth rate decreased again, but this time it was a matter of economic resources. In the words of Lewis Coser (1979), the family is a greedy institution – especially for women. For careerists, contemporary working life is also a greedy institution. These two – family and work – compete for people's time, energy and commitment. The claims of working life are normally given priority over domestic work and the needs of family members. There is still collective, organized, quality care for children and the elderly in Sweden, funded by the public purse. The lifestyle of particularly dual-career families, though, presupposes more help than is offered by the state. For instance, to avoid children spending more than eight to ten hours in a child-care institution, some parents need someone to collect them and bring them home. There are also parents who need even more help than that, and for them an au pair might be the best alternative (Platzer 2002). Even though dual-career families are most interested in employing care workers, it is obvious that the worker replaces the woman/wife. She has the main responsibility and is the one who, for instance, gives the employee work instructions, oversees the performed work and keeps in touch with the employee (Anderson 2000; Platzer 2007).

A number of private solutions have been introduced as complements to fill the gap between the services the public sector provides dual-career families and the actual needs they experience. Domestic services are price sensitive, however, and the taxes are still comparatively high. There are therefore some strategies being used to lower the cost, such as employing a worker without paying any taxes or hiring an au pair.

Another solution became available with the tax deduction scheme introduced in 2007 (*Skattereduktion för hushållsarbete* 2007, 346). This came after years of ideological debates about whether it should be acceptable to employ domestic workers at all, and if so, who was going to pay for it – the employer alone, or the employer subsidized by the taxpayer (Platzer 2004). Those in favour of introducing the scheme expected it to diminish the black market and improve gender equality. There are, however, only a few signs of such changes. Some employers who used to buy domestic services without paying taxes now use the scheme instead, and some women have found it easier to compete with men in the labour market. The share of all households in Sweden who received the deduction is only around 2 per cent (SCB 2010), which is far less than was expected. There is no real evidence that the scheme has contributed to a decrease of the black market; instead the tax deduction has probably made the domestic-service market larger. As concerns the gender-equality issue, studies show that women still take the main responsibility for the children and domestic work. Employers seem to prefer to buy domestic services from migrants on the irregular market. They are considered to be more cooperative, cost less, be more prepared to work flexible hours, and to stay for a longer time than the native workers (Anderson 2000).

In contrast to previous periods, the demand for domestic workers has been met by a supply of migrant labour that to a large extent is already resident in Sweden. As previously mentioned, these migrant women work as domestic care workers on the irregular market, are partners to Swedish men, or just expected to become care workers because of their social position. Additionally, as already mentioned, there are migrants either on tourist visas or without any papers at all, nannies with temporary work permits, and au pairs.

The relationship between migration and labour market polices does not belong to history. On the contrary, the relationship has been strengthened. One explanation is Sweden's membership of the EU, and later the enlargement of the EU first and foremost with several Eastern European countries. In a public inquiry in 1997 into the free movement of labour (SOU 1997:153), the consequences of Sweden's joining the EU in 1995 were discussed. A conclusion was that labour migration to Sweden would probably increase and a presupposition for female migration was that these women would accept wages and labour conditions below standard in Sweden. Temporary work permits, particularly in the manual-service sector, are considered an appropriate employment alternative for migrant women. In this way, such women would be able to support and care for their own families without posing a threat to traditional gender patterns in their sending countries.

Another example of welcoming migrant workers in Sweden, but only under certain conditions, was a discussion that took place when the EU was enlarged by ten more countries in 2004. Ever since the 1980s, immigration to Sweden has increased by around 3 per cent a year and this seems to be a continuing trend (Globaliseringsrådet 2008). Because of low birth rates and the need for labour, some Swedes wanted to increase immigration. In January 2004, a parliamentary commission was appointed to look into the formal principles of labour migration. The purpose was to create new formal principles that would allow greater labour migration from countries outside the EU/EES, and also to find ways to present Sweden as an attractive country in the eyes of potential migrants. The commission's report (SOU 2005:50) was published in 2005. Three years later, in 2008, the prime minister Fredrik Reinfeldt and the former minister of judicial affairs, Tobias Billström, presented a proposition with new rules for labour migration (Prop. 2007/08). The new rules are expected to create a more effective and flexible system of labour migration. The employer's needs are supposed to propel the recruitment process, and employment of migrants from countries outside the EU/EES is no longer going to be controlled by the authorities. If there are special reasons, temporary work permits can be prolonged and even converted into permanent residence permits. The temporary work permit will be tied to a specified employer and a specified kind of work. After two years it will be possible for the worker to look for employment elsewhere. Some actors in the labour market were sceptical about the migrant's dependence on one employer, but overall the proposal was met with wide support (Prop. 2007/08).

At the same time as it is becoming more difficult for refugees to obtain residence permits in Sweden, labour migration is increasing. When recruiting, it is now easier to get the employees who are needed. At the end of 2008, new regulations were introduced to make it easier for employers to recruit employees from countries outside the EU. It also became easier for individuals to enter the country in order to look for work (Department of Justice, June 2008). The Swedish government wants increased collaboration between representatives from sending, receiving and transit countries in order to meet the stated aim of creating a system in which it is easier to recruit labour (Department of Justice, August 2008).

Discussion

The organization of care work has varied according to the different social, economic, and political settings. Furthermore, there is a clear connection between these variations and the changing migration regime. It is obvious that at times when the demand for care workers is high, the migration policies have been adjusted, and vice versa. One conclusion is that there is a strong connection in Sweden between the demand for care workers and the migration laws. This is also stated by the economic historians Christer Lundh and Rolf Ohlsson (1999), who have studied labour and refugee migration to Sweden in the second half of the twentieth century. They conclude that the economic and political situation in Sweden has been the most important factor in shaping the migration regime – and not the needs of asylum seekers, for example. The various categories of migrant workers in Sweden show, nonetheless, that migration is not only an effect of state policies. Instead it must be viewed in the context of global capitalism. A precondition for increasing labour migration is the wide economic gaps between countries and regions on the global level.

It is obvious that the migrant care worker is replacing native women. In competing with male colleagues, women in professional careers can get help from domestic workers. In that respect, the adjustment of the migration regime can be considered to contribute to maintaining gender equality in Sweden. It may mean liberation for some women, but it does not create gender equality in general. Instead men can continue to avoid responsibility for housework and caring for children and the elderly (Ehrenreich & Hochschild 2002). The surplus value that care workers create is also a benefit to the welfare state as a whole. When taking care of children and the elderly in institutions, for low wages, the migrants help preserve the welfare system.

Migrants have to a large extent been expected to take low-status work, but on the other hand until the 1980s at least they did have full access to the welfare system. Migration policies have long been adjusted to reflect the needs of the labour market. On the other hand, the number of refugees who obtain a residence permit is decreasing. Furthermore, at the same time as migrants and their children are among the most exposed to the decline of the welfare system, the work of migrant labour creates a surplus value in rich countries.

References
Literature

Ahrne, Göran & Roman, Christine (1997), *Hemmet, barnen och makten. Förhandlingar om arbete och pengar i familjen* (SOU 1997:139; Stockholm: Fritzes).

Anderson, Bridget (2000), *Doing the Dirty Work. The Global Politics of Domestic Labour* (London: Zed Books).

Broman, Erik, Flodin, Tim & Platzer, Ellinor (2008), 'Den nya anknytningsinvandringen och efterfrågan på omsorgsarbetskraft', in S. Lundberg & E. Platzer (eds.), *Efterfrågad arbetskraft?* (AMER Årsbok 2008; Växjö: Växjö University Press).

Calleman, Catharina (2006), *Regleringen av arbetsmarknad och anställningsförhållanden för hushållstjänster* (Rapport 2006:7; Uppsala: IFAU).

Calleman, Catharina (2007), *Ett riktigt arbete? Om regleringen av hushållstjänster* (Säter: Pang förlag).

Coser, Lewis (1974), *Greedy Institutions. Patterns of Undivided Commitments* (New York: Free Press).

Ehrenreich, Barbara & Hochschild, Arlie Russell (2003), *Nannies, Maids and Sex Workers in the New Economy* (New York: Metropolitan Books).

Elmhorn, Camilla (2008), 'Framväxten av en avancerad tjänsteekonomi och en ny urban elit i Stockholm', in H. Lindgren & T. Petersson (eds.), *Tillväxt och tradition: perspektiv på Stockholms moderna ekonomiska historia* (Monografi utgiven av Stockholms stad; Stockholm: Stockholmia).

Florin, Christina (1999), 'Skatten som befriar. Hemmafruar mot yrkeskvinnor i 1960-talets särbeskattningsdebatt', in C. Florin, L. Sommestad & U. Wikander (eds.), *Kvinnor mot kvinnor. Om systerskapets svårigheter* (Stockholm: Norstedts).

Frank, Denis (2005), *Staten, företagen och arbetskraftsinvandringen – en studie av invandringspolitiken i Sverige och rekryteringen av utländska arbetare 1960–1972* (Växjö: Växjö University).

Hochschild, Arlie Russell (2000), 'Global care chains and emotional surplus value', in A. Giddens (ed.), *On the Edge: Living with Global Capitalism* (London: Jonathan Cape).

Khosravi, Sharham (2006), 'Territorialiserad mänsklighet: irreguljära immigranter och det nakna livet', in Paulina de los Reyes (ed.), *Om välfärdens gränser och det villkorade medborgarskapet* (Rapport av Utredningen om makt, integration och strukturell diskriminering; Stockholm: Fritzes).

Lundh, Christer & Ohlsson, Rolf (1999), *Från arbetskraftsimport till flyktinginvandring* (Stockholm: SNS Förlag).

Moberg, Kerstin (1978), *Från tjänstehjon till hembiträde. En kvinnlig låglönegrupp i den fackliga kampen 1903–1946* (Uppsala: Historiska institutionen, Uppsala universitet).

Nilsson, Linnéa (2006), 'Vägen till karriären – en polska', *Kvinnofrontens nyhetsbrev på nätet*, 1, <http://home.swipnet.se/kvinnofronten/Nyhetsbrev/1_06/linneanilsson.htm>, accessed on 27 September 2009.

Olsson, Lars (1995), *På tröskeln till folkhemmet. Baltiska flyktingar och polska koncentrationslägerfångar som reservarbetskraft i skånskt jordbruk kring slutet av andra världskriget* (Lund: Förlaget Morgonrodnad).

Platzer, Ellinor (2002), 'Kulturellt utbyte eller billig arbetskraft? Au pair i Sverige', *Sociologisk Forskning,* 3–4, 32–57.

Platzer, Ellinor (2004), *En icke-lag i sökljuset. Exemplet hushållstjänster i Sverige* (Research Report in Sociology of Law, 2004, 4; Lund: Lund University).

Platzer, Ellinor (2006), 'From Private Solutions to Public Responsibility and Back Again: The New Domestic Services in Sweden', *Gender & History,* 2, 211–221.

Platzer, Ellinor (2007), *Från folkhem till karriärhushåll. Den nya husliga arbetsdelningen* (Lund: Arkiv).

Schierup, Carl-Ulrik, Paulson, Sven & Ålund, Aleksandra (1993), 'Den interna arbetsmarknaden – etniska skiktningar och dekvalificering', in id. (eds.), *Arbetets etniska delning* (Stockholm: Carlssons).

Williams, Fiona & Gavanas, Anna (2008), 'The Intersection of Childcare Regimes and Migration Regimes: A Three-Country Study', in H. Lutz (ed.), *Migration and Domestic Work. A European Perspective on a Global Theme* (Hampshire & Burlington: Ashgate).

Sources

Globaliseringsrådet (2008), *Den stora utmaningen: internationell migration i en globaliserad värld.*

Justitiedepartementet [Swedish Ministry of Justice] (2008a), *New rules for labour immigration,* June.

Justitiedepartementet (2008b), 'Europarådskonferens om migration i Kiev'. Press release 29 August.

Proposition 2007/08:147 *Nya regler för arbetskraftsinvandring.*

Roks rapport 2/2009, *Täckmantel: äktenskap – Kvinnojourernas erfarenhet av fruimport,* Emma Wilén.

SCB [Statistics Sweden] (2010), Press release, No 2010/27, 11 February.

Skattereduktion för hushållsarbete. Lag 2007:346.

SOU 1997:153, *Arbetskraftens fria rörlighet – trygghet och jämställdhet. Betänkande av Kommittén om EUs utvidgning – konsekvenser av personers fria rörlighet m.m.*

SOU 2005:50, *Arbetskraftsinvandring till Sverige. Befolkningsutveckling, arbetsmarknad i förändring, internationell utblick. Delbetänkande av Kommittén för arbetskraftsinvandring (KAKI), Stockholm.*

III
THE NATION, CITIZENSHIP
AND DEMOCRACY

CHAPTER 9

Global care and Finnish social policy

Minna Zechner

Child-care and eldercare are pivotal social policy issues that have become increasingly international. The reason for internationalization is the increased international mobility of both those who give care and of those who need care. Care is here understood as activities and relationships involved in meeting various kinds of needs of children and older persons (see Daly & Lewis 2000). Despite the mobility of people, social policies framing care are predominantly national. Moreover, transnational actors such as the EU have yet to formulate explicit policies regarding social care. Instead the EU has a great influence on migration and on the international mobility of people to, from and within Europe, and hence it does have an essential role in shaping the internationalization of child- and eldercare.

The majority of child- and eldercare is done informally, by families and close relatives, even in developed welfare states such as the Nordic countries. Denmark may be an exception, where official services provide the bulk of care for older persons (Timonen 2008). Averaged across the fifteen EU countries and Norway, informal care of older people in 2000 was five times more prevalent than formal care (Daly & Rake 2003). Social (care) policies frame implicit and explicit expectations about responsibilities that individuals, families and public bodies have within social care. Most research on the globalization of care focuses predominantly on migrants, and especially on the care work they do (for example Parreñas 2001; Escrivá 2004;

Lutz 2008). In this study, care policies, and more specifically Finnish child- and eldercare policies, are taken as the starting-point. I shall scrutinize certain care policies and see if they avert or bolster international elements or activities in child- and eldercare.

The possible international elements and activities in child- and eldercare assessed here are (*i*) recruiting care workers from outside the country; (*ii*) getting children or the elderly to Finland to be cared for; (*iii*) caring for them across the national borders; (*iv*) sending them to be cared for outside Finland; and (*v*) getting family members or other close relatives to Finland to give care. These activities are considered against the backdrop of Finnish care policies, but equally the norms and values in which social policies are embedded are considered when possible.

Migration and care in Finland

For a long time Finland was a country of emigration. Only after the collapse of the Soviet Union did the number of immigrants begin to increase. In 1990s the majority of immigrants arrived for humanitarian reasons. In the beginning of the twenty-first century, labour migration has become more common. That said, in 2009 the most common reason to migrate to Finland was family-linked. Despite increasing numbers of immigrants, the number of foreign-born inhabitants is still fairly small compared, for example, to other Nordic countries: in 2007 13.4 per cent of the population in Sweden was foreign born, in Norway 9.5 per cent, in Denmark 6.9 per cent, and in Finland 3.8 per cent (OECD 2009).

Even if Finland deviates from the Nordic norm in this respect, it shares many common features in care policies. Public responsibilities in relation to child- and eldercare are extensive. Policies are designed to boost female workforce participation and gender equality by relieving mainly women from their caring responsibilities. Certain policies also specifically encourage men to participate in caring activities, especially child-care.

Mary Daly (2002, 255) has stated that the provision for care entails the meeting of three needs: services, time and money. To provide for these needs, social policy responses resort to four types of measures:

monetary social security benefits; employment-related provision; services; and incentives for job creation. The Finnish child- and eldercare policies analysed here also fall into these four types, as Table 1 demonstrates. For a closer look, I have picked the most used benefits and services supporting child- and eldercare. Policies supporting families with children who have disabilities or long-term illnesses are not included here. A more detailed description of policy responses presented in the table will be found below. There is a national body of legislation that guides the provision of care benefits and services. Local councils or groups of local councils are obliged to organize sufficient health and social services for their inhabitants, using their own tax revenues with some support from the state purse. The rule of thumb is that in Finland all kinds of child-care receive more open public support than does care for the elderly.

Table 1: Four types of Finnish child-care and eldercare policy measures

Policy response	Child-care	Eldercare
Employment-related provision	Maternity, paternity, parental, and child home-care leave	Temporary leave of absence for urgent family reasons
Financial benefits	Child benefit, maternity, paternity; and parental allowances; child home-care allowance; private day care allowance	Care allowance for pensioners, carer's allowance
Job incentives	Au-pair system	Tax rebate
Services	Day care services	Home-based and institutional care services, vouchers

The EU has, to some extent, the ability to shape national policy responses. The free movement of labour, capital, goods and services amongst the member states are the EU's cornerstones. The right of its citizens to move and reside freely within the territory of the member states is also granted to their family members, irrespective of nationality (Directive 2004/38/EC). These issues have a great impact on the internationalization of care. In 2002 in Barcelona, the member states pledged to step up the provision of child-care so that by 2010 it would be available to 90 per cent of children between three and six years of age and 33 per cent of children under three years of age (Commission 2006).

Regardless of whether this goal has been achieved or not, it is clear that the EU's impact on eldercare policies is less direct than on child-care policies. Still, at least two main areas of EU impact are visible. Firstly, there has been a gradual move towards applying internal market and competition laws in the field of social protection (Saari & Kvist 2007). Hence the EU sets guidelines for how public entities are supposed to procure goods and services, and issue tenders for services that are open to outsourcing. Secondly, a common EU policy on legal and illegal immigration is under way (Council of the European Union 2008). This means that the international movement of essential actors in care – namely family members and care workers – is becoming more standardized than earlier throughout the EU member states.

Time for care

A central employment-related policy response to care is to offer leave of absence for care purposes. This sends the message that people may, or are supposed to, care for their close relatives themselves, and that it is acceptable to be absent from work for such reasons. In Finland this possibility is given only to parents of young children, since there is no such scheme for caring for an adult. Only a temporary leave of absence for acute family reasons is available for very short-term eldercare.

The question of whether child-care leave is conducive to global care arrangements can be answered by looking at whether it allows parents to (*a*) care for a child who lives abroad or (*b*) to care for a child who comes from abroad. Parental leave (maternity, paternity and parental leave) is designed so that parents can care for their own children until each child turns one. This leave attracts an income-related benefit at a level of about 65 per cent of the recipient's previous year's income. Parents are eligible for leave and related benefits only when the mother has lived in Finland and has been eligible for Finnish social security payments a minimum of 180 days before the baby is due. Leave is also available to parents adopting a child from Finland or from abroad (Kela). Finnish social security eligibility is mainly based on residency that is intended to be permanent. For example, asylum seekers do not fulfil this criterion (Law on residence-based social security).

Having gained the right to parental leave, it is possible to travel abroad at least temporarily to provide care and, for example, combine caring for one's child with caring for somebody else's child or for an older person. There is some evidence that Finnish mothers who are on parental or care leave use the time to care for elderly relatives as well (Zechner 2004). It seems that parental leave is also used to care for older family members across national borders (Zechner 2008). A number of Norwegian mothers on maternity or parental leave have stayed in Spain where their parents live as retired migrants. At best the arrangement can be mutually beneficial: older parents get company and care, and daughters receive help with child-care. With Finnish parental leave, generally the rule is that living more than one year outside Finland results in falling outside the Finnish social security system. Temporary international arrangements are thus possible with the help of parental leave.

Child home-care leave is available for parents with children under three years of age. Payments are flat rate and will be discussed in detail in the next section. It is possible to take child home-care leave abroad within the EU or in European Free Trade Association (EFTA) member countries and Switzerland. This leave is available to expatriate families if they still are covered by the Finnish social security system, while those sent overseas to work for Finnish-based companies are usually eligible. Whether in Finland or abroad, those on leave may, in addition to their own children under the age of three, care for other children or for the elderly. There are no definite short-term travel restrictions on parental and child home-care leave. Recipients of child home-care leave are expected to inform the Finnish Social Insurance Institution if they are to be abroad for longer than three months. By contrast, for example, unemployment benefit and income maintenance do impose explicit restrictions on international travel (see Zechner 2008).

For eldercare there are very few employment-related policy responses in Finland. Temporary leave of absence is available for employed people at times of unexpected family occurences such as accidents, death or terminal illness. There are no fixed limits to how long such leave of absence may last, but it is meant only to cover short-term crises, and no monetary benefit is attached to this right. There are no specific geographical restrictions regarding the use of temporary leave of absence for family emergencies. The notion of family embraces the immediate family and members of elder generations (Kröger 2005). This right of absence may thus also be used when family members in need of care and help are abroad, but only for very short spells of care, and thus visits to those living very far away are difficult. It may be also used when accompanying older relatives to Finland in times of a family crisis, as long as travel restrictions (visas, costs, etc.) or immigration policies (residence permits) do not pose obstacles to this option.

In all, one may conclude that since there is no actual leave to care for older relatives, Finnish policy responses do not support global arrangements of eldercare by giving carers time for such activities. Instead, care leave supports parental care for one's own children, and eligibility is tied to permanent residency in Finland. Since there is little control over the use of time once leave has been granted, parental and child-care leave do make it possible to spend time caring for someone else in addition. Beneficiaries may travel abroad to care for for someone, an elderly relative for example, or they may give care across nation-state borders, or care for someone who comes to Finland to be cared for. The one-year rule of absence, related to eligibility to social security, must be kept in mind.

Money for care

A number of countries have chosen cash benefits as the main policy measure for child- or eldercare. When there is little monitoring of the use of cash benefits and an available pool of migrant care workers, benefits are often used to buy care on the grey market (Da Roit 2007; Egger de Campo 2007; Gori & Da Roit 2007). By migrant care workers I mean immigrants who are doing care work, live-in or live-out, often for low pay and outside the formal economy. In Europe, Austria and Italy for example have chosen this kind of policy response to eldercare, while in Spain a great deal of child- and eldercare is provided by immigrants working in the homes of care recipients but mainly without the support of cash benefits (Escriva & Skinner 2008).

Finland offers two kinds of allowance for eldercare. One of them is the care allowance for pensioners, which is paid to the individual according to the long-term need for assistance. There are three, needs-assessed rates: the level of the benefit in 2010 is € 57 a month where weekly assistance is needed; € 143 for daily assistance; and finally € 302 for round-the-clock assistance. The allowance is usually paid abroad only if you live abroad temporarily (in other words, for less than a year); hence this allows the person to, for example, travel abroad temporarily in order to receive care. Another issue, of course, is whether a person with extensive care needs would be able to travel abroad in the first place.

There are no further restrictions on the use of the benefit, and it may be used to pay a migrant carer either formally or under the counter. The benefit levels are fairly low compared to the amount of care needed, so they would not cover the expenses entirely if a migrant carer was hired. In Italy, where wage levels are lower than in Finland, a live-in migrant carer providing round-the-clock care can expect to earn anything between € 450 and € 1,500 a month on the grey market (Degiuli 2007). Buying formal cleaning services in Finland from a company costs € 25–€ 35 an hour, and care-related help is usually more expensive than cleaning. This means that the Finnish care allowance for pensioners would not cover many hours of help. By the same token, it is questionable whether elderly Finns would be willing to have a migrant working and possibly even residing in their homes for care reasons. The elderly in Finland generally think that especially when care needs become extensive, public services should step in (Vaarama et al. 2006). Moreover, Finns tend to live in small dwellings compared to other Western Europeans (Juntto 2008). This means that at the very least, having a live-in carer would increase the crowdedness of one's home.

The second eldercare allowance is the carer's allowance, which is paid to the person providing informal care for a relative or for somebody otherwise close. Carer's allowance is paid by the local council where the elderly person in need of care resides. The need for care must be extensive, and the carer may only be a relative or otherwise close to the person. The level of reimbursement depends on the care needs and on how demanding the care work is. The minimum payment is € 300 a month (in 2010), but there are no fixed maximum levels. In most cases a care package is planned in connection with informal care (Law on carer's allowance).

There are two restrictions on carer's allowance that limit the global element in its use. The first is that the local council where the elderly person resides pays the benefit, which means that if a migrant managed to get an elderly parent to Finland to be cared for, he or she would not be eligible for the benefit since they are not already permanent residents in any local council. There have been a few cases when a legally resident migrant has attempted to bring an elderly parent to be cared for in Finland (Radiosuomi, Yle). Since the laws on family reunification only cover minors (Kofman 2006), the elderly people concerned have not been granted residence permits. However, as a result of the individuals' ailing health, media coverage, demonstrations, and appeals to the higher courts, some of them have been able to stay. For example, amongst the Chinese the family care norm is very strong and sponsoring the elderly to migrate abroad to where their children live is fairly common (Lan 2002; Lunt 2009). If the elderly person were to migrate from another EU country, such restrictions would not apply regarding their right to reside in Finland – although their eligibility to health and social care would still be a contested issue, as the cases of retired migrants with emerging care needs have demonstrated (Gustafson 2001; Legido-Quigley & La Parra 2007; Warnes et al. 1999).

The second restriction on carer's allowance that limits global care is the requirement that the carer must be a relative or otherwise close to the person in need of care. Recruiting migrants for care work and using the carer's allowance to cover the expenses is thus not an option. It might work for a relative to move to Finland to care for an elderly person already resident in Finland if immigration policies permit their entry into the country. To receive the allowance, the carer produces a written agreement describing the care she or he will provide, and stating whether the elderly person is receiving help from a public service. To receive the allowance one must pass a strict needs test, which means that care needs and the care given must be extensive (Kalliomaa-Puha 2007). There is no income-related means testing for the benefit.

For child-care there is a wider variety of monetary benefits than there is for eldercare. Child benefit is a monthly flat-rate benefit paid to the mother for each child under the age of 17. The sum increases with each subsequent child. In 2010 a mother receives € 100 a month for the first child, a sum that increases to € 182 a month for the fifth child or more. Single parents are entitled to a € 50 supplement for each child. There is no means or needs testing (Kela). For example, a two-parent family with two children receives € 210, and a single parent € 310 monthly. There is no control on the use of child benefit. For example, the minimum amount for au-pair pocket money, in addition to food and lodging, is according to the ministry of labour € 252 a month. Hence the child benefit for two children received by a single mother would cover such an expense. One still has to wonder why families would opt for an au pair when they have a right to day care services. I shall return to this issue later on.

Child-care leave (maternity, paternity, and parental leave) comes with an income-related benefit. If the leave is not taken, the benefit is also lost. Since such leave has already been discussed (pp. 178–180), I shall move on to the child home-care allowance, which in 2010 is a € 314 flat-rate benefit, with a possible supplement of € 168 if the family income is below a certain threshold. The benefit is paid until the child turns three-provided that she or he is not in a public day care institution. In addition, some, but not all, local councils pay their own supplements, which range from € 50 to € 250 per month and child (Haviseva-Lahtinen 2008). The reason for paying supplements is that it is cheaper for local councils than providing the day care services if the loss of tax revenues from parents outside the labour force when caring for their children is not counted.

Child home care allowance, paid by the Social Insurance Institution of Finland, is a benefit widely used by mothers in Finland (Kilpeläinen 2009). Finland has the most extensive subjective right to child-care of all the Nordic countries, but it is least used and children are cared for longest full-time at home (Haataja 2005). A similar benefit is available also in Norway, but it is not nearly as widely used (Gulbrandsen 2009). The allowance can also be paid for children accompanying a parent who is posted to another EU or EEA country, provided the family continues to be covered by the Finnish social security system (Kela).

There are no restrictions on how the benefit may be used, and parents may be on child home care leave or be employed while receiving the benefit. It is possible to use the benefit to hire an au pair, and it would cover more than the minimum level of au-pair pocket money. The benefit may also be used to cover the expenses of flying relatives to Finland to care for the child, most likely grandparents. These international child-care helpers are referred to in previous studies as 'swallow grandparents' (Escrivá 2004), 'international flying grannies' or 'transnational grannies' (Plaza 2000).

Child home-care allowance may be used to send the child to be cared for outside Finland as well. However, child home-care allowance has changed the norms of care for young children. Professionals and parents have started to see the home-care of children younger than three as normal and desirable. Long periods of care leave and mothers' commitment to care are seen as essential parts of motherhood (Anttonen 2003). Hence, at least for native Finnish parents, sending a child under three to be cared for abroad by, say, grandparents, is not necessarily an attractive option. The nuclear family norm is also strong and prevents young children from being sent away from parents for care reasons (see also Dahl & Spanger in this volume).

Instead, for certain groups of people, sending children to another country as a strategy to ensure them a better future is a feasible option. For example, a number of Korean and Chinese parents have been sending their children to the US to attend local schools in order later to get into an American university. They may reside either with a paid carer, in boarding-houses, or with relatives and friends (Zhou 1998; Orellana et al. 2001). These children are often referred to as parachute kids.

Children as well as the elderly may also migrate as part of a stage or chain migration when family members migrate at different times. Usually one or more adult members migrate first, followed later by children and the elderly. It is possible for the first ones to migrate to be children, as with parachute kids, who may eventually be the first step in a chain migration (Orellana et al. 2001). Terms such as satellite kids, satellite families and astronaut families refer to fairly similar phenomena where one or two parents live elsewhere than their children (Tsang et al. 2003). Reverse migration is also taking place, especially among teenage children who may not be behaving in the expected manner and are sent 'back home' to learn to behave in a desired manner. Some migrant parents also prefer their children to be educated in their country of departure (Orellana et al. 2001); while migrants may send their children to school in the country of departure when there are plans for the entire family to return (Goulbourne et al. 2010). In Somali families it is not at all uncommon for children to live apart from their biological parents since children are considered to be mobile and to belong to a larger group of relatives than a nuclear family (Johnsdotter 2007).

The last monetary benefit paid for child-care is private day care allowance. This is paid directly to the private day care provider that parents choose for their child. The rationale is to even up the care expenses between parents using private or public day care services and to ease the pressure on public services. The benefit is € 160 per child and month plus a means tested care supplement of up to € 135 per child and month (figures for 2010). Some local councils pay additional supplements ranging from € 70 to € 800 a month (Haviseva-Lahtinen 2008). The allowance is paid as long as private child-care provision is used. In order to receive the benefit, care must be formally arranged, and thus be liable for social security fees and taxes. The issue of services will be discussed later in more detail. Parents who are working abroad in Finnish diplomatic missions have recently complained that their child-care arrangements are not equally supported, since they are not getting the same levels of support for their day care arrangements as families residing in Finland (*Helsingin Sanomat* I). The private day care allowance is only paid to care providers in Finland.

Paradoxically, monetary benefits for child-care allow much more room for global arrangements than similar benefits for eldercare. The paradox stems from the fact that at the same time Finnish families have a subjective right to day care services, whereas the rights for older persons with care needs are not defined as subjective. Fairly generous cash benefits with virtually no control on their use give parents the possibility to use the money for sending children to be cared for abroad, or for paying, for example, grandparents to come to Finland to care for the children, hiring an au pair from abroad, or bringing a child or an older person in need of care to be cared for in Finland, immigration restrictions permitting.

Creating care employment

The third type of policy response to care covers incentives to create jobs. Since Finnish care – and especially eldercare – traditionally relied heavily first on informal and later also on publicly provided care, there have until now been very few incentives for individuals to employ care workers directly. With the recent trends in the marketization of care and commercial management influences in the public sector, the care sector has been identified as a lucrative area for job creation. Domestic help credit is a policy response aimed to boost job creation in private enterprises, as well as to encourage people to buy services on the white market. Domestic help credit is a tax rebate available if one employs somebody to do care work (or renovations, cleaning, etc.) at one's home or in the home of one's parents, parents-in-law, adopted parents, foster parents, or other members of elder generations of the family. The rebate cannot be claimed for child-care. It covers up to 60 per cent of the actual work, excluding travel expenses and materials. In 2010 the maximum rebate is € 3,000 per person (Taxation).

Domestic help credit has contributed to the increase of domestic service hire, especially of legal cleaning services (Tommiska 2005). For example, in 2005 the majority (65 per cent) of the domestic help credit users used it for renovations and construction, 30 per cent used it for housework, 4 per cent for gardening and only a small minority used it for care purposes (Melkas 2008). Also, only 2 per cent of the Finnish households applying for the tax deduction in

2004 bought services for their parents or grandparents (Niilola & Valtakari 2006). In addition, the rebate, no matter the purpose, was mainly used by people with high incomes, especially entrepreneurs and administrative staff (Melkas 2008). The same trend is visible in Sweden (see Carlsson and Platzer in this volume). It is not possible to use the rebate to buy services for the elderly living outside Finland, since the company that provides the services must be registered in the Finnish preliminary taxation register. However, a Finnish company providing such services to the elderly residing abroad may make it possible for the client to use the rebate. It is possible that Finnish companies would offer such services abroad in the future, given the EU principle of the free movement of services.

The au-pair system could also be seen as a policy to increase employment, even though strictly speaking au-pairing is a cultural exchange, not employment. The au-pair system is not officially supported but is still permitted. It gives families the possibility to have someone from abroad look after the children and do light housework for a maximum of 30 hours a week. In exchange the au pair receives free board and lodging, and a minimum of € 252 pocket money a month (see Calleman in this book). Au pairs do not need work permits. Those from inside the EU need to register with the police; au pairs from outside the EU have to apply for a residence permit. The host family and the au pair are not supposed to be related (ministry of labour), effectively precluding international family care possibilities.

Since many au pairs do not generally need residence permits, there are no statistics on their numbers. It is assumed that in Finland there are only small numbers. In Sweden, for example, the estimate is that there are around a thousand au pairs a year; there, au pairs help to bring greater flexibility to family life. Families with working parents and young children have au pairs to transport children to and from day care, school and activities. Having au pairs allows parents to work longer hours, relieves them of domestic chores and enables them to spend quality time with children (Platzer 2002) (see also Bikova, Calleman and Stenum in this volume).

Generous cash benefits for care could be interpreted as an implicit policy of incentives to create jobs in care work. If there is little surveillance in the use of these benefits, job creation mainly takes place in the grey or undeclared labour market (see Theobald 2008). For example, in Italy and Austria there are such cash benefits for eldercare as well as plenty of migrant labour available within their national borders. They are also willing or forced to work outside the formal economy.

Considering Finland's eastern border with Russia, there is also a large potential for grey market care workers if they were allowed to enter. Another requirement for such arrangements would be that Finns would see grey market care as a feasible way to solve the dilemmas of care. With tightening means testing for eldercare services, this could become an alluring option. For the time being, small homes, negative attitudes towards Russians, strict immigration policies, few cash benefits and the habit of turning to public services when needs become extensive serve to inhibit the use of grey market eldercare.

Help to care

The last policy response to be reviewed consists of services. Unlike child-care, for eldercare the right to services is not subjective even though older persons do have a general right for services. A clearly defined right that older people have is a needs assessment if they are over 80 years of age. In practice, elderly people with care needs face increasingly restrictive needs testing for both home-based and institutional care (Anttonen 2009). Social care services are provided in institutions such as health care centres, nursing homes and sheltered housing. All public eldercare services, be they institutional or home-based, are strictly needs tested. Fees for long-term institutional care are income-related so that a maximum of 82 per cent of a person's monthly income may be channelled to payments. Outside institutions, one of the most important forms of eldercare service is home-help, where fees are also adjusted to income (Law on social and health care customer fees).

Care services free women in particular from caring responsibilities. Nordic countries such as Finland have been called social service states, where public agencies have a strong role in social care service provision (Anttonen 1990). As mentioned before, families have a subjective right to child day care services, and local councils are responsible for organizing both child- and eldercare services. Public child day care provision is extensive and the fees reflect the family income: the highest fee for full-time day care in 2010 is € 254 a month, and families on low incomes get reduced prices or may even receive the service free of charge.

To be eligible to use public care services, a child or an elderly person must reside permanently in Finland. Through the family reunification measures, legally resident immigrant parents are allowed to bring their biological children (minors) to Finland. Grandparents or other relatives are not usually included in the definition of family. In Spain and Denmark the older generation may be included in family reunification measures if they are dependents; in Germany they can be for humanitarian reasons; and in the Netherlands if they are in serious difficulties (Kofman 2008, 75). The availability of services may have an impact on international activities. If child-care is not available and/or affordable in the migrant's country of residence, child shifting may become an interesting option, meaning, for example, that children are left with a grandmother when their mother migrates (Toro-Morn 1995). Children may be sent to a place where care or schooling is either available or most appropriate to the parents' way of thinking. Domestic servants may be hired for their language skills. Filipina domestic servants were appreciated during a certain era in Spain because they could teach and communicate with the children in English (Escrivá & Skinner 2008).

Affordable and available day care services in the country where the migrants live lessen the need for international moves in child-care. If parents are not content with the quality of the services or with the fact that children become socialized into the mainstream culture where they are resident, they may want to send their children abroad to be cared for or to be educated (see Toro-Morn 1995; Orellana et al. 2001). For example, in Somali families it is a common practice to look after children from other families in the same clan family (Johnsdotter 2007).

Culturally or linguistically appropriate services may not always be available for the elderly, either (Lunt 2009). Emilia Forssell (2004) has studied care practices of elderly people who have migrated to Sweden at an advanced age. Younger generations tend to act as filters between the service system and the care receiver. The longer the time lived in Sweden, the more willingly especially the younger generation is to use outside services to assist them in their eldercare activities. Whether for care reasons parents are sent back to their country of departure or to a third country is not known. Lack of care services may influence the younger generation's return migration when older relatives in need of care are living in the country of departure (Baldassar et al. 2007).

Public eldercare services are becoming increasingly sparse in Finland. Eldercare policies have actively been geared towards encouraging people to buy care services on the open market instead of relying on public services. Care managers may offer the tax rebate as a cheaper option than public services for the elderly with few care needs and a good financial situation. Getting used to choosing and buying services on the open market may pave the way to buying grey market services to be used at home. For example, having a cleaner has become more common – and more acceptable – than before (Tommiska 2005; Rahikainen & Vainio-Korhonen 2006). This phenomenon is also visible in other Nordic countries (see Fjell in this volume).

In August 2009 Finland saw a new law come into force by which local councils may offer vouchers instead of social and health services. Inhabitants can use the vouchers to buy services from a variety of pre-determined private producers instead of using publicly produced or outsourced service provision. The same means testing and fees apply to vouchers as to other publicly supported services. Since service providers are pre-selected by the local council, it is not possible to use the vouchers to buy services abroad.

The international element in public services generally comes by attracting immigrants to work in the care sector. In the UK it has been estimated that the National Health Service would collapse without immigrant doctors and nurses. Attracting care labour from abroad is a new phenomenon in Finland. So far only a few companies have brought in a handful of nurses from the Philippines, China and Hungary (*Helsingin Sanomat* II). Immigrants do not as yet dominate in the care occupations on the Finnish labour market. For example, in 2006 fewer than 2 per cent of the assistant nurses or nursing aides had a foreign background (Space–Time Research 2006). Still, like the other Nordic countries, Finland is gearing its immigration policies towards labour migration in order to secure an available labour force in, for example, the care sector (Työvoiman maahanmuuton ... 2008). For the time being these measures have only been implemented on a very small scale.

Conclusions

Welfare states exert influence on people's lives beyond national borders (Righard 2008). In a world where international movement and transnational activities are increasingly common, it is important to consider the consequences that national policies on child- and eldercare have – and might have – in relation to international activities when organizing care for children and the elderly. This is an issue that not only affects migrants and their families, but also the entire population, as the numbers of immigrants increase in the care services as employees or as care recipients.

In this chapter five types of international activity have been evaluated: (*i*) recruiting care workers from outside the country; (*ii*) getting care receivers – children and the elderly – to Finland to be cared for; (*iii*) caring for them across national borders; (*iv*) sending them to be cared for outside the country; and (*v*) getting family members or other close relatives to Finland so that they can provide care. These activities have been considered in terms of Finnish child- and eldercare policies.

It became evident that even if eldercare policies are far more limited than child-care policies, they also have less room for international activities, except for the recruitment of carers to formal services. Finland has plans to recruit health care personnel, and to a lesser extent social care personnel, from abroad (Työvoiman maahanmuuton ... 2008, 13), but so far little has been done. The economic recession and the strict training and language requirements for staff in social and health care services have hindered the plans until now.

In contrast to eldercare policies, child-care policies offer greater scope for international activities. The cash benefits are far more generous for child-care than for eldercare, and there is very little follow-up on their use. The money may be used for hiring an au pair or flying in a grandparent to give or receive care. Leave of absence, which is only on offer to parents of young children, gives them time to spend on caring for their children and/or elderly family relatives abroad, or on bringing them to Finland to be cared for. Families with young children have more freedom to have international activities in child-care arrangements than the elderly in need of care and their family members. It must be borne in mind that immigration policies have a restrictive role, especially when carers or care receivers are to be brought to Finland from outside the EU, EFTA or Switzerland. It is far easier to bring in a minor, especially if biological offspring, to join a migrant family in Finland than it is to bring in an elderly person.

One reason for having such a large variety of options for child-care is that policy responses are the result of political compromises, and parties emphasize different kinds of solutions. At any rate, right across the political spectrum children are seen as a social investment in the future, and there is a strong consensus on the need to support child-care arrangements. Eldercare is more difficult to frame in terms of a social investment, and political parties in general show less interest in it. I believe that the policy support for international elements in child-care is unintended. It is usual for social policies to have unintended consequences or for people to use policies in an unexpected manner. Care policies are in this sense not exceptional.

Internationally, there are some indications of specific migration for reasons related to the social care of the elderly. For example, overseas nursing homes have been established in Spain for retired Norwegians or Britons. In Kenya, some hotels have been converted into care homes for Africans retiring and returning from the UK, and there are also examples in Thailand and the Philippines of care apartments that are marketed to older people in Japan. The need for care, and especially for health care, may also elicit temporary international mobility in the form of medical tourism, which typically refers to patients travelling abroad for surgical operations. Popular destinations for medical tourism include countries such as Thailand, Singapore, India and South Africa. The direction of movement in care migration and medical tourism is from rich countries to poor ones (Connell 2006; Kröger & Zechner 2009). The direction of movement in care provision is the opposite, from poor to rich countries.

References

Anttonen, Anneli (1990), 'The feminization of the welfare state. The welfare state in transition: From the social insurance state towards the social service state', in Leila Simonen (ed.), *Finnish Debates on Women's Studies* (Working Papers 2/1990; Tampere: Centre for Women's Studies and Gender Relations, Research Institute for Social Sciences, University of Tampere), 3–25.

Anttonen, Anneli (2003), 'Lastenhoidon kaksi maailmaa', in Hannele Forsberg & Ritva Nätkin (eds.), *Perhe murroksessa. Kriittisen perhetutkimuksen jäljillä* (Helsinki: Gaudeamus), 159–185.

Anttonen, Anneli (2009), 'Hoivan yhteiskunnallistuminen ja politisoituminen,' in Heli Valokivi & Minna Zechner (eds.), *Hoiva – tutkimus, politiikka ja arki* (Tampere: Vastapaino), 54–98.

Baldassar, Loretta, Baldock, Vellenkoop Cora & Wilding, Raelene (2007), *Families Caring Across Borders. Migration, Ageing and Transnational Caregiving* (Basingstoke: Palgrave Macmillan).

Commission of the European Communities (2006), *The demographic future of Europe – from challenge to opportunity*, COM(2006) 571 final, Brussels, 12 October 2006, <http://europa.eu/legislation_summaries/employment_and_social_policy/situation_in_europe/c10160_en.htm>, accessed on 8 October 2009.

Connell, John (2006), 'Medical tourism: Sea, sun, sand ... and surgery', *Tourism Management*, 27/6, 1093–1100.

Council of the European Union (2008), *European pact on immigration and asylum*, Brussels, 24 September.

Daly, Mary (2002), 'Care as a good for social policy', *Journal of Social Policy*, 31/2, 251–270.

Daly, Mary & Lewis, Jane (2000), 'The concept of social care and the analysis of contemporary welfare states', *British Journal of Sociology*, 51/2, 281–298.

Daly, Mary & Rake, Katherine (2003), *Gender and the Welfare State: Care, Work and Welfare in Europe and the USA* (Cambridge: Polity Press).

Da Roit, Barbara (2007), 'Changing intergenerational solidarities within families in a Mediterranean welfare state: Eldercare in Italy,' *Current Sociology*, 55/2, 251–269.

Directive 2004/38/EC, of the European Parliament and of the Council, 29 April 2004, 'On the right of citizens of the Union and their family members to move and reside freely within the territory of the Member States'.

Degiuli, Francesca (2007), 'A Job with No Boundaries: Home Eldercare Work in Italy', *European Journal of Women's Studies*, 14/3, 193–207.

Egger de Campo, Marianne (2007), 'Exit and voice: An investigation of care service users in Austria, Belgium, Italy and Northern Ireland', *European Journal of Ageing*, 4/2, 59–69.

Escrivá, Anna (2004), *Securing care and welfare of dependants transnationally: Peruvians and Spaniards in Spain* (Working Paper no. WP404; Oxford: Oxford Institute of Ageing), <http://www.ageing.ox.ac.uk/files/workingpaper_404.pdf>, accessed on 9 October 2009.

Escriva, Angeles & Skinner, Emmeline (2008), 'Domestic work and transnational care chains in Spain', in Helma Lutz (ed.), *Migration and Domestic Work: A European Perspective on a Global Theme* (Aldershot: Ashgate), 113–123.

Forssell, Emilia (2004), *Skyddandets förnuft. En studie om anhöriga till hjälpbehövande äldre som invandrat sent i livet* (Stockholm: Stockholms universitet, Institutionen for socialt arbete, Socialhögskolan).

Gori, Cristiano & Da Roit, Barbara (2007), 'The commodification of care – The Italian way', in Clare Ungerson & Sue Yeandle (eds.), *Cash for Care in Developed Welfare States* (Basingstoke: Palgrave Macmillan), 60–80.

Goulbourne, Harry, et al. (2010), *Transnational Families. Ethnicities, Identities and Social Capital* (Abingdon: Routledge).

Gulbrandsen, Lars (2009), 'The Norwegian cash-for-care reform. Changing behaviour and stable attitudes', *Nordic Early Childhood Research*, 2/1, 17–25.

Gustafson, Per (2001), 'Retirement migration and transnational lifestyles', *Ageing and Society*, 21/4, 371–394.

Haataja, Anita (2005), *Äidit ja isät työmarkkinoilla 1989–2002/2003* (Sosiaali- ja terveysministeriön selvityksiä 2005, 29: Helsinki).

Haviseva-Lahtinen, Anna-Maija (2008), *Lasten kotihoidon ja yksityisen hoidon tuen kuntalisät*, Kunnat.net, kuntatiedon keskus <http://kunnat.net/k_perussivu.asp?path=1;29;353;10336;49069;140175;140176>, accessed on 19 November 2009.

Helsingin Sanomat I (2009), 'Ulkoministeriön virkamiehet kantelivat lastensa päivähoidosta' [newspaper article about Foreign Ministry civil servants' complaints at not receiving public support for childcare], <http://www.hs.fi/politiikka/artikkeli/Ulkoministeri%C3%B6n+virkamiehet+kantelivat+lastensa+p%C3%A4iv%C3%A4hoidosta/1135250396042>, accessed on 16 November 2009.

Helsingin Sanomat II (2007): 'Filippiiniläisiä hoitajia palkataan Tilkkaan hoitamaan vanhuksia' [newspaper article about a company hiring Filipina nurses to care for the elderly], <http://www.hs.fi/kaupunki/artikkeli/Filippiinil%C3%A4isi%C3%A4+hoitajia+palkataan++Tilkkaan+hoivaamaan+vanhuksia/HS20070912SI3KA03mye>, accessed on 10 December 2009.

Johnsdotter, Sara (2007), '"Släktträdet är långt." Somaliska familjer och de nationella regelverken', in Erik Olsson et al. (eds.), *Transnationella rum. Diaspora migration och gränsöverskridande relationer* (Umeå: Boréa Bokförlag), 115–136.

Juntto, Anneli (2008), *Asumisen muutos ja tulevaisuus* (Helsinki: Suomen ympäristökeskus).

Kalliomaa-Puha, Laura (2007), *Vanhoille ja sairaille sopivaa? Omaishoitosopimus hoivan instrumenttina* (Helsinki: Kansaneläkelaitos).

Kela, The Social Insurance Institute of Finland, <www.kela.fi>.

Kilpeläinen, Riitta (2009), 'Pienen lapsen hoiva valinta- ja neuvotteluprosessina', in Pertti Koistinen (ed.), *Työn hiipuvat rajat. Tutkielmia palkkatyön, hoivan ja vapaaehtoistyön muuttuvista suhteista* (Helsinki: Tilastokeskus), 84–97.

Kofman, Eleonore (2006), 'Migration, ethnicity and entitlements in European welfare regimes', in Audrey Guichon, Christien van den Anker & Inna Novikova (eds.), *Women's Social Rights and Entitlements* (Houndmills, Basingstoke: Palgrave), 130–154.

Kofman, Eleonore (2008), 'Gendered migrations, livelihoods and entitlements in

European welfare regimes', in Nicola Piper (ed.), *New Perspectives on Gender and Migration. Livelihood, Rights and Entitlements* (New York, Routledge), 59–100.

Kröger, Tarja (2005), *Perhevapaasäännösten toimivuus*, (Työhallinnon julkaisu 358; Helsinki: Ministry of Labour), <http://www.mol.fi/mol/fi/99_pdf/fi/06_tyoministerio/06_julkaisut/07_julkaisu/thj358.pdf>, accessed on 11 November 2009.

Kröger, Teppo & Zechner, Minna (2009), 'Migration and care: Giving and needing care across national borders', *Finnish Journal of Ethnicity and Migration*, 4/2, 17–26.

Lan, Pei-Chia (2002), 'Subcontracting filial piety: Elder care in ethnic Chinese immigrant families in California', *Journal of Family Issues*, 23/7, 812–835.

Law on carer's allowance 937/2005.

Law on residence-based social security 1573/1993.

Law on social and health care customer fees 734/1992.

Legido-Quigley, Helena & La Parra, Daniel (2007), 'The health care needs of UK pensioners living in Spain: An agenda for research', *Eurohealth*, 13/4, 14–18.

Lunt, Neil (2009), 'Older people within transnational families: The social policy implications', *International Journal of Social Welfare*, 18/3, 243–251.

Lutz, Helma (ed.) (2008), *Migration and Domestic Work: A European Perspective on a Global Theme* (Aldershot: Ashgate).

Melkas, Perttu (2008), 'Hyvätuloiset käyttävät eniten kotitalousvähennystä', *Hyvinvointikatsaus*, 1, 38–39.

Ministry of Labour, <www.mol.fi>.

Niilola, Kari & Valtakari, Mikko (2006), *Kotitalousvähennys* (Työpoliittinen tutkimus 310), <http://www.mol.fi/mol/fi/99_pdf/fi/06_tyoministerio/06_julkaisut/06_tutkimus/tpt310.pdf>, accessed on 26 November 2008.

OECD (2009), *International migration outlook 2009*, <www.oecd.org/els/migration/imo>, accessed on 11 November 2009.

Orellana, Marjorie Faulstich, Thorne, Barnio, Chee, Anna & Ewa Lam, Wan Shun (2001), 'Transnational childhoods: The participation of children in processes of family migration', *Social Problems*, 48/4, 572–591.

Parreñas, Rhacel Salazar (2001), *Servants of Globalization: Women, Migration and Domestic Work* (Stanford: Stanford University Press).

Plaza, Dwaine (2000), 'Transnational grannies. The changing family responsibilities of elderly African Caribbean-born women residents in Britain', *Social Indicators Research*, 51/1, 75–105.

Platzer, Ellinor (2002), 'Kulturell utbyte eller billig arbetskraft? – Au pair i Sverige', *Sociologisk forskning*, 3–4, 32–55.

Radiosuomi (2008), 'Onko venäläisen kansalaisoikeusaktivistin karkottaminen oikein?' [A radio broadcast about the deportation of a Russian civil rights activist], <http://radiosuomi.yle.fi/node/1548>, accessed on 16 November 2009.

Rahikainen, Marjatta & Vainio-Korhonen, Kirsi (eds.) (2006), *Työteliäs ja uskollinen. Naiset piikoina ja palvelijoina keskiajalta nykypäivään* (Helsinki: Suomalaisen kirjallisuuden seura).

Righard, Erica (2008), *The Welfare Mobility Dilemma. Transnational Strategies and National Structuring at Crossroads* (Lund: Lunds universitet, Socialhögskolan).

Saari, Juho & Kvist, Jon (2007), 'European Union developments and national social protection', in Jon Kvist & Juho Saari (eds.), *The Europeanisation of Social Protection* (Bristol: Policy Press), 1–20.

Space–Time Research (2006), (SuperCROSS, 1993–2008 Space Time Research Pty Ltd.), <www.str.com.au>, accessed on 15 January 2009.

Taxation, the official tax office website with Finnish tax information, <www.tax.fi>.

Theobald, Hildegard (2008), 'Elder care policies, care work and the intersection of inequalities: A cross-country comparison', paper presented at the ISA RC 19th conference, *The Future of Social Citizenship: Politics, Institutions and Outcomes*, Stockholm, 4–6 September.

Timonen, Virpi (2008), *Ageing Societies. A Comparative Introduction* (Berkshire: Open University Press).

Tommiska, Katja (2005), *The users and providers of informal work. A qualitative perspective. National report: Finland* (EU project report on formal and informal work in Europe; Hamburg: University of Hamburg).

Toro-Morn, Maura I. (1995), 'Gender, class, family and migration. Puerto Rican women in Chicago', *Gender & Society*, 9/6, 712–726.

Tsang, A. Ka Tat, Irwing Howard, Alaggia, Ramona, Chau, Shirley B. Y. & Benjamin, Michael (2003,) 'Negotiating ethnic identity in Canada', *Youth & Society*, 34/3, 359–384.

Työvoiman maahanmuuton edistämisen yhteistyömuodot lähtömaiden kanssa (2008), (Sisäasiainministeriön julkaisuja 31/2008; Helsinki: Ministry for Interior Affairs), <http://www.poliisi.fi/intermin/biblio.nsf/A9AF8FF1470F65D4C22574DBo 04DB30D/$file/312008.pdf>, accessed on 17 November 2009.

Vaarama, Marja, Luoma, Minna-Liisa & Ylönen, Lauri (2006), 'Ikääntyneiden toimintakyky, palvelut ja koettu elämänlaatu', in Mikko Kautto (ed.), *Suomalaisten hyvinvointi* (Helsinki: Stakes), 104–136.

Warnes, Anthony, King, Russell, Williams, Allan, M. & Patterson, Guy (1999), 'The well-being of British expatriate retirees in Southern Europe', *Ageing and Society*, 19/6, 717–740.

Yle: Hallinto-oikeus, 'Egyptiläinen isoäiti ei saa jäädä Suomeen' [A news article about an Egyptian grandmother who was not allowed to stay in Finland with her adult children], <http://yle.fi/uutiset/teksti/kotimaa/2009/09/hallinto-oikeus_egyptilainen_isoaiti_ei_saa_jaada_suomeen_977526.html>, accessed on 16 November 2009.

Zechner, Minna (2004), 'Family commitments under negotiation: Dual carers in Finland and in Italy', *Social Policy and Administration*, 38/6, 640–653.

Zechner, Minna (2008), 'Care of Older Persons in Transnational Settings', *Journal of Aging Studies*, 22/1, 32–44.

Zhou, Min (1998), '"Parachutekids" in Southern California: The educational experience of Chinese children in transnational families', *Educational Policy*, 12/6, 682–704.

CHAPTER 10

Public care work in private contexts

A historical perspective on the Swedish welfare state

Karin Carlsson

In 1944 the first 512 council-employed, state-subsidized home carers entered the homes of Swedish families;[1] they cleaned, cooked and took care of children. They had undergone training and were dressed in uniforms. They earned a fixed salary and their working conditions were regulated by the state. The home carers constituted the workforce of the Social Home Help Programme, which offered households temporary domestic assistance when a housewife was ailing, ill, or for some other reason unable to perform her domestic work (SFS 1943:947 1§). This workforce can be interpreted as a creation of a new category of domestic workers. Although based on a traditional understanding of gender, the occupation was modified and dressed in new clothes, and as such it became a part of the emerging Swedish welfare state. In 1952, when the Commission on Collective Housing published its report *Home Help*, the programme was recognized as one of the most valuable socio-political reforms of the 1940s (SOU 1952:38, 63). By then domestic work had become an important political issue, and the economic value of care was recognized.

The implementation in Sweden in 2007 of new legislation that introduced tax deductions for the purchase of household domestic services illustrates new conceptions of this sphere of work. The attempt to professionalize the domestic workforce had been abandoned, and at the same time the reform mirrored a new approach to how welfare should be distributed. Sweden and the Nordic countries have been known for using a model of welfare in which economic resources are redistributed through high taxation, and where care assignments aimed at children and the elderly are subsidized and made available through a large public sector. However, since the late 1970s this system of welfare distribution has been under reconstruction, and public services have increasingly been replaced by private solutions. The negotiation of the boundaries between public and private has been, and is continuously, at stake.

In this chapter I will compare the politics and arguments behind the launching and organization of Sweden's Social Home Help Programme, with those behind the implementation of tax deductions on domestic services in 2007. Through this comparative approach, I will first of all be able to identify shifting discourses regarding how welfare should be distributed and how this both mirrors and enforces specific gender structures. Secondly, I will pay attention to the domestic workers, and how their historically vulnerable situation in the labour market has been dealt with within the two settings studied here.

The reason for choosing an empirical example from the 1940s for a comparison with the present situation is primarily twofold. First, the Social Home Help Programme existed during a period from which the popular image of the Swedish and Nordic welfare state is commonly drawn, which makes it a fruitful starting-point for an understanding of changes within the welfare system. Second, the 1940s and 1950s were a period when domestic work to a unique extent became a central theme in public and political discussions. The political debates that followed the proposal for tax deductions in 2007 – as well as the arguments behind it – also revealed period-specific discourses surrounding domestic work: in part in the social and economic value ascribed (or not) to the work performed, in part with regard to how, and by whom, it supposedly could and should be performed.

The main sources consist of official commission reports from the respective periods, as well as governmental bills and legislative documents. When portraying the development of the Social Home Help Programme, documents regulating its operation have been used, as well as sources produced by the National Board of Health and Welfare.[3] From this it follows that it is mainly the authorities' perspective that will be highlighted. These sources are moreover primarily viewed through the prism of welfare, which consequently constitutes the central contextual frame.

An emergent welfare state

In an international political setting, the concept of a Nordic model of welfare has been widely accepted. In general this is used when referring to a welfare system consisting of a strong state where comprehensive welfare benefits and services are made possible through high taxation. Even though this image has been both criticized and nuanced it can still function as a starting-point for the socio-political context necessary here (Christiansen & Petersen 2001, 154).[4]

According to a common interpretation, the path towards a 'Swedish model' had already started in the late 1920s when the prime minister and leader of the Social Democratic Party, Per Albin Hansson, used the concept of the 'People's Home'. This concept embedded a vision of a future society which would know 'no special favourites and no stepchildren', nobody 'privileged or unappreciated', where everybody was to be considered equal (Åmark 2005, 65; Agius 2006, 75).[5] Hansson's politics, as well as his vision, must be understood as a reaction to the contemporaneous situation in which the battle against poverty was a prioritized political task. It was then thought of as a social problem with structural and societal origins – not individual ones – and as such it became a public responsibility (Andersson 2009, 106–107). This view was central to the policies pursued by Gustav Möller, the minister of social affairs, during the 1940s. Möller aimed to abolish the stigmatization that he claimed was associated with receiving poor relief, an objective that could be reached through the introduction of universal benefits (Åmark 2005, 70). He believed in the possibility of creating a good society by building a working relationship between a capitalist economy and the welfare state (Hilson 2008, 105). Economic growth – through consumption and expanding markets – was accepted as long as the state made sure that part of the surplus was shared and spent on common needs (Andersson 2009, 21). This meant that health services, child-care, education and social security increasingly became a part of the public sector's responsibility.

Within this setting, the often vulnerable situation of the domestic workforce became highlighted in political discussions. Apart from the idea that the shortage of domestic workers made women hesitate about having children (see below) it was also thought of as a democratic problem. To hire domestic workers was expensive and something only a few could afford. According to Möller, it was not enough to create better working conditions through legislation and thereby try to attract more women to this sphere of work. Instead he pictured the future domestic workforce as an integrated part of the public sector. Education and state intervention was, in his perspective, the best way to secure the survival of the occupation. In addition, this would assure that those families that most needed the help – meaning those of less means – also received the help they required (Lundqvist 2007, 125–6). The launching of the Social Home Help Programme was one step towards this vision.

Clean, care and educate – and solve society's 'problems'

Compared to other European countries of the early 1930s, Sweden had a remarkably low fertility rate. This issue became an important political question,[6] and also constituted one of the early arguments behind the implementation of the programme. In 1935 a commission was appointed to investigate the reasons behind the negative population trend, and to present solutions to the problem. After an interruption, due to the outbreak of the Second World War, it re-established its work in 1941. Within this commission, a group of female experts was assembled to investigate the need for a Social Home Help Programme, and deliver a proposal for its design. Two years later they presented their conclusions (Hatje 1974, 15; Lundqvist 2007, 47; Åmark 2005, 228). At that time the birthrates were no longer a crucial issue, but there were still other problems to be solved. The commission argued that the care of children, and the maintaining of households, should not be jeopardized in those cases where the mother was frail or sick (SOU 1943:15, 53). If the housewife could be replaced by a home carer, families could be kept intact and children remain in the home. And if the sick mother moreover could be treated within the household, state finances could furthermore be lowered in other sectors (SOU 1943:15, 49). In the commission's own words, the programme aimed to offer housewives temporary domestic aid through an assigned home carer 'in homes in which disease, child-birth or suchlike circumstances have created a need thereof' (SFS 1943:947 1§). Even though home help was meant to reach all families, families with children – and particularly families with low incomes – were to be prioritized. In other words, the programme was also to be used to actively counteract differences between classes.

The National Board of Health and Welfare became the monitoring authority for the Social Home Help Programme, but the direct and implementing responsibility fell to each local council. In order to understand the extent and development of the Social Home Help Programme it can be noted that parliament originally allocated funds for the first 512 home carers. The following year the number increased to 1,038 and by 1960 it had reached approximately 3,700.[7] In 1952 88,000 families received help, and that same year only 8 (of 1,037) local councils lacked some kind of Social Home Help. Until the 1960s the programme underwent a steady expansion, and yet the capacity was constantly considered insufficient. To provide one example, in 1955 10,000 applications were rejected due to the shortage of trained labour; a problem that would become a main theme in repeated discussions both within the Home Carers' Association and at the state level (Stencil 1963:8, 4; SOU 1955:29, 37–39; SOU 1952:38, 50, 95; *Sociala Meddelanden* 1954:1, 31; Motion AK 1957:345).

In terms of occupational 'content', the home carer's work was closely connected not only to the domestic worker's, but also to that of nurses and social workers. Her assignments were threefold. Her primary task comprised practical domestic work such as cleaning, washing, doing the dishes and cooking (RoA 1944:5, 12–13; SOU 1943:15, 53). Furthermore, she had a caring assignment that first and foremost was directed towards the children and their upbringing. At the same time she was perceived as a complement to the nurse and was expected to have some competence related to healthcare (SOU 1943:15, 53). The third task was linked to the government's ambition to improve public health. The commission of 1943 considered the Social Home Help Programme, and the home carers, as a way to influence, educate and – when necessary – change families' everyday behaviour and hygienic practices. As a part of a larger public health movement, the idea was that the home carer – simply through her mere presence and her behaviour – would serve as a good example and thereby inspire housewives and families to a better way of living (RoA 1946:42 §2).

The main help-receiving groups came to shift over time. Initially families were seen as the main recipients, but after the mid-1950s the focus was directed towards the elderly. This shift can be understood as a pragmatic solution to demographic changes, as a significant increase in the number of elderly was noticed after the 1940s.[8] The public responsibility for caring for the elderly, and how this responsibility was to be implemented, became an important political and public topic, and the Social Home Help Programme came to be used as a quick, ready solution.

From the start, one of the main problems was the difficulty in finding competent recruits. When the family as the primary help-receiving group was substituted by the elderly, this problem became less severe. The educational demands for taking care of the elderly were considered less important and no training was needed.

The state subsidies for the Home Help Programme were withdrawn in 1960, but only four years later they were in fact reinstated – although in a different version. The most important changes were that the elderly this time explicitly had out-conquered 'the families' as the prime help-recipients, and that the general educational requirement had been reduced (Prop. 85 1964, 48 ff; cf. Protokoll FK 25:31d, 65).

The Home Help Programme as such was not unique to Sweden. The other Nordic countries had similar arrangements, where home-help programmes were supported by the state and governed by the local councils. In Norway a state subsidy was introduced in 1948;

one year later it was implemented in Denmark; and Finland started a home-help programme in 1950 (Skjelbred 2004, 44; Dahl 2000, 27; Simonen 1990, 71). In all of the Nordic countries the programmes stipulated that the women receive training on joining, and according to the state commissions the aim was also to offer full-time employment and good benefits (Szebehely 2003, 25–26), even if this was difficult to fully achieve in practice, as in the Swedish case.

The Nordic countries, except Finland, followed a similar pattern when families were replaced as help recipients by the elderly during the 1950s, which in turned was followed by a decrease in the demands for occupational training. Difficulties in finding recruits were furthermore a general trend. Finland, however, did not face the same problems. According to Wærness, this was due to the difficulties for Finnish women to enter other occupations; something that made working as a home carer more attractive. Furthermore, Finland – to a larger extent compared to the other Nordic countries – widened the assignments of the home carers and included social work with families with 'problems' as well as additional help-receiving groups such as the elderly and disabled (Szebehely 2003, 26 ff; Wærness 1995, 126–7).[9]

Changing welfare system – a third way

The Social Help Programme, then, was introduced as part of the emerging Swedish welfare state. During this period Sweden came to be known as a country that found a way to navigate between economic growth and social equality, often spoken of in terms of a middle way between capitalism and communism (Andersson 2009, 51). Some decades later this 'middle way' was to become 'the third way'. In her book *The Nordic Model*, Mary Hilson explores, among other things, how the image of this model – among scholars and in the media – came to be described as a nearly unreachable and glorified socialist utopia. At the same time, a parallel image emerged where it instead was interpreted as an over-regulated 'quasi-totalitarian nightmare' (Hilson 2008, 12, 20, 23). The latter approach surfaced in the 1980s along with the entrance of neo-liberalism. Right-wing politicians argued that the welfare system, with its generous subsidies

and benefits, along with its expansive public sector, hindered economic efficiency, productivity and flexibility (Hilson 2008, 109–110;
Greve 2006, 1 ff.). This critical approach was also visible in academic
scholarship at the time. Moreover, studies for example focusing on
governmental policies of sterilization and migration[10] all pictured a
society where, as Henrik Stenius puts it 'all doors were open ... and
they [were] not just open: society march[ed] in and intervene[d],
sometimes brusquely.' (Stenius 1997, 171) The use of 'grand narratives' of this type has been criticized on the grounds that such research
often embeds normative readings in which ideological preferences
easily affect the resulting interpretations (Lundberg & Tydén 2007,
28 ff., 32 ff.). Nevertheless, the critique advanced in the 1980s was
in fact, as Jenny Andersson demonstrates, embraced by the Social
Democratic Party who turned to the British New Labour and their
'third way' for inspiration. And this was a way where the reality of
market economy, globalization and individualism was seen to be
wholly compatible with the politics of social democracy (Andersson
2008, 19, 23, 9, 48, 70–71). In comparison to the 1950s, when the
public sector was thought of as necessary for economic efficiency,
the rhetoric now changed. Effectiveness and cost efficiency were
placed at the centre of debates (Andersson 2008, 80). Among the
consequences was an effort to privatize schools, healthcare and culture
(Andersson 2008, 77–78; Lundberg & Åmark 2001, 175). Even
the pension system – a political solution that was long considered
the 'jewel in the crown' of the Social Democrats' politics – became
dependent on the market and the fluctuations of the stock exchange
(Andersson 2008, 102; Lundberg 2003).

The very ideology underpinning how welfare should distributed
shifted – not least through the Social Democratic Party's embrace
of private solutions. When a centre–right coalition gained a majority of the seats in parliament in 2006, reforms towards increased
privatization became even more explicit, all of them – according to
the new government's own rhetoric and political ambitions – aiming to extend individual freedom of choice. This political vision is
clearly traceable when one examines family policies introduced in
the early twenty-first century.

Tax-deductible domestic services

Previous research has emphasized how the private and public are in constant negotiation when it comes to responsibilities of care. Furthermore, policy implementation has been shown to have a great impact on how households choose to organize their work (Leira 2005, 68). With this in mind, we now turn to one of the socio-political plans launched in July 2007: the introduction of a tax deduction on purchases of private, domestic services. This meant that private households could buy services such as cleaning, washing, gardening, child-care and eldercare at considerably reduced prices. For the purchase to be eligible for the tax deduction, the services had to be bought from registered companies (SFS 2007: 346 §4).[11]

One of the arguments behind the implementation of the new reform was to make it possible for parents to participate in the labour market by relieving them of unpaid care responsibilities and domestic work at home. The government explicitly addressed the situation for women, arguing that they took the greatest responsibility within the domestic sphere. Therefore, the reform was argued to have general positive effects in terms of gender equality – meaning that women would be able to compete with men in the labour market on more equal terms (Prop. 2006/7:94: 31). Besides, it was thought the new tax deduction would decrease the black-market economy by making the open market less expensive (Prop. 2006/7:94).

This was not the first attempt to implement such a policy. The 1990s had seen two commissions present their proposals for tax deductions. None of them made it through parliament. In 1994 the centre–right government proposed tax deductions on purchases of cleaning, gardening, property maintenance, child-care and the like (SOU 1994:43, 9–10). By making the formal market compatible with the black-market economy, the commission argued that new jobs could be created and that unemployment rates would be decreased (SOU 1994:43, 101, 103). As argued in the commission of 2007, it was also seen as a way for women to increase their chance of pursuing a career by reducing the burden of domestic work. Finally, the 1994 commission emphasized that all this would increase market production and therefore benefit society as a whole (SOU

1994:43, 11). The same year, the Social Democratic Party regained a majority in government and with this the proposal disappeared from the political agenda, at least for a few years (Platzer 2004, 32)

In 1996, the Social Democratic Party nevertheless appointed a commission to investigate how a tax deduction could be implemented. With a slightly broadened understanding of what was to be covered by the deductions, the arguments were in part an echo of the earlier centre–right proposal: new legislation would reduce unemployment among the young and those with low levels of education. With reference to a former commission – which had dealt with immigration issues – they also argued that this could lower the unemployment rates among immigrants as well. Furthermore, it was argued that the bill would facilitate an increase in women's participation in the paid labour market (SOU 1997:17, 220 ff., 13, 167–8, 355; cf. SOU 1996:55). At the same time, the proposal actually echoed parts of the argument behind the later, 1950s version of the Social Home Help Programme, when it was seen to be a way to handle a growing population of elderly people in need of care. The commission of 1997 concluded that care assignments, which earlier had been seen as a public responsibility, increasingly had become a private undertaking. Without problematizing why such a development had occurred, the proposal was presented as an adjustment to the present situation and to social practices that already were widespread (SOU 1997:17, 15, 273 ff., 278, 293–4; cf. SOU 1952:38, 17, 42–3, 52 ff.).

Even though several Social Democratic members of parliament welcomed the work of the commission, the proposal of 1997 never made it past the government. Ellinor Platzer has shown how the question in fact was ignored. It was either considered to be too expensive, or was dismissed in anticipation of further investigations (Platzer 2004, 48–9).

The commission reports of the 1990s were followed by intense media debates. Opposing voices frequently used arguments about how class structures would be petrified; how general gender equality risked deteriorating; how the gap between immigrants and those born in Sweden would widen, and finally how the proposals would extend the privatization of child-care and eldercare (Platzer 2004, 113). The post-war Swedish setting, with the Social Democratic

Party and trade unions dominating the political scene, has been used to explain the widespread resistance to implementing policies of this kind (Öberg 1999). In the literature the debate has also been described as having an ideological bias, in which the image of the mistreated domestic worker was effectively used; something that in turn has been interpreted as the deliberate obstruction of any implementation of the proposals of the 1990s (Öberg 1999, 19–20).[12]

Returning to the tax deductions launched in 2007, a survey by the official agency Statistics Sweden showed that 46,000 persons (equivalent to 0.6 per cent of the people paying taxes in Sweden) had made use of the tax deduction during its first six months. According to the survey, the deduction was mostly used by single, female old-age pensioners and couples with children. It was furthermore overwhelmingly used by high-earners (Sköld 2009, 24). Even if these statistics were gathered only shortly after the implementation of the reform, they can nevertheless indicate some trends of importance.

Welfare solutions and changing spheres of care

A comparative historical analysis is always a challenging task. The comparison of different discursive settings, political structures and economic situations calls for constant awareness of what is being compared. Not only two different time periods have been placed beside each other in this chapter, but also distinctly different types of family policy. Firstly, the Social Home Help Programme was launched during a period when the traditional nation-state was fairly intact. Moreover, the welfare state was being established, which meant that – among other things – care responsibilities, social security and health services increasingly became a public responsibility. The economic situation at the time moreover favoured these political goals, as it was creating numerous job opportunities. This economic expansion in turn came to be one of the explanations for the shortage of domestic workers at the time. The construction of the Social Home Help Programme was gendered, mirroring a traditional understanding of relations between the sexes; it was a solution in which a trained woman was to replace the housewife in the home, thus keeping the family intact without jeopardizing gender relations or the well-being of the children.

The situation of the early twenty-first century is in some ways reversed. The borders of the nation-state have become considerably more porous, not least through the increasingly integrated economy of the world's nations (Christiansen & Markkola 2006, 27; Giddens & Hutton 2000, vii). At the same time, a new approach towards *how* welfare should be redistributed has occurred, meaning an increase in private solutions. In some ways gender equality has been achieved, but at the same time an increased gap between different ethnic groups can be noted. And if the welfare state of the 1950s managed to come to terms with the poverty within its largely homogeneous national setting, poverty has now taken new forms and must be discussed from a global perspective (Lister 2009, 242, 246). Nevertheless, in both these empirical examples state subsidies were given to households for the hiring of domestic help. This was, however, done in different ways – ways which mirrored period-specific family policy discourses, and as such they can be used as a foundation for a discussion about changing welfare systems and gender relations, as well as aspects of how domestic work has been interpreted and performed through history.

Welfare solutions and gender discourses

I would like to begin by reflecting on changing gender discourses, and the impact of family policies when private households chose how to deal with care work and domestic work. Returning to the 1940s, it should be noted that the Social Home Help Programme was not the only proposal for how to ease the burden of the housewives at the time. Suggestions concerning how to organize child-care were put forward, as were proposals concerning collective solutions for both laundry and cooking arrangements. Some of these solutions came to be realized, such as the technical development of household equipment and the rationalization of the domestic work in general. Other proposals were tougher to implement. For example, when the commission for expanded public child-care presented its proposal in 1951, it encountered resistance in the form of arguments that it was jeopardizing the well-being of children. Twenty years would pass before such a solution won broader acceptance (Lundqvist 2007, 178). In contrast, then, the Social Home Help Programme can be interpreted as a more traditional way of solving these problems, by introducing a hybrid between the traditional role of the 'mother', and a modern version of the domestic worker. This solution was in fact completely in line with what at the time still was a strong bread-winner norm, and the associated 'housewife contract' which made economic and socio-political programmes favour the organization of family life around one single provider. These ideological norms and structural incentives were strong. The prime responsibility of women was the home, family and children. But just as commissions, political groups and individuals were arguing for easing the everyday life of housewives, for example by proposing paid vacation for housewives and compulsory training in home economics for all women, this housewife ideal was being challenged – at the same time as it was at its most widespread. Debates and discussions both in media and parliament raised questions concerning how to make it easier for women to work outside their homes. Thus it truly was, in the words of Åsa Lundqvist, an era of ambivalent family ideals (Lundqvist 2007, 107–108). In this setting the Social Home Help Programme can be interpreted as a semi-public solution. Although a public representative entered the private home, neither existing gender discourses, nor the understanding of the private sphere as the main place for child-care, were challenged. It was a pragmatic solution combining the traditional private sphere with modern notions of public responsibility.

After the 'prime time' of the Social Home Help Programme, other state solutions also aiming to facilitate domestic work were tried out. Apart from attempts to address the value of sharing domestic work between household members, the primary focus during the 1970s was to enlarge the public sector charged with taking care of children and the elderly. This, in turn, introduced women to employment that brought with it social security, colleagues and an entry into union membership (Öberg 1999, 189). During this period several structural incentives that hindered gender equality were removed. Maternity leave became parental leave in 1974. The tax system was changed in 1971, making it more financially beneficial for married women to work. Yet another reform came in 1989 when women were legally accepted in all military positions. This meant that the last structural obstruction – hindering women's equal participation on the labour market – was removed. (Sundevall forthcoming 2011).

Ideologically, gender equality has been widely accepted in Sweden. Men and women do participate in the labour market to the same extent, and the number of women representatives in parliament has risen from 5 per cent in the 1940s to 45 per cent in 2000 (SCB 2004, 59, 84). But still a gender gap remains. Compared with men, part-time employment is more common among women, women also earn less even within female dominated occupations, and in 2002 only 24 per cent of those in executive positions were women (SCB 2004, 68, 94).

As noted above, the gender perspective was used by the commission and the government when they introduced the proposal for tax deductions. The government explicitly addressed the situation for women who, they argued, generally took a greater responsibility within the domestic sphere, which in turn hindered them from competing with men in the labour market (Prop. 2006/7:94, 31). In public debate this was referred to as 'the time puzzle', referring to the seemingly impossible challenge of combining a career with family life. According to the commission, a substitute for the mother was needed if the puzzle was to be solved. Instead of a professional substitute as in the 1940s, however, the domestic worker was now to be recruited from youngsters, social groups with low education or immigrants. The aim of the post-war commission to turn domestic work into a profession was no longer considered an option, which indicates an important discursive trajectory surrounding the values associated with domestic work.[13] And the 'woman-friendly welfare state', which the Norwegian political scientist Helga Maria Hernes was calling out for in 1987 (Hernes 1987), must today be extended to include perspectives on class and ethnicity. For with policies such as those discussed here, we risk creating a society that in part is constructed to exempt some groups of women from domestic work by presupposing that it will be carried out by other groups of women. This suggests how a class perspective once more becomes crucial to the analysis of policy outcomes – as does, clearly, the question of ethnicity.

The two empirical examples also shed light on changes in relation to spheres of care. The 1950s were not ready for public solutions to care assignments, especially when children were involved. Instead, the private household was still the most important space for those assignments. Bringing up children outside the private sphere was seen by many to jeopardize their future. Changes came in the 1970s with the extended public sector, and in 2002 90 per cent of all children aged between three and five attended public day care. The existence of public spaces for child-care is now far from being a controversial issue. At the same time, these newly implemented social policies do suggest that the private home might return to being a central place for day care. Besides tax deductions, a home care allowance was introduced in 2008, meaning that the state rewarded families financially for taking care of their children at home instead of using public arrangements (SFS 2008, 307). Even if most Swedish children still attend public day care, these policies point in a new possible direction, when tax deductions and home-care allowances can increase the demand for both care and domestic workers. What, then, of the legislative situation for domestic workers in the labour market?

Working in spheres of care

When Gustav Möller in the 1940s argued that domestic workers would be best off if they were integrated into the public sector, the argument had its own specific context. It was a proposal built on historical knowledge of the working conditions for domestic workers. Compared to other occupations, the legal protection for domestic workers was weaker when it came to maximum hours of work and protection for minors. Historically, the reason for this vulnerable position had been a resistance towards regulating family life and private spheres. Another frequent argument was that the content of domestic work was so varied that it was unsuitable for legislation (Calleman 2007, 105–106, 201). Furthermore, the fact that the private home was not seen as a workplace complicated any prospect of legally enforcing labour laws (Moberg 1978, 152 ff., 173). Catharina Calleman has pointed out how legislation on domestic work mirrored the particular power relationship between employer and employee in this area; a relationship that in comparison with other occupations gave the employee markedly less influence and control over the situation (Calleman 2007, 202).

The law of 1944, which regulated the terms of employment for the domestic workers, was modified in 1970, yet differences in relation to general labour laws were still apparent. Legislation regulating employment security, supervision, overtime and hours of work was still relatively weak for domestic workers. Calleman argues that the reason for this was the specific discourse of the 1970s. The general understanding was that the hiring of domestic workers was about to vanish, partly due to the shortage of labour, partly due to an increased public sector for child-care and eldercare. The risk of employees being exploited was quite simply considered less acute (Calleman 2007, 113–114, 195–6, 200). The legislation for workers employed by companies offering domestic services more closely resembles the terms of general labour legislation (Calleman 2007, 178).

This brief historical outline indicates the exceptional position of the domestic workforce in the labour market, a position further complicated if one looks at the unionization of these workers. Sweden has a history of a high degree of trade union membership. In the mid-1990s, 88 per cent of all workers were organized.[14] The reason for the high degree of unionism in Sweden is connected to a tradition of collective agreement between organizations representing employers and employees. These agreements regulate wages, employment security and suchlike. Consequently there is, for example, no legislation concerning minimum wages in Sweden (Calleman 2007, 135, 203–204). In the last fourteen years, the degree of unionism among Swedish workers has declined. In 2009, 71 per cent of the workers were unionized. Among those employed within the private service sector the degree of unionism was 61 per cent. In fact, a study made by Calleman shows that the degree of organization among those employed within domestic services was as low as 20 per cent in 2006. Even if this negative trend in unionism has been visible since the 1990s, a more drastic drop was immediately apparent in 2006 when the cost of union membership soared following the centre–right Alliance government's abolition of the state subsidization of union membership fees (Calleman 2007, 181; Larsson 2009, 2–3, 17).

In a historical perspective this low degree of unionization among domestic workers is not a new phenomenon, and trade unions representing domestic workers employed in private homes are, and have been, rare. In Sweden, efforts have been made to organize the domestic workers since 1902. A more thorough attempt was made through the creation of the Trade Union of Domestic Workers in the 1920s. Even though they received economic support from *Landsorganisationen* (the Swedish Trade Union Confederation) the organization faced several difficulties. The turnover rates among members were high, and it was also hard to reach out to the domestic workers and inform them about their existence. In addition they did not have an organized counterpart to negotiate with (Moberg 1978, 142 ff.). These problems were acknowledged by the commission working with the design of the Social Home Help Programme. If this was to be an attractive occupation, they argued, it was of importance that the home carers worked under formal terms of employment, which meant that they had fixed salaries, paid vacation and regulated working hours (SOU 1943:15, 56 ff.). In comparison, in the proposal of 2007, workers' rights were touched upon only at a single point, in the context of addressing the workers' conditions on the informal, black market. Here the commission argued that an introduction of subsidies would have positive effects by formalizing such jobs and thereby giving workers increased economic independence (Prop. 2006/07:94, 55; Prop 2006/07:94, 56). But besides this, the workers' perspective was absent. Instead, the work of the commission can be read as an uncritical echo of the assignment given by the government, as a promotion of the policy at hand, disregarding both historical and present knowledge of the often complex situation of the domestic workforce.[15]

Today, Sweden's largest trade union, *Kommunal*, represents workers employed within the domestic service sector. The two largest companies offering domestic services also accept collective agreements.[16] But if the degree of unionization among these workers in general is as low as 20 per cent, the negotiations of terms of employment are consequently mostly done without the support of an organization representing the worker. When the government in addition predicts that this employment mostly attracts those with a shorter education, youngsters and persons born abroad, the situation becomes – in this perspective – even more problematic; not least when self-employment is expected to increase, meaning that there is no organization behind the worker at all.

The Swedish welfare state is changing. The launching of the tax deduction in 2007 is only one example of a larger project of privatization. Schools, healthcare, child-care and eldercare are increasingly becoming a part of the private market. Even if everything in society is always under reconstruction, it is of great importance to acknowledge how different changes affect one another. If an increase in privatization in a sector that throughout history has had a weak legislative position in the labour market is followed by a decrease in trade union membership, the historical perspective provided here suggests that we are facing what in Swedish would be called a *nygammalt problem* – 'a new old problem'. This development demands further investigation, which in turn calls for a historical awareness of how similar problems and solutions have been dealt with in the past.

Notes

1 In Swedish they are called *hemvårdarinnor*, translated here as home carer, something akin to what in English would be called a home-help. Home-help, however, is the term often used in Sweden when referring to people who assist the elderly; and, given the Social Home Help Programme in its initial phases, concentrated its efforts on families, it is important to draw a distinction between the two occupations.

2 Omitted.

3 The National Board of Health and Welfare was, and still is, a government agency under the Ministry of Health and Social Affairs.

4 Gøsta Esping-Andersen is the standard reference and starting-point for scholars discussing models of welfare. Besides the liberal and conservative welfare states, as Esping-Andersen writes, there is the Social Democratic system (Esping-Andersen 1990).

5 Jenny Andersson has pointed out that the concept also communicated an emotional dimension of belonging, a 'home' in which material safety was provided and in which everybody had a place. In practice, though, everyone did not 'belong', and everyone did not have the same rights (Andersson 2009, 57, 105, 114–115). It should also be noted that some scholars emphasize that 'The People's Home' was not in common usage during the period. See, for example, Björck (2008) where he examines the concepts and also shows how '*folkhem*' was in use in an earlier period.

6 Alva and Gunnar Myrdal's *Crisis in the Population Question* (1934) is often

referred to as the starting-point for the discussion. In their book they presented several proposals for social reforms intended to facilitate families' everyday life; reforms which in turn would combat the negative trend (Myrdal 1934/1997).

7 During this period Sweden had approximately 7 million inhabitants (<http://www.scb.se/Pages/TableAndChart_224772.aspx>).

8 In 1948, for example, Sweden had 693,000 people over the age of 65; a decade later the number had increased to approximately 852,000 (Wersäll 2006, 60).

9 An international study beyond the Nordic countries would be useful, not least because such a comparison could help shed light on how different welfare arrangements affect intersections of class, gender, ethnicity, etc., but such a historical perspective is still to be explored in detail. Forthcoming work by Elin Kvist and Elin Peterson will provide a contemporary European perspective in this field. See also Cobble (2009) on transnational movements of ideas connected to Social Home Help, and for an American perspective Boris and Klein (2006, 84) and Palmer (1989, 102).

10 See, for example, Runcis 1998; Zaremba 1999.

11 On 1 January 2008 this was changed to *Lagen om skattereduktion för hushålls-arbete*; see SOU 2008:57 *Skattelättnader för hushållsarbete*, 45.

12 For further reading regarding tax-deducible domestic services in Sweden, see for example Gavanas, Anna (2006), 'De onämnbara: jämlikhet, "svenskhet" och privata hushållstjänster i pigdebattens Sverige', in *Arbetslivets osynliga murar* (SOU 2006:59); Nyberg, Anita 'Hemnära tjänster – kvinnornas befriare?', *Kvinnovetenskaplig tidskrift* 1999:3; Strollo, Emma (2009), 'Från Pigjobb till hushållsnära tjänster – ett historiskt perspektiv', *Arbetarhistoria* 2009:1–2; Platzer, Ellinor (2007), *Från folkhem till karriärhushåll. Den nya husliga arbetsdelningen* (Lund: Arkiv förlag).

13 Note, however, that some of the home carers' assignments did transform into professions, such as child-care and the work that later came under social services.

14 Denmark and Finland also have a tradition of strong trade unionism, while Norway's rate is around 50 per cent. Compared to the US, where four states had a union membership that just topped 20 per cent in 2009, the Swedish figures must be considered high (Calleman 2007, 135, 203–204, <http://www.bls.gov/ro2/unionnynj.htm>).

15 Sweden, along with Finland, is known for having a distinctive political system that relies heavily on independent commissions, made up of a broad spectrum of politicians, civil servants and academics, to formulate possible political reforms. The period between 1930 and 1970 has been described as the heyday of the state commission. However, in the mid-1970s questions were raised about their objectivity as well as their working methods, which were thought to be both time-consuming and expensive. Even though the system of commissions is still in place, they should now be understood as briefer surveys of different possible political options (Johansson 1992, 246; Lundqvist 2007, 13–14).

16 <http://www.kommunal.se/Kommunal/Medlem/Branscher-och-yrken/Kok-och-stad/Branschen-idag/>.

References
Literature

Agius, Christine (2006), *The Social Construction of Swedish Neutrality. Challenges to Swedish Identity and Sovereignty* (Manchester: Manchester University Press).

Åmark, Klas (2005), *Hundra år av välfärdspolitik. Välfärdsstatens framväxt i Norge och Sverige* (Umeå: Boréa).

Andersson, Jenny (2009), *När framtiden redan hänt. Socialdemokratin och folkhemsnostalgin* (Stockholm: Ordfront).

Björck, Henrik (2008), *Folkhemsbyggare* (Stockholm: Atlantis).

Boris, Eileen & Klein, Jennifer (2006), 'Organizing Home Care: Low-waged Workers in the Welfare State', *Politics & Society*, 34, 81–108.

Calleman, Catharina (2007), *Ett riktigt arbete? Om regleringen av hushållstjänster* (Säter: Pang).

Christiansen, Niels-Finn & Markkola, Pirjo (2006), 'Introduction', in id. et al. (eds.), *The Nordic Model of Welfare. A Historical Reappraisal*, (Copenhagen: Museum Tusculanum Press).

Christiansen, Niels-Finn & Petersen, Klaus (2001), 'Preface', *Scandinavian Journal of History*, 26/3, 153–156.

Cobble, Sue (2009), 'Vänskap bortom Atlanten. Arbetarfeministernas internationella kontakter efter Andra Världskriget', *Arbetarhistoria*, 1–2, 12–20.

Dahl, Hanne Marlene (2000), *Fra kitler til eget tøj – diskurser om professionalisme, omsorg og køn* (Århus: Forlaget Politica).

Esping-Andersen, Gøsta (1990), *The Three Worlds of Welfare Capitalism* (London: Polity Press).

Giddens, Anthony & Hutton, Will (2000), 'Preface', in id. (eds.), *On the Edge. Living with Global Capitalism* (London: Random House).

Greve, Bent (2006), 'Introduction: The Social, Political and Economic Future of the European Welfare States', in id. (ed.), *The Future of the Welfare State. European and Global Perspectives* (Aldershot: Ashgate Publishing).

Hatje, Ann-Katrin (1974), *Befolkningsfrågan och välfärden. Debatten om familjepolitik och nativitetsökning under 1930- och 1940-talen* (Stockholm: Allmänna förlaget).

Hernes, Helga (1987), *Welfare State and Woman Power. Essays in State Feminism* (Oslo: Norwegian University Press).

Hilson, Mary (2008), *The Nordic Model. Scandinavia since 1945* (London: Reaktion).

Hirdman, Yvonne (1989/2000), *Att lägga livet till rätta. Studier i svensk folkhemspolitik* (Stockholm: Carlsson).

Hirdman, Yvonne (2001), *Genus. Om det stabilas föränderliga former* (Malmö: Liber).

Johansson, Jan (1992), *Det statliga kommittéväsendet. Kunskap, kontroll, consensus* (Stockholm: Stockholm University).

Leira, Arnlaug (2005), 'Omsorgsstaten och familjen', in Anne Lise Ellingsæter & Arnlaug Leira (eds.), *Velferdsstaten og familien. Utfodringer og dilemmaer* (Oslo: Gyldendal Akademisk).

Lizter, Ruth (2009), 'A Nordic Nirvana? Gender, Citizenship, and Social Justice in the Nordic Welfare States' Social Politics', *International Studies in Gender, State and Society*, 16/2, 242–278.

Larsson, Mats (2009), *LOs arbetslivsenhet. Facklig anslutning år 2009. Facklig anslutning bland anställda efter klass och kön år 1990–2009*, <http://www.lo.se/home/lo/home.nsf/unidview/A267C47E973B60C9C125761500360F01/$file/Facklig_anslutning_2009.pdf>, accessed on 20 October 2010.

Lundberg, Urban (2003), *Juvelen i kronan. Socialdemokraterna och den allmänna pensionen* (Stockholm: Hjalmarson & Högberg).

Lundberg, Urban & Tydén, Mattias (2007), 'Stat och individ i svensk välfärdspolitisk historieskrivning', in Marika Lundberg Hedin, Urban Lundberg, Jens Rydström & Mattias Tydén (eds.), *Staten som vän eller fiende? Individ och samhälle i svenskt 1900-tal* (Stockholm: Mattias Institutet för framtidsstudier).

Lundberg, Urban & Åmark, Klas (2001), 'Social Rights and Social Security. The Swedish Welfare State 1900–2000', *Scandinavian Journal of History*, 26/3, 157–176.

Lundqvist, Åsa (2007), *Familjen i den svenska modellen* (Umeå: Boréa).

Lövgren, Brita (1993), *Hemarbete som politik. Diskussioner om hemarbete, Sverige 1930–40-talen, och tillkomsten av Hemmens Forskningsinstitut* (Stockholm: Almqvist & Wiksell International).

Moberg, Kerstin (1978), *Från tjänstehjon till hembiträde. En kvinnlig låglönegrupp i den fackliga kampen 1903–1946* (Uppsala: Acta Universitatis Upsalaiensis).

Myrdal, Alva & Myrdal, Gunnar (1997), *Kris i Befolkningsfrågan* (first published 1934; Stockholm: Nya Doxa).

Öberg, Lisa (1999), 'Ett socialdemokratiskt dilemma', in Christina Florin, Lena Sommestad & Ulla Wikander (eds.), *Kvinnor mot kvinnor. Om systerskapets svårigheter* (Stockholm: Norstedt).

Palmer, Phyllis (1989), *Domesticity and Dirt. Housewives and Domestic Servants in the United States, 1920–1945* (Philadelphia: Temple University Press).

Platzer, Ellinor (2004), *En icke-lag i sökljuset. Exemplet hushållstjänster i Sverige* (Sociology of Law Research Reports; Lund: Lund University).

Runcis, Maija (1998), *Steriliseringar i folkhemmet* (Stockholm: Ordfront).

Simonen, Leila (1990), *Contradictions of the Welfare State, Women and Caring. Municipal Homemaking in Finland* (Tampere: Acta Universitatis Tamperensis).

Skjelbred, Frode (2004), *Husmorens storhetstid. Arbeiderpartiets kvinnesekretariat og innføringen av husmorvikarer och husmorferie* (Hovedfagsoppgave i historie; Oslo: Oslo University).

Sköld, Lovisa (2009), 'Välfärd 2009: 2', *Statistics Sweden*, 24–25.

Statistiska Centralbyrån/Statistics Sweden (2004), *På tal om kvinnor och män. Lathund om jämställdhet* (Stockholm: SCB).

Stenius, Henrik (1997), 'The Good Life is a Life of Conformity. The Impact of the Lutheran Tradition on Nordic Political Culture', in Øystein Sørensen & Bo Stråth (eds.), *The Cultural Construction of Norden* (Oslo: Scandinavian University Press).

Sundevall, Fia (forthcoming 2011), *Det sista manliga yrkesmonopolet. Genus och militärt arbete i Sverige 1865–1989* (Stockholm: Makadam)

Szebehely, Marta (ed.) (2003), *Hemhjälp i Norden. Illustrationer och reflektioner* (Lund: Studentlitteratur).

Wersäll, Margareta (2006), *Fattighusliv i ensamhetsslott. Ivar Lo-Johansson och de äldre i samhällsdebatt och dikt* (Uppsala: Avdelningen för litteratursociologi vid Litteraturvetenskapliga institutionen i Uppsala).

Wearness, Kari (1995), 'Den hjemmebaserte omsorgen i den skandinaviske velferdsstat. En offentlig tjenste i spenningsfeltet mellom ulika kulturer', in Stina Johansson (ed.), *Sjukhus och hem som arbetsplats. Omsorgsyrken i Norge, Sverige och Finland* (Stockholm: Bonnier Utbildning).

Zaremba, Maciej (1999), *Det rena och det andra. Om tvångssteriliseringar, rashygien och arvssynd* (Stockholm: Bokförlaget DN).

Sources

<http://www.scb.se/Pages/TableAndChart_224772.aspx>, accessed on 10 January 2010.

<http://www.bls.gov/ro2/unionnynj.htm>, accessed on 2 April 2010.

<http://www.kommunal.se/Kommunal/Medlem/Branscher-och-yrken/Kok-och-stad/Branschen-idag/>, accessed on 2 April 2010.

Motion AK 1957:345.

Protokoll FK 25:31d, 65.

Proposition 1964:85.

Proposition 2006/7: 94.

Råd och Anvisningar i Socialvårdsfrågor 1946: 42.

Stencil 1963:8 Social hemhjälp Promemoria avgiven av Familjeberedningen.

Svensk författningssamling (SFS) 1943:947 Om Statsbidrag till social hemhjälpsverksamhet.

Svensk författningssamling (SFS) 1951:225 Om Statsbidrag till social hemhjälpsverksamhet.

Svensk författningssamling (SFS) 2007:346 Lagen som skattereduktion for utgifter for hushållsarbete.

Svensk författningssamling (SFS) 2008:307 Om kommunalt vårdnadsbidrag.

Sociala Meddelanden 1954:1.

SOU 1943:15 Utredning och förslag angående statsbidrag till social hemhjälpsverksamhet.

SOU 1952:38 Hemhjälp.

SOU 1955:29 Samhället och barnfamiljerna.

SOU 1994:43 Uppskattad sysselsättning. Om Skatternas betydelse for den private tjänstesektorn.

SOU 1996:55 Sverige, framtiden och mångfalden. Slutbetänkande från invandrarpolitiska kommittén.

SOU 1997:17 Skatter, tjänster och sysselsättning.

SOU 2008:57 Skattelättnader för hushållsarbete.

CHAPTER II

Global domestic workers in Denmark

Labour market regulation, union representation, and solidarity strategies

Lise Lotte Hansen

In the Nordic welfare states, taking care of children, the sick, and the elderly is to a large extent carried out within the public sector. Nevertheless, there is an increasing demand for cleaning in private homes, taking care of private gardens, assistance at parties, and childcare outside nursery and kindergarten hours. This is most likely to be done by workers responsible for only one task such as cleaning, and only for a couple of hours each week or when needed. Another solution is to get an au pair. An increasingly large number of the domestic workers, including au pairs, are female migrants from the global East or South, and some of these are working in the informal sector. On a global scale, non-standard jobs and jobs in the informal sector are increasing (Vosko 2007). A major problem is that labour market regulation either does not protect informal sector workers, or it only does so to a limited degree; another problem is that trade union membership is rare among these workers. Different strategies are called for. These include organizing and union renewal strategies and the development of new forms of regulation.

In comparison to most other countries, the Danish labour market is thoroughly regulated and most workers are trade union members. Nevertheless, labour market regulation, workers' interest representation and trade union strength are challenged by these new developments, which also include 'bad' employers, decreasing interest in union membership and activism, diversity among workers, and union-hostile regulations. Consequently, Danish trade unions have to develop new strategies to include all workers in their interest representation *and* to stay in power.

The research on global domestic workers has only to a limited extent been concerned with the role of trade unions and not at all with non-state labour market regulation. Instead, the focus has generally fallen on welfare-state regulation and on care and gender regimes (for example Williams & Gavanas in Lutz 2008), or on global care chains and new forms of cultural, social and economic inequality (for example Ehrenreich & Hochschild 2002; Isaksen, Devi & Hochschild 2008). But if non-state labour market regulation and the role of trade unions are left out, then pluralism in labour market regulation will be overlooked and an important social justice agency, the labour movement, ignored. This is a problem especially in regard to the Nordic labour markets, because much regulation is based on agreements between the labour market parties. Moreover, trade unions represent workers' interests not only in the labour market, but also on the broader political agenda regarding welfare.

This chapter concerns the responses from trade unions to the challenges of regulation, interest representation and workers' solidarity that follow the presence of global domestic workers in the Danish labour market. The focus is on au pairs from the Philippines and ethnic minority women in private sector cleaning in both declared and undeclared jobs. The trade unions involved are LO (the Danish Confederation of Trade Unions), FOA (Trade and Labour) and 3F (United Federation of Danish Workers).

Danish industrial relations

The Danish labour movement is well organized, with federation offices at national level, branches in local communities and employee representatives in the workplace. The organizational structures of the trade unions and the confederations are hierarchical, with democratic representation and elected leaders. Nevertheless, in general the form and content of initiatives are tailored to the specific context and depend on those who participate in it. This results in a great variation in ways of approaching problems, although most policies and strategies are decided centrally. I have therefore chosen to study three organizational settings which in different ways are all involved in the interest representation of global domestic workers: LO, FOA, and 3F.[1] LO is the national confederation of trade unions for unskilled and skilled workers. I have interviewed two officers at LO, one male and one female, who are both involved in policy-making relating to domestic workers. FOA is the trade union for public employees. They have taken a specific interest in au pairs and their working and living conditions. I have interviewed a senior male trade union leader from the national office. 3F is the trade union mainly for those working in the private sector, and I have interviewed two female leaders from a local branch that has many ethnic minority members who work in cleaning. The ethnic minority workers they speak about are members or potential members who have a work contract and who sometimes work in private homes, but more often in offices, in hotels and the like. Some are self-employed, others employed by a cleaning company and others again directly by the employer in the workplace.[2] LO officers also refer to a broader group of ethnic minority workers. For that reason, and because there are many similarities between the strategies concerning the inclusion of temporary migrant workers and other groups of ethnic minority workers, I have chosen to focus on both. I have also included informal sector workers and workers from both elsewhere in the EU and from the Global South. The discussion also builds on policy documents and research reports.

At the very core of industrial relations research is the question of how trade unions can develop new forms of workers' solidarity and interest representation. This new form of solidarity should rest on diversity instead of homogeneity and pave the way for different living and working conditions as well as interests. This contrasts with the definition of common interests by the most powerful groups that were – and are – mainly male, white and in ordinary jobs in big industrial plants (Hansen 2004;, Hyman 1999). Both research and the trade unions primarily focus on the organization and participation of all workers. However, as Hyman makes plain, a clear response to the new ideological challenges is also needed – the labour movement has to re-strengthen its ideological base and reclaim the central themes of flexibility, security and opportunity (Hyman 1999).

In the UK, US, Canada and Australia in particular, union renewal is still on the trade union agenda; this includes seeing women and now ethnic minority groups as a resource that can be used to regain power in the labour market. The renewal strategies include new forms of organizing and stronger cooperation with networks and non-governmental organizations (NGOs), and, in some unions, changes in democratic structures, interest representation and policy-making (see also Hansen 2004). Briskin (2002) has discussed the creation of inclusive trade union structures that both give women a political base *and* do not lead to separatism. This approach focuses on women's self-organized groups and interest representation. Moreover, she discusses coalition-building both among women across trade unions, the women's movement, community organizations *and* across different equity-seeking groups (for example women, ethnic minorities, gays and lesbians) within trade unions. She shows how coalition work among women in Canada has redefined both the ideology and the practice of union solidarity. Ledwith (2006) argues that the same is the case on a more global scale. Another concern is that given globalization, coalition-building must expand both nationally and transnationally in order to create resistance. Yet this is complicated because of the organizational, cultural and demo-cratic differences between national labour movements (Ferdinand 2008, also Hyman 1999). To this Vosko (2007) adds that trade unions and labour market regulation have never been strong in the Global South, and partly therefore workers have developed a wide range of organizations and networks that are more directly related to different living and working conditions, and to informal sector work. Vosko argues that trade unions could learn from this wide variety of organizational forms so they are better able to include migrant workers.

New British research shows how structural barriers such as im-migration regulation influence the representation and collective organization of migrant workers. It also shows that the lack of trade union engagement by migrant workers is just as much the result of an absence of branch activities – which influences all workers negatively – as it is of exclusionary mechanisms. Moreover, the research emphasizes that workers' identity changes depending on the context, leading to an awareness of the need to avoid essentialism both in policy-making and in actual activities on the ground. It also means that work should be stressed as the basis for collective identity (Moore et al. 2010).

The work in question here is domestic work that is female-gendered, reproductive work. This is often carried out in small workplaces, in non-standard employment and with lower wages than in most parts of the labour market. Moreover, the intimate character and the logic of care work, together with the special relationship between employer and employee, which is highly emotional, personalized and characterized by mutual dependence, make the working conditions for domestic workers very different from, for example, factory work (also Lutz 2008). Nevertheless, migrant care workers' working and living conditions vary too, depending on the type of job and how this is regulated. According to Yeates (2004) domestic workers are in the least regulated part of the labour market; their work is often based on individual arrangements and informal recruitment. These workers are the most vulnerable, with only a few, if any, rights, and also the most difficult to organize and protect because of the character of their work and (lack of) contracts.

The Danish labour market

In comparison to most other countries, the Danish labour market is thoroughly regulated and trade unions are strong. The Danish labour market is mainly regulated through agreements made between the employers' organizations and the trade unions. In addition, some areas are fully or partly covered by legislation; for example, health and safety, parental leave and holiday regulation. The labour market has strong independent institutions developed and controlled by the parties; for example, the Industrial Court and the Conciliation Board. Moreover, there is a tradition of negotiations and policy-making between the labour movement, the employers' organizations and the state both on labour market policy and on broader welfare problems. The labour market is well organized both on the employers' and the employees' sides. Trade unions mainly organize in relation to trade and education and most trade unions are affiliated to one of three confederations: LO, FTF (the Confederation of Unions for Salaried Employees and Civil Servants), or AC (the Danish Confederation of Professional Associations). Most employees are union members, 76.8 per cent in 2005, equally divided in terms of men and women, manual workers and salaried employees. Coverage by agreements is almost total in the public sector and 71 per cent in the private sector (Scheuer 2007). Crucial to the model is the existence of both 'real' and organized employers *and* strong trade unions. Just as important is a bargaining culture based on trust, consensus and mutual respect (Bredgaard 2007). Furthermore, trade union membership is decisive, because labour market legislation is only marginal. In addition, trade union membership gives access to direct interest representation not only in the labour market, but also in regard to a broader welfare policy agenda.

However, neo-liberalism, together with the globalization of work and employment, has not left the Danish labour movement untouched. Most affected by these changes are the trade unions affiliated to LO. They are losing members due to growing competition from the cheaper independent unions and the general tendency among younger people to be less interested in trade union membership and activism. Moreover, union-hostile regulations have affected manual workers' unions the most. In addition, unskilled and low-skilled jobs are more often out-sourced than other types of jobs. And finally, these jobs also attract the highest share of ethnic minority and migrant workers. LO and the affiliated trade unions are therefore also concerned about organizing and renewal, as are, for example, the British trade unions. However the Danish strategies are not as developed and comprehensive as the British.

So on the one hand, global domestic workers meet a bargaining system and a labour movement that have been able to ensure a high level of protection, pay and welfare for all workers. On the other, both are predominantly male and white. This is reflected in representation, culture, democratic structures, policies and bargaining results

(Hansen 2004; Kolstrup & Ibsen 2007). The labour movement acknowledges some of these problems, and LO and the affiliated unions have made policies and strategies directed at improving equal representation, reforming bargaining agendas, fighting discrimination and including different members; yet, there are huge differences in both strategies and results between unions and even within the same union. In general, the labour movement is becoming more diverse both in forms of solidarity and interest representation. This is, however, more in terms of changes in policies than in democratic structures (also Wrench 2004).

Au pairs and ethnic minority cleaners

In Denmark, most 'domestic workers' are home-helpers and therefore public employees. The rest are either au pairs or cleaners who are employed in small companies, self-employed or working in the informal economy. For the latter group, the work is undeclared. At one end of the regulation continuum (Yeats 2004), public sector work is fully regulated both by legislation *and* agreements, and most employees are members of a trade union and have an elected employee representative at the workplace. Private sector cleaners with a working contract are almost as well protected as public employees. At the other end of the regulation continuum, we find au pairs and cleaners in the informal sector. They are either not at all or only partly protected by legislation, not covered by labour market agreements, and they have no direct access to membership and interest representation by trade unions.

The number of au pairs from outside the EU has more than doubled since 2002 and is now a little over 2,500, of which Filipinas make up the by far the largest group, 1,987 in 2009 (Ministeriet for Flygtninge, Indvandrere og Integration, 2010). The au-pair arrangement is a cultural exchange programme, but the Filipina au pairs are spoken about and treated as workers, and they identify themselves as such too. The au pairs are taxed as if they were workers and protected by holiday regulations; moreover, they are covered by Danish public health insurance and the host families are urged to sign an industrial injury insurance (see also Stenum 2008). According to the FOA trade union leader, most au pairs are treated well. However, because of the difference between the idea of the au-pair arrangement and the actual use of it, some fundamental problems arise that affect almost all the au pairs: salaries are low, the working conditions are unclear and uncertain, and the management of the work is unprofessional. Moreover, the au pairs experience the difficulties and dilemmas of care work and of living-in with the family. All this is difficult to change because of the status of the au-pair contract, which means that they are not covered by labour market agreements and have no channel of direct interest representation. Additional problems arise as a few au pairs are misused in relation to either working time or pay.

Migrant and ethnic minority women in private service cleaning are a diverse group in regard to the regulation of their work, cultural background and personal resources. Undeclared work is quite widespread in jobs in private homes, and not only among migrants – ethnic majority workers also moonlight (Kjær 2010a; Rezai 2005). However, regular cleaning and home-service companies operating on the formal labour market also offer their services to private households. Women working in these companies are organized in 3F.

The Undocumented Workers Transitions report (2008) on Denmark estimates that there are about 1,000 to 5,000 undocumented migrants in Denmark, although the figures are by their nature very uncertain. They are refugees who have had their application for asylum turned down, or people who have entered the country as students, au pairs or on tourist visas. Another group of workers in the informal economy are women who come from the new EU member states. Research shows that 12 per cent of all Polish workers in Copenhagen are working in the 'informal' labour market, which is characterized by 'moonlighting', lack of contracts and undocumented workers (Hansen & Hansen 2009, 60). About 5 per cent of all Polish workers are women working as cleaners in private homes and they do not have a civil registration number, their contracts are only oral, and they get their pay 'in hand'. Most of the women are overqualified for the job and their working conditions and pay are poor (Hansen & Hansen 2009, 77). The report also shows that the Polish workers (both women and men) only have a very limited knowledge about the Danish labour market model and that almost 75 per cent have never been in touch with a Danish trade union. Only 11 per cent are members of a trade union and only 10 per cent of an unemployment insurance fund. On the other hand, they have very strong networks with other Polish immigrants whom they turn to for support and for helping to find a job.

All the interviewees agreed that both the numbers of workers in the informal economy and the 'grey zone' in between the formal (declared) and the informal sector (undeclared work) are increasing (see also Kjær 2010b). The two women leaders in the 3F branch also expressed their concerns about both increasing exploitation of ethnic minority women workers *and* a strong pressure on pay and working conditions in private service cleaning in general. As a rule, cleaning is placed lowest in the job hierarchy: it is female-gendered, unskilled, often extremely part-time, and low-paid. Furthermore, it suffers from having fewer organized workers, and unprofessional and unorganized employers.

Some of the ethnic minority women only have poor labour market qualifications. Moreover, some have full responsibility for the family, and others have a husband who, because of the immigration regulations, is only allowed to stay in Denmark if his wife can support him. In addition, some are also very lonely and do not know if, how, and where they can get help. However, this is not the case for all workers. According to the two 3F branch leaders, the Filipinas and the Thais are regarded in general as 'good' workers by the employers and are connected to strong networks of other immigrants, especially from their home country.

Another challenge is that the open market in the EU and the free movement of labour have brought about an increasing number of employers who are circumventing rules and agreements or are unqualified to take care of a business. Furthermore, self-employment is rising in the cleaning business. Self-employment means that the individual cleaner has her/his own company, which is then hired by a contractor. It has become a way to avoid the regulations attached to a regular employment relationship, so it poses some new challenges to the trade unions.

LO's response: membership and agreements

The two LO officers approach the domestic worker problem like they would go about any other problem in the Danish labour market: it is a question of membership and good agreements. New regulations should mainly be made through bargaining with the employers over regulations that protect members against 'bad' employers. Nevertheless, the male officer offers a tiny opening for considering more legislation similar to that in Norway, because some workers' pay and rights are difficult to secure by agreements only.

The two officers do not know about any specific problems and interests among domestic workers, but stress the need to know more. A major concern is how to solve the au-pair problem: should the au-pair arrangement be ended and replaced with one that fits the present situation better, or should the au-pair arrangement continue and be supplemented with other arrangements?[3]

The female officer believes that there is a need for help in the home as some women have problems combining a working career and family responsibilities and, in the future, we will all have to work more. She suggests that the 'home-service arrangement' should be reintroduced.[4] Besides fighting moonlighting and solving work-related family problems, the 'home-service arrangement' would be able to ensure there were regular, professional employers with whom the trade unions could enter into agreements, and, moreover, would reduce both unregulated working conditions and 'extremely part-time' jobs. Another main solution is trade union membership, yet this has turned out to be a difficult strategy as some workers fear trade unions, others choose the cheaper independent unions, and others again have never been approached by trade unions. Moreover, it is difficult to organize domestic workers because of the very nature of their work. The male officer says:

> It is clear that, like all other workplaces, the bigger they are, the more surveillance and control. But it is more difficult at the small hotel where a couple of girls run around – not many come looking for them. It is a little like these Polish girls, they do private cleaning, there you don't have a chance, it will ... always be poorly organized

because the union representative or the local branch leaders will not know that somebody works in that home … But of course you have to work for a better coverage, and make some arrangements for them – where they can come and get information and know how they can get support.

The male officer is hesitant about working together with NGOs – the strong Danish unions do not need them. On the contrary, he believes that new ways of organizing are less important than a direct, high-visibility approach from employee representatives and local branch leaders. In contrast, the female officer emphasizes that the labour movement has had good experience of working together with women's and other types of NGOs. The female officer meets with the Norwegian and Swedish LOs, takes part in the International Trade Union Confederation (ITUC) especially in their Women's Committee, and negotiates agreements in the International Labour Organization (ILO). The ITUC also cooperates with domestic workers' organizations in Europe. The male officer stresses that international cooperation can mainly be used for putting forward the 'nice demands'. Partly in contrast, the female officer adds that,

> It is very important for the labour movement, especially in the Third World, that these international things exist … Now, I have just been together with all these women in Brussels, and they say that often the right things are in their own legislations but they lack the power to implement them. And then I try to say, but the labour movement is among other things a force for implementation. In Denmark they have that role.

LO is involved in tripartite policy-making to fight discrimination against ethnic minorities, and has taken several initiatives to better integrate minority workers both in the labour market and in the labour movement. According to the male officer, a gender perspective is not included in these policies: 'It is more, in reality, to get them in as members. And to get them engaged in trade union work. That's what's important … '. In contrast, the female officer introduces some gender issues and refers to the former Women Workers Union as being successful in getting ethnic minority members to stand for leadership positions, and get elected too.

The motivating drive for both officers is the experience of social injustice in relation to global workers, and the importance of solidarity with the weak. Their main concerns are the marginalization and discrimination of ethnic minorities and a worry that the result of the recent developments in the labour market will be an underclass without decent pay and equal rights. The male officer adds that another reason is that labour is needed to maintain the welfare society in the future.

FOA's response: inclusion and networking

'Someone has to do something', the male leader says when asked why FOA is involved in representing the interests of the au pairs. Representing interests is possibly an exaggeration because the status of the au pairs limits the service to bringing cases to court in the public legal system or writing letters to families who abuse their au pair's rights and conditions. Regarding the first, FOA has been less successful because it is difficult to prove the abuse and because the legal system is very slow. Regarding the latter, some families accept that they have to change attitudes. At the same time, and maybe just as important, FOA offers a 'room' for inclusion in the sense that the au pairs can be members of FOA despite not being acknowledged as workers *and* that the FOA leader takes part in a large number of meetings and other social events together with the au pairs. FOA works together with different organizations especially among the Filipinas and with one of the Catholic churches in Copenhagen, too. Cooperation with these organizations has been decisive in terms of knowing about the problems and being able to get in contact with the au pairs. The leader says,

> It has placed us in the middle of a network ... in which you know the au-pair field, and it means that we continuously get notifications about what the terms are like, and we intervene in cases too ... in reality we are now in a situation where we are trying to bring

some test cases to court to be able to document that it isn't possible
to defend the au pairs' conditions.

Moreover, networking has also been important for removing the au
pairs' fear or distrust of the trade union. On another level, FOA has
been active in raising the au-pair problem within the labour movement as well as in public debate. Nevertheless, the leader adds that
it is also challenging: these are not democratic organizations with
elected leaders and strategic policy-making; moreover, the informal
hierarchies within and between different groups sometimes create
problems, and finally it is very time-consuming. For all that, working together with the different organizations has been very valuable
and personally exciting, so for the leader it is mainly a question of
learning how to navigate in a different context.

Besides the experience of injustice, the leader gives other reasons for commitment to the case, namely that the type of work is
within FOA's area of interest and that it is necessary to be known
as a force to be reckoned with so as to prevent the development of
a 'grey zone' of workers who have no contact with trade unions.
It is important to get the area organized if, in future, the welfare
institutions in Denmark are dismantled and care work privatized.
And then, of course, an important reason is solidarity. At present,
the au pairs do not take part in trade union democracy. This is not
because of resistance within the trade union, but because they are
only in Denmark for a short period of time, which makes it difficult
to get them interested in building up and maintaining a network
within the trade union. Moreover, most of the au pairs do not have
any severe problems while they are in Denmark and therefore they
are less interested in becoming trade union activists. In that sense,
they are similar to many of FOA's younger members.

The leader suggests a lot of different initiatives that could be
undertaken to improve the situation of the au pairs. In the short
run, it is important to get the legislation changed so that the au
pairs are better protected, and to make it possible for au pairs to
stay on and get an education in Denmark, which would also be a
way to ensure enough labour in the future. In the longer run, he
is in favour of some kind of Green Card arrangement. Moreover,

he thinks that if Denmark accedes the ILO convention on 'Decent work for domestic workers', it will be easier to distinguish between au pairs and domestic work as all jobs that exceed 30 hours a week (the limit in the au-pair arrangement) will be treated as domestic work, and consequently will be covered by agreements. But first and foremost, it is important to ensure a real employment relationship, which would also demand some kind of professionalization of the employers. In addition, he points out that FOA works together with trade unions in the Nordic countries.

The leader has not considered whether the problems the au pairs have are similar to problems faced by other members of FOA. He is aware that it is 'women's work' and the 'invisibility' of the au pairs, in contrast to, for example, Eastern European builders, that is part of the problem, but he has not reflected on how this is related to the kind of work most of the other members of FOA do or on the gender power relations linked to cleaning, caring and cooking. However, when asked he says,

> the problems the au pairs have are typically about working hours, that it goes beyond normal limits in regard to the au-pair rules. And then this business of being underpaid. But there … is just exactly that about that it is an intimate relationship, because it is person to person, and it is care about something that actually is valuable both when it is in eldercare and about the children. Really, it is the same relationship, no doubt about that.

3F's response: women's solidarity and new representation

The two female 3F branch leaders have taken care of ethnic minority women cleaners' interests for more than twenty years. They can see changes both in problems and policies, but also in ethic minority cultures. The major problem is no longer only a need to learn Danish, but that of the legislation on family reunion. Moreover, labour market policy has changed so it is less about education and training and more about how to apply for a job and, all in all, more restrictive. In regard to the women as a group, their Danish is not improving, some have only a few personal resources and severe social problems; they are busier and less interested in trade union activities than earlier and some are met with cultural restrictions imposed by their families. The trade union has also changed; a major shift being a result of the merger between the KAD (the Women Workers Union in Denmark) and the SiD (the General Workers Union in Denmark). Previously, more ethnic minority women took part in the branch activities, contact with the women was better, and the service less complicated. Furthermore, the fact that it was a women-only union made it easier for the immigrant women to join and even sometimes created room for liberation. The two leaders were used to considering special needs and wishes that respected cultural norms. The cleaning sector has also changed from being mainly women's work to now, when it is mainly ethnic minorities, both women and men who are employed.

The two leaders are aware that they have to be better at coming in contact with all the women, and men, working in cleaning:

> I think that if we are to protect the old members and try to get new ones then the best thing for us leaders is to get out to gatherings, out into their churches, their services or into some clubs. (Leader B)

Another step is to get more ethnic minority members elected as leaders or appointed to a post in the branch. The branch is involved in different forms of activities in which ethnic minority members are trained for leadership and have the possibility to build networks with each other and senior leaders. Support from other ethnic minority leaders is important for getting the women to stand for election, just as support after being elected is significant so both branch officers act as mentors. But new approaches are also necessary. The branch has to change the way the work is organized so it is possible for those ethnic minority women who so wish to have their cases handled by other women.

A gender perspective is integrated in most of what the two leaders do. For them, this is also about being in a common situation as women:

But you know it's also about something else. We women can speak
… we speak together in a different way … we have a lot of things
in common despite where we come from. Most of us experience
being mothers. We have that in common and will have the rest
of our lives. And it means a lot if you're going out and trying to
motivate them to become members in this trade union. (Leader B)

On the one hand, this is about a need for solidarity among women.
On the other, it is a concern about gender power relations both
in the labour market and in the trade union. The first, of course,
is partly a response to the second, but it is also something more:
a kind of affectional solidarity. In the labour market, cleaning is
placed at the lower end of the job hierarchy – and moreover is
invisible in two ways. First, many workplaces are small and so are
the companies which employ them. Secondly, it is not high on the
trade union agenda:

> It is an all-women area. And there is no one else than women who
> are involved … and it has a low priority, because it is only 'the
> ethnics', and it is not something that covers the whole country, it
> is only in the capital and the big cities. And these women can deal
> with it. And it's only cleaning, and that's something with bad pay,
> so this is a woman's job. (Leader A)

Just recently the branch has decided to prioritize the work they do,
mainly for organizational reasons. The two leaders are proud that
they have been able to achieve that change in priorities and that
their branch will be able to show a new way forward for the trade
union. To begin with they will suggest that the organizers' work will
be directed at visiting women's clubs. But they also dream about
starting a women-only and ethnic-minority-only conference,

> Because then they could speak from the heart. They could see that
> they're not alone. Many times 'the ethnics' come, one, maybe two.
> And then we sit, a hundred people, and there's only one or two of
> them, and God knows how they must feel alone. (Leader A)

Challenges, changes and conflicts

It is clear that the Danish labour movement is searching for new ways in a complicated terrain where domestic workers' rights and representation are only some of many challenges. The ways are numerous: some supplement one another well, others are rather radical, and others again reproduce a traditional union agenda. In general, the strategies address most of the challenges. However, it is also clear that gender power relations are still present, and in some cases even reflected in the strategies.

In general there is strong pressure on pay and working conditions in the cleaning area, and both the cleaners and the au pairs have problems with unprofessional employers who in some cases also bend or ignore regulations, agreements and the tradition of cooperation among the labour market parties. Moreover, union-hostile policies have meant a reduction in economic resources and consequently in trade union staff and activities. Despite that, the three organizations in question are all increasing their activities in regard to organizing and representing migrant and ethnic minority workers.

The au pairs, the Polish cleaners and other undocumented workers in the informal sector *and* the ethnic minority cleaners who are organized in 3F are in similar yet dissimilar situations. On the one hand, they all enter a well-regulated labour market where trade unions are strong and have been able to ensure a high level of protection, pay and welfare for all workers. However, both the labour movement and the labour market are highly gendered, and, moreover, segregated in terms of ethnicity. Cooking, caring and cleaning are regarded as women's jobs and all the workers in question struggle with low pay, and some with bad working conditions and job insecurity, too. At the very bottom of the ladder one finds cleaning, which has low status, including in the labour movement. One can talk about jobs changing gender. Cleaning has also changed ethnicity and is now mainly a job area for ethnic minority workers, both women and men. Moreover, the au pairs, the undocumented workers in informal sector jobs, and the ethnic minority women cleaners all belong to the minority – they are culturally Others. However, the two groups are different, too. Both the au pairs and the Polish cleaners are described as generally resourceful, well educated and having strong networks to other migrants. In contrast, some of the ethnic minority cleaners in 3F have few personal resources and poor labour market skills. Nevertheless, they have a working contract, many are Danish citizens, and all are covered by labour market regulation. This is not the case for either the au pairs or the cleaners in the informal sector; some of the latter group are undocumented workers, and may even lack residence permits.

In general, none of the three groups is involved in trade union activism, but for different reasons: the au pairs regard their job as transitional; the Polish women and other undocumented workers have no access to trade union membership; and some of the ethnic minority workers in 3F have few personal resources and/or many family responsibilities, while others are not interested. However, the 3F branch is working to get more ethnic minority workers to stand for election as leaders. Another related problem is that domestic workers are regarded as difficult to organize because of the character of their work – they are 'invisible'. However, this invisibility is also a result of gendered power relations embedded in organizing strategies. FOA has already developed new ways of organizing and incorporating these workers, and the 3F branch wants to do so, too. All officers and leaders say that solidarity, but also the need to get more members, is an important reason for their work.

Conclusion

In general, the officers and leaders in LO, FOA and 3F are all follow-ing the path of the established labour market model both in present practice and in ideas for future strategies. New forms of regulation are discussed mainly in the form of agreements, though there is a little openness to more legislation in limited areas. Moreover, there are discussions about how to change informal sector work into formal jobs and how to create 'real' and professional employers with whom to bargain. The labour movement is also putting effort into organizing in both new and traditional ways. However, a more comprehensive process of union renewal is not on the agenda. On the other hand, FOA works together with migrants' networks, and in the 3F branch they want to do the same. Furthermore, they wish to create self-organization structures for ethnic minority groups. FOA has made it possible for au pairs to be members, while the 3F does not offer membership to workers without a work contract.

It is clear that the strategies – if implemented – will lead to a much better protection of global domestic workers and to better pay and working conditions. It will also give them direct influence on interest representation and welfare policy strategies. However, there are a number of issues to consider. The downsides are that undocumented workers will have even fewer job opportunities and that women from the global South might not get access to these jobs because of restrictions on immigration. Moreover, it could be questioned whether activities and strategies include answers to the specific working and living conditions faced by domestic workers. In addition, trade unions have to consider which form their interest representation and trade union activities should take when the migrants regard their jobs as transitional. Another unsolved problem concerns the protection and inclusion of undocumented and/or informal sector workers: should they have access to trade union membership? Finally, the question is whether these initiatives will be sufficient to redefine the ideology and practice of union solidarity, and change gendered and ethnic power structures within the labour movement and in the labour market.

Notes

1 LO, with its membership made up of individual trade unions, represents the labour movement in tripartite agreements and on bodies such as boards, think tanks, commissions and committees at international, national and regional levels. It is involved in general policy-making, media campaigning and the development of such things as new labour-organizing strategies. The labour movement's internal training system (FIU) also comes under LO's aegis. FOA organizes, for example, cleaners, home-helps, nursing assistants, child-care assistants, and caretakers. 3F organizes industrial workers, cleaners, gardeners, maids, waiters, kitchen staff, painters, lorry and taxi drivers, and railway workers, among others.
2 Members or potential members only include women working in the informal economy if they also have a regular job, and excludes workers without a contract.

3 At the ILO congress in June 2010, the female LO officer was the negotiating partner on behalf of the Danish labour movement at the convention concerning 'Decent work for domestic workers'. The convention is going to be ratified at the next ILO congress in June 2011. The convention does not include au pairs, so the fundamental problems related to working au pairs are not solved.

4 The home-service arrangement offered publicly financed economic support to provide services to private households.

References
Literature

Bredgaard, Thomas (2007), 'Interview med Ton Wilthagen', *Tidsskrift for Arbejdsliv*, 9/4, 94–98.

Briskin, Linda (2002), 'The equity project in Canadian unions. Confronting the challenge of restructuring and globalisation', in Fiona Colgan & Sue Ledwith (eds.), *Gender, Diversity and Trade Unions. International Perspectives* (New York: Routledge), 28–47.

Ehrenreich, Barbara & Arlie R. Hochschild (eds.) (2003), *Global Women. Nannies, Maids, and Sex Workers in the New Economy* (New York: Metropolitan Books).

Ferdinand, Amalie V. V. (2008), 'Internationalt fagforeningssamarbejde – hvad skal der til?' (Upubliceret speciale Scient. Adm. ISG; Roskilde: Roskilde Universitetscenter).

Hansen, Lise Lotte (2004), *Ligestillingspolitiske problemer – og mulige løsninger. Køn, magt og forandring i LO og UNISON* (Ph.D. dissertation; Roskilde: Institut for Samfundsvidenskab & Erhvervsøkonomi, Roskilde Universitet).

Hyman, Richard (1999), 'Imagined Solidarities: Can Trade Unions Resist Globalization?', in Peter Leisink (ed.), *Globalization and Labour Relations* (Cheltenham, UK; Northhampton, MA., USA: Edward Elgar), 94–115.

Isaksen, Lise et al. (2008), 'Global Care Crisis: A Problem of Capital, Care Chain, or Commons?', *American Behavioral Scientist*, 52/3, 405–425.

Kolstrup, Ane & Sanne Ipsen (2007), *Etniske minoriteter i det fagpolitiske arbejde – muligheder og barrierer* (Fagbevægelsens Videnscenter for Integration; Copenhagen: CASA).

Ledwith, Sue (2006), 'The Future as Female? Gender, Diversity and Global Labour Solidarity', in Craig Phelan (ed.), *The Future of Organised Labour: Global Perspectives* (Oxford; Bern; Berlin; Bruxelles; Frankfurt am Main; New York; Vienna: Peter Lang), 91–134.

Lutz, Helga (ed.) (2008), *Migration and Domestic Work. A European Perspective on a Global Theme* (Aldershot: Ashgate).

Moore, Sian, Thomson, Greg & Watson, Max (2010), 'The true spirit of self-organisation? Migrant worker activists in UNISON', paper presented at the 9th European Congress of the IIRA: 'European Employment Relations – Crisis and Visions', Copenhagen, 28 June–1 July.

Rezai, Shahamak (2005), *Det duale arbejdsmarked i et velfærdsstatsligt perspektiv – et studie af dilemmaet mellem uformel økonomisk praksis og indvandreres so-*

cioøkonomiske integration (Hovedrapport og anbefalinger; Roskilde: Institut for Samfundsvidenskab og Erhvervsøkonomi, Roskilde Universitet).

Scheuer, Steen (2007), 'Dilemmas of Collectivism – Danish Trade Unions in the 21st Century', *Journal of Labor Research*, 28/2, 233–254.

Vosko, Leah F. (2007), 'Representing Informal Economy Workers: Emerging Global Strategies and Their Lessons for North American Unions', in Dorethy Sue Cobble (ed.), *The Sex of Class: Women Transforming American Labor* (New York: Cornell University Press), 272–291.

Wrench, John (2004), 'Trade Union Responses to Immigrants and Ethnic Inequality in Denmark and the UK: The Context of Consensus and Conflict', *European Journal of Industrial Relations*, 10/1, 7–30.

Yeates, Nicola (2004), 'Global Care Chains. Critical Reflections and Lines of Enquiry', *International Feminist Journal of Politics*, 6/3, 369–391.

Sources

Interview, FOA leader, 22 October 2009.

Interview, LO officers, 22 October 2009.

Interview, 3F leaders, 10 November 2009.

Hansen, Jens A. & Nana W. Hansen (2009), *Polonia i København. Et studie af polske arbejdsmigranters løn-, arbejds- og levevilkår i Storkøbenhavn* (LO-Dokumentation nr. 1).

Kjær, Jakob S. (2010a), 'Hver tiende dansker køber sort rengøring', *Politiken*, 21 July 2010.

Kjær, Jakob S. (2010b), 'Omfattende svindel i rengøringsbranchen', *Politiken*, 25 July 2010.

Ministeriet for Flygtninge, Indvandrere & Integration (2010), *Tal & fakta på udlændinge området 2007 & 2009*, <www.nyidanmark.dk/da-dk/Statistik/Search-Statistics.htm?searchtype=statistics>, accessed on 15 April 2010.

Stenum, Helle (2008), *Au pair i Danmark: Billig arbejdskraft eller kulturel udveksling* (Copenhagen: FOA).

UWT (2008), *Denmark, Country Report*, Undocumented Workers Transitions, EU Sixth Framework Programme, <www.undocumentedmigrants.eu>, accessed on 11 November 2009.

About the authors

Mariya Bikova is a Ph.D. student at the Department of Sociology, University of Bergen, Norway. Her research interests relate to questions of gender and migration, with a special focus on au-pair schemes and the way they influence gender relations in both receiving and sending families. As part of her Ph.D. thesis, 'Gender and the global production of welfare in a Norwegian context', she is conducting an analysis of female migration by studying the long-term effects of au-pairing on both the au pairs and the family members they leave behind. The project is due to be completed in 2014.

Catharina Calleman is an assistant professor at the Department of Law, University of Umeå, Sweden. Her teaching and research interests primarily concern labour law, both general labour law issues and issues with a gender perspective. In recent years she has been working on the project 'Labour Law in the Twilight Zone between Private Law and Public Law', which aims to analyse the regulation of domestic work and care work performed in private homes. Her next project will concern labour migration to the Nordic countries.

Karin Carlsson is currently writing her Ph.D. thesis at Stockholm University, Sweden, on the history of the Swedish social home help-programme of 1944 and its skilled workers. She focuses on the problems involved in professionalizing domestic work. Her research interests mainly relate to questions of gender and welfare.

Hanne Marlene Dahl is an associate professor in the Department of Society and Globalization at Roskilde University, Denmark. She works on care, gender and the state, with a special focus on new public management, professionalization, globalization and Europeanization. Her current research is on the different logics of new public management and professionalism in the institutional set-up of Danish eldercare, and on the situation of au pairs in the EU.

Tove Ingebjørg Fjell is professor of Cultural Studies at the University of Bergen, Norway. Her research has focused on gender, culture, medical technology and contextual interpretations of genetics and inheritance. She has examined how people make gender equality in families, and is currently working with a project on partner violence against men.

Lise Lotte Hansen is an associate professor at the Department of Society and Globalization at Roskilde University in Denmark. She works with issues of gender, diversity, leadership and democracy in trade unions, worker solidarity in a new world of work, employment and organizations, ethnic minority women, cleaners' rights, and interest representation.

Lise Widding Isaksen is a professor at the Department of Sociology at the University of Bergen, Norway. Her research interests are gender, migration, welfare and globalization. She has written extensively on gender, power and the welfare state, with special emphasis on the social organization of care work. Her current research focuses on the impact of globalization and international migration on Nordic welfare states.

Ellinor Platzer, Ph.D., is a senior lecturer and researcher in sociology at Linnaeus University, Växjö, Sweden. Her research interests are migration, gender, social equality and welfare, and her current research focuses on the migration of medical professionals.

Marlene Spanger is a Ph.D. student at the Department of Society and Globalization at Roskilde University, Denmark. Her research interests are migration, gender, sexuality and sex work. She is just finishing her Ph.D. thesis on Thai migrants selling sex in Denmark.

Helle Stenum is a Ph.D. student at the Academy for Migration Studies in Denmark (AMID), Ålborg University, Denmark. She has worked on migration management, focusing especially on temporary and illegalized migration. Her empirical studies include research on migrant positions, au-pairing as an institution, homeless migrants, and rejected asylum seekers in Denmark. She is currently working as an independent researcher and consultant, and is an external lecturer at the Department of Culture and Identity, Roskilde University, Denmark.

Minna Zechner, Ph.D., works as a researcher at the Department of Social Research at the University of Tampere, Finland. She researches on eldercare and social policy. Her recent work focuses on globalization and transnational care, migration and social policy, and global movements of care.